DATE DUE

MAY 5 79		
MAY 7 79		
NOV 1 9 80		
JUN 3 81		
DEC 9 81		

FEB 24 81

Chile
&
Allende

Chile
&
Allende

Edited by Lester A. Sobel

Introduction by Jordan M. Young
Professor of History, Pace University (New York)

Contributing editors: Chris Hunt and Joanne Edgar

FACTS ON FILE, INC. NEW YORK, N.Y.

Chile
&
Allende

Library of Congress Catalog Card Number 74-81148
ISBN 0-87196-215-2
9 8 7 6 5 4 3 2 1
PRINTED IN
THE UNITED STATES OF AMERICA

Contents

Introduction

THE DEATH OF PRESIDENT SALVADOR ALLENDE GOSSENS Sept. 11, 1973 ended a 1,042-day political experiment in Chile but did not halt the controversy over the Marxist leader, his policies and his meaning for Latin America. Both Allende's death and his election to the presidency of Chile Sept. 4, 1970 will be the center of historical dispute for years.

It is worth noting, however, that although Allende was the first Marxist to win a country's presidency in a democratically conducted election, Marxist and Communist elements had achieved occasional prominence in Chilean government and politics for at least four decades. A Marxist government had been imposed briefly by a coup in 1932, and Communists had won positions of power in 1947, when three Communists were appointed to the cabinet. The Communist party had helped form coalitions that elected non-Communist presidents in 1938 and 1946.

The September 1970 election that brought Socialist candidate Allende to power was very close:

Candidate	Votes	Percent	Political Grouping
Salvador Allende	1,075,616	36.3%	UP (Popular Unity), a 6-party coalition of the Socialist, Communist, Radical and Social Democratic parties, MAPU (left-wing splinter group from the Christian Democrats) and API (Independent Popular Action)
Jorge Alessandri	1,036,278	34.9%	Independent (conservative) coalition
Radomiro Tomic	824,849	27.8%	Christian Democrats

1

Narrow election victories are not unusual in Chilean presidential elections. Allende had lost the 1958 presidential election to Jorge Alessandri by 33,516 votes, so his 1970 victory by 39,338 votes was not an extradordinary event. Close presidential elections in Chile did not necessarily lead to revolution.

Yet there was deep concern both nationally and internationally when Allende won the presidency in 1970 because he had campaigned on a Marxist platform and had promised, if elected, to carry out deep economic and social reforms that would restructure the existing political system of Chile.

Soon after his inauguration, President Allende went before the Chilean Congress May 21, 1971, and said: "At the commencement of this legislative period, I must raise this problem. Chile now has in its government a new political force whose social function is to uphold, not the traditional ruling class, but the vast majority of the people. The change in the power structure must be necessarily accompanied by profound changes in the socioeconomic order, changes which Parliament [Congress] is summoned to institutionalize.... In the revolutionary process which we are living through there are five essential points around which we shall concentrate our social and political campaign: (1) the principle of legality, (2) the development of institutions, (3) political freedom, (4) the prevention of violence, (5) the socialization of means of production."

As a professional historian, I have tried to pull together the most important events of the period insofar as they have been revealed by September 1974. Unfortunately, what emerges is not a clear-cut or precise picture.

President Allende became an actor in a modern Greek tragedy, unable to control forces on the extreme left and extreme right that tore his administration to pieces. Allende, a member of the Chilean Congress in 1937, until his election to the presidency in 1970 had spent almost 33 years as an opposition politician. The transition from a member of the opposition to chief executive of a nation that he had to govern with a coalition of political forces was not simple or easy. Allende may have been a political exile within his own country and perhaps resembles to some extent Juan Bosch of the Dominican Republic, who after 27 years of foreign exile returned to win the presidency of his country in 1961—only to be overthrown by revolution 9 months after he took office.

Both left- and right-wing opposition hardened their positions in the final months of the Allende administration. Sen. Carlos Altamirano, secretary general of the Chilean Socialist Party, threatened to expose the president as a weakling or traitor to the revolution if Allende did not move more swiftly to carry out political and economic reforms demanded by the extreme left wing. Southern Chile had become a political no-man's-land, as farms were taken over without legislative or legal sanction. Industrial plants, both large and small, began to fall under state control as credit disappeared.

The depth of the right-wing opposition cannot be completely documented. Attitudes of the left wing, on the one hand, and of middle-class Chileans (a majority, in mental attitude at least), on the other, gradually polarized as standards of living began to fall, food shortages developed and political liberties eroded. After Allende began to ignore the Supreme Court and the Congress, he found himself forced to call in the Chilean military to shore up his regime.

The North American business community was probably linked to the downfall of the Allende government. Copper nationalization, although approved by the previous Christian Democratic administration and ratified by most Chilean politicians ranging from the left to the right, resulted in heavy economic pressure on the Allende government as it moved ahead with its program. Chile was short of dollars as the world price of copper tumbled after Allende's election. Funds from international lending agencies disappeared, and legal blockades trapped Chilean copper when it arrived in European ports.

Perhaps a successful Allende posed more of a threat to the right and center than did Fidel Castro. Armed revolutions frightened people, but success at the ballot box could be understood and possibly accepted by the Latin American middle class.

To understand why Chile could elect the first freely chosen Socialist president in Latin America and why the armed forces overthrew him 1,042 days later requires some examination of Chile's geography, people and history. Chile has always been out of step with other Latin American countries. The uniqueness and difference of Chile from its neighbors is easily pin-pointed.

Geography

Chile was, and still is, to a large extent sealed off and isolated from the rest of South America. An island on the continent, Chile is 2,600 miles long and rarely more than 150 miles wide. The western border of Chile, the Andes Mountains, blocks passage to Argentina. Desert and mountains seal off the northern frontier and keep the Peruvians and Bolivians at arms length. To

CHILE

— International boundary

⊛ National capital

○ Provincia capital

╄╄╄ Railroad

— Road

| 0 | 100 | 200 | 300 | 400 Miles |
| 0 | 100 200 | 300 | 400 Kilometers |

the East is the Pacific Ocean, and to the South the continent splinters into the nothingness of the Antarctic region.

The internal geography of the country has fragmented Chile and has made nation-building difficult.

Northern Chile is 1,000 miles of barren, arrid, mineral-rich land that punishes its inhabitants in the day with blazing temperatures and freezes them at night.

Immediately south is the 400-mile-long Central Valley. This is the heartland of the nation. Santiago, the capital, is located here with its population of 3,120,000, while the seaport town of Valparaiso, with 350,000 inhabitants, and the mining-and-industrial town of Concepcion, with 200,000, combine to make this the most important part of Chile.

The third area, southern Chile, stretches 1,200 miles from the Central Valley to the Straits of Magellan. It resembles the U.S. Pacific Northwest in climate and geography. Chile claims the O'Higgins Peninsula in the Antarctic region and also controls Easter Island, 2,300 miles west of Valparaiso.

The strange geography has indeed set Chile apart from the Latin American world.

People

The midyear estimate of the Chilean population for 1973 was 9,247,000, with 72.9% considered urban. The population reflects the fact that the early Indian inhabitants, estimated at approximately one million in the 16th century, were gradually wiped out so that today (1974) in Chile, perhaps 150,000 pure, Araucanian-speaking Indians remain—and play no significant role in the body politic. The early Spaniards that came to Chile, primarily military men assigned to one of the few hostile Indian frontiers in Spanish America, did not bring families with them. The Basque section of Spain contributed the greatest number of immigrants in the post-colonial period, and their taciturn, dour yet industrious life styles left a deep imprint on the nation. Europeans from other nations were also attracted to Chile in the 19th century, and Germans, Danes, Italians, Scots, French, English and Yugoslavs mixed with the earlier settlers. Thus in the mainstream of Chilean life today, it is not unusual to encounter such names as O'Higgins, Mackenzie, Tomic, Alessandri, Grove, Dalgren and Gozzens mixed with Irarrázaval, Errázuriz and Eyzaguirre.

Chile: Military Expenditures[1] in Current Prices in Relation to Gross Domestic Product (GDP) and Fiscal Sector Expenditures, and Military Expenditures on a Constant Price Basis, 1967-72

Values in Millions of Escudos and U.S. Dollars

Year	GDP	Expenditures		Military expenditures as:		Military expenditures on constant price basis[2] (1967 = 100)	
		Fiscal sector	Military	% of GDP	% of fiscal sector	Escudos	US$[3]
		— In current escudos —					
1967	32,811	8,929	1,080	3.3	12.1	1,080	187
1968	44,283	9,682	1,272	2.9	13.1	977	169
1969	64,551	13,669	1,807	2.8	13.2	1,016	175
[4]1970	[4]92,194	22,282	[5]3,356	3.6	15.1	1,386	239
[7]1971	[6]126,306	36,020	5,235	4.1	14.5	1,834	317
[7]1972	—	56,067	[8]9,089	—	16.2	—	—

[1] Data are based on expenditures of the Ministry of Defense plus social security expenditures for the armed forces.

[2] Current prices converted to constant prices by using the general price index from International Monetary Fund, *International Financial Statistics*, August 1971.

[3] Values in constant escudos converted at 5.79 escudos to the U.S. dollar, the trade rate at the end of 1967.

[4] Provisional data.

[5] Social security expenditures estimated on the basis of budgetary data.

[6] Estimated on the basis of the reported rate of growth in the gross national product.

[7] Budgetary data.

[8] Social security expenditures estimated on the basis of the percentage relationship of expenditures for social security to expenditures of the Ministry of Defense in 1971.

Sources: Data on GDP as follows: 1967-70 Banco Central, *Boletin Mensual*, July 1972; 1971, estimated on the basis of data in Agency for International Development, Division of Statistics and Reports, *Economic Data Book*, Chile: Revision sheet No. 310, June 1972.

Expenditure data as follows: 1967 from Contraloria General de la Republica, *Memoria de la Contraloria General y Balance General de la Hacienda Pública*; 1968-69 data on total expenditures from Banco Central, *Memoria 1969*, and data on military expenditures from the budget of the following year, i.e., *Ley de Presupuesto Fiscal de Entradas y Gastos de la Nacion para el año 1969 and . . . para el año 1970*; 1970-71 from Direccion de Presupuestos, *Exposicion sobre el Estado de la Hacienda Pública . . . 16 de Noviembre de 1971*, supplemented, for 1970, with budgetary data on social security expenditures and, for 1971, with preliminary data on social security expenditures from American Embassy, Santiago, telegram No. 1553, April 3, 1972; 1972 budget estimates in Organization of American States, Inter-American Committee for the Alliance for Progress (CIAP), Report No. 541, April 21, 1972.

From Latin American Military Expenditures 1967–1971 (U.S. Department of State)

The Economy

Much of Chile's economic and political history is linked to copper as formerly it had been tied to nitrate exports. Dollars for servicing the foreign debt and the purchase of food and petroleum imports are obtained primarily through copper exports. Chile is the world's fourth largest producer of copper, and it ranks second in copper exports. Most of Chile's copper output comes from five large mines. The three largest, Chuquicamata, El Salvador and El Teniente, account for 85% of the nation's production. Before their nationalization, they were owned by U.S. corporations. Production was 570,000 tons in 1971 and 590,000 tons in 1972, according to the 1973 annual report of the Inter-American Development Bank. Copper prices have been erratic in the past few years, ranging from 67¢ a pound in 1969 to 49¢ a pound in 1972, but they nearly doubled in August 1973, when they reached 97¢.

Nitrates, formerly Chile's biggest money earner, have dropped in importance drastically. Chile accounted for 65% of the world nitrate production at the beginning of the 20th century but for only 4% in the 1970s, when synthetic nitrates met most of world demand. Chile's average annual production of nitrate in the 1960s was 1.02 million tons, but the world market has been shrinking, and most of the large multinational corporations such as Anglo-Lautero have sold their holdings to the Chilean government. Nitrate output declined in the early 1970s, and in 1972 only 660,000 tons was produced.

The decline in mineral exports, coupled with decreased manufacturing (starting in September 1972), plus poor agricultural performance that forced increased wheat, sugar and beef importation, created great inflationary pressures in 1973. In the first eight months of 1973 consumer prices went up 150% and real wages declined by more than 50%.

According to the Inter-American Development Bank's report for 1973, Chile also had a serious balance-of-payments problem. The annual report said: "Chile's external performance suffered a major turnabout in 1971–72 after three years of reserve accumulation averaging $145 million. In 1971 the net international reserves of the banking system fell $305 million despite the suspension of foreign debt servicing in November and the second special allocation of $16 million of Special Drawing Rights (SDR). Reserves declined another $328 million in 1972 even though the country obtained debt servicing relief equivalent to $361 million and another allocation of SDR $17 million."

Chile's outstanding public and private debt with official guarantee rose from approximately $2.04 billion at the end of 1969 to an estimated $2.75 billion in 1972. The Chilean economy had not been a healthy one before the election of Allende in 1970, and conditions did not improve during his 600 days in office.

History

Chile entered world history in 1535 when Diego de Almagro, one of Francisco Pizzaro's lieutenants, led an expedition south from Peru to explore the area. He had hoped to find wealth and an empire equal to that of the Incas. His band of Spanish conquistadores found nothing to conquer and returned in 1537 to Peru, bitter, poor and angry. Almagro and his followers, known later as "the Men of Chile," turned against Pizzaro and fought a losing battle for control of the Inca empire.

A few years later, in 1540, Pedro de Valdivia received permission from Pizzaro to attempt another conquest of the Chilean area. Valdivia Feb. 12, 1541 founded Santiago, which ultimately became the capital of the nation. The Spanish garrison battled the Araucanian Indians constantly, and in 1553 Valdivia died in an Araucanian ambush. The man who ambushed him, his former Indian aide, Lautaro, used all the knowledge he had gained of Spanish fighting techniques to destroy the founder of the Chilean territory.

Thus early, it was established that Chile was an area that had to be fought over, and Spain created a special permanent army paid for from the Peruvian treasury to serve on the southern frontier. The Araucanians were tough, and the Arauco Wars (also called the Indian Wars) conditioned the Spaniards who went to Chile. They were tough soldiers and tough administrators.

Chile was under direct control of the viceroyalty of Lima, Peru in the 17th and the 18th centuries, but in 1778 a slight gesture toward more independence for the area was made when a captain generalcy of Chile was created, with local government to be managed by the town council (the *Cabildo*) of Santiago. The last viceroy of Peru, Don Ambrosio O'Higgins, made this grant to his favorite province.

European events triggered the independence movement in Chile. Chileans would not obey the orders of the puppets of

Napoleon, and between 1811 and 1817 Chilean patriots and Spanish soldiers fought for control of the country. In 1817 Chile finally broke free from Spain after the battle of Chacabuco. Gen. José de San Martin from Argentina, in the company of a young Chilean, Bernardo O'Higgins, defeated the Spanish royalist army. As Chile was always considered a secondary area in the Spanish-American empire, Spain did not feel that the area was worth holding to the bitter end. When independence came to Chile in 1817, no great and deep struggle had torn the nation, no great social, economic or political upheaval had taken place. Chile was an independent country with most of the same people who ruled the country before still in control.

Bernardo O'Higgins ruled Chile as "supreme director" from 1817 to 1823, but his advanced social and political ideas soon alienated the most powerful members of Chile's establishment. The conservative, land-holding class was willing to let O'Higgins lead Chile to independence but not rule the country. O'Higgins was forced to resign in 1823, and he went into exile. Liberals and conservatives, both basically from the same economic and social class, fought for control of the nation from 1823 to 1830. Little difference existed between the two groups; both were from the small landed oligarchy. But neither trusted the other. The turning point came in 1830 when Conservative and Liberal military forces met in the Battle of Lircay. The Conservatives won.

A tough centralized constitution adopted in 1833 became the law of the land for nearly 100 years. The constitution provided for high property qualifications for voting and generally favored the upper income groups. The Conservatives, however, permitted political opposition, and in 1842 a Liberal Party emerged. The basic program of the party included a mildly anticlerical position and some reforms of the land-holding system.

While the rest of Spanish America went from dictatorship to *caudillo,* to petty tyranny, Chile was governed by elected presidents who gradually extended the political system to include more and more citizens.

Chilean territory was enlarged in 1879 when its armies invaded Peru and Bolivia during the War of the Pacific (1879–83). The roots of the war are to be found in the precious nitrate regions of the north. Chilean businessmen in the early 1870s began to invest money in these areas in Bolivian and Peruvian territory.

Peruvian and Bolivian authorities, apprehensive over Chilean economic expansion, signed a secret offensive and défensive treaty and, contrary to earlier agreements, raised taxes on

Chilean nitrate producers. Chileans charged that this was clearly a conspiracy to deprive them of property, and Chile declared war. The Chilean army invaded the two countries and defeated both. Bolivia lost its portion of land on the Pacific Ocean and became a land-locked nation. Peru also lost valuable land. As a result of the war, the Chileans earned the title of the "Yankees of Latin America."

New wealth from the nitrate fields now poured unhindered into Chile and aided its economic development. It also resulted in the formation of a new political party. In the 1880s the Radical Party emerged and challenged both the Liberals and Conservatives with more advanced social programs. The Radical Party's economic base was mineral wealth, so it was not adverse to land reforms. Yet its challenge was a peaceful one.

A sharp break in Chilean history took place when José Manuel Balmaceda, president from 1886 to 1891, split the conservative classes, who felt threatened by his social and economic programs. Revolution broke out in January 1891. A strange situation developed as the Chilean army remained loyal to the president while the Chilean navy rallied to the support of the Congress. The two sides were locked in a desperate struggle for nearly 9 months.

The navy was generally the most conservative force in the countries of Latin American, and Chile was no exception. The Chilean navy sailed north, easily landed a few battalions of marines and took control of the northern nitrate regions. Nitrate sales to Europe quickly provided funds to build and recruit a new army, which the navy transported to Southern Chile. Here it defeated the presidential army. 10,000 lives were lost, and President José Manuel Balmaceda committed sucide in September 1891 when he learned that his forces had been defeated.

Chilean politics from 1891 to 1920 was marked by an uneasy struggle for power among many groups. The defeat of President Balmaceda meant that Congress controlled the country. With Congress in power, political parties had to appeal more and more to the people for support. The net result was a sharp politicization of the middle class and the development of an articulate labor movement.

The man who was able to capitalize on this development in Chilean history was a dramatic and dynamic populist leader, Don Arturo Alessandri, who ran for the presidency in 1920. The "Lion of Tarapaca," as his contemporaries called him, was the direct forerunner of such later figures as Juan Perón, Getulio

Vargas and Fidel Castro. Alessandri appeared to the people as a radical reformer, and he won the 1920 election. But much as in 1891, Congress blocked his reform program. After bickering with Congress for nearly four years, President Alessandri made a fatal mistake and asked the Chilean army for help in pressuring Congress to pass the reform legislation he had promised. The younger military men jumped at the opportunity. Congress quickly enacted the legislation demanded as the young officers watched in the galleries and demonstrated their determination by literally rattling their sabers in their sheathes. In 1925 a new, more liberal constitution was prepared for Chile.

But the army had tasted power. A military man, Col. Carlos Ibanez del Campo, elected president in 1927, took control of the nation and gradually eliminated opposition until nearly all the powers for governing were concentrated in his hands. By 1930 Ibanez was a complete dictator as the Chilean Congress voluntarily gave up its rights (power to control the budget, to act in political parties, to enjoy press freedom, to hold elections) in a search for stable government.

The world depression at this time resulted in the decline of nitrate and copper sales and increased social tension. Strikes and social agitation were answered by sharp and unpopular repressive measures by the Ibanez administration. In July 1931, when the medical profession went on strike against Ibanez, the dictator found no defense against this weapon, and he left the country.

1931 and 1932 were chaotic years in Chile. A military-civilian coup imposed a Marxist government, which collapsed in 12 days and was followed by more political chaos. Nearly all political elements then united behind former President Arturo Alessandri, who was now considered a conservative and trustworthy. Alessandri was elected to a six-year term of office late in 1932 and served successfully until 1938.

In 1938 the Popular Front Forces, made up of the Radical, Socialist and Communist parties, won the presidency with a coalition candidate. Radical Party politician Pedro Aguirre Cerda narrowly defeated Conservative candidate Gustave Ross by 222,700 votes to 218,609.

The Popular Front broke up in January 1941 when the parties failed to reconcile their differences. The Radical Party, however, was able to maintain control over the government.

President Aguirre Cerda died of a heart attack Nov. 25, 1941. New elections held in January 1942 produced another Radical Party president, Juan Antonio Rios, who defeated Carlos Ibañez by a vote of 260,034 to 204,635. Rios died in 1946, and new presidential elections were held.

The parties fragmented in the presidential elections of 1946, but the Radical Party managed to secure another victory at the polls with Gabriel González Videla by allying itself with the Communist Party.

In recognition of the Communist Party aid in winning the election, President González Videla appointed three Marxists to cabinet posts. Thus the first official participation of Communists in a Latin American government began when Carlos Contreras Labarca became minister of communications and public works, Miguel Concha minister of agriculture and Victor Contreras minister of land and colonization.

The coalition, however, quickly fell apart as the Communists used their positions inside the administration to hinder effective government and were dismissed. The Radical Party of President González Videla took over most of the cabinet positions.

The next government to put Communists in power in Chile was Allende's.

Throughout 1947 González Videla was faced with sharp labor hostility. One result was an Aug. 21 decision by the Chamber of Deputies to suspend individual liberties to deal with a crippling strike in the coal mines. The Chilean government deported 2 Yugoslav diplomats Oct. 8 on charges of responsibility for the strike. Yugoslavia broke relations with Chile Oct. 11, and Chile Oct. 21 severed relations with the USSR and Yugoslavia, accusing both nations of inspiring unrest in the coal mines. Stepping up his attacks on the Communists, González Videla Oct. 22 announced the arrest of 200 Communist leaders.

In 1948 González Videla managed to obtain Congressional approval for the "Law for the Permanent Defense of Democracy," which made the Communist Party illegal and removed Communist voters from the electoral registry. But González Videla failed to mobilize the Chilean voters behind him, and the 1949 Congressional elections gave the Radical Party only tenuous control of the country.

Carlos Ibañez returned triumphantly to power in the 1952 presidential election. He polled 446,439 votes to Matte Larraín's 265,357. Lack of a majority sent the election into Congress, where Ibanez was selected president as the candidate with the most votes. Ibañez' six-year term was a complete failure, however, and his disastrous administration resembled the second Getulio Vargas period in Brazil.

The 1958 presidential elections pitted Jorge Alessandri, a conservative, against left-wing Salvador Allende and Eduardo Frei of the Christian Democrats. The results:

Candidate	Votes	Percent	Candidate	Votes	Percent
Jorge Alessandri	389,909	31.6 %	Luis Bossay	192,077	15.6 %
Salvador Allende	356,493	28.9 %	Antonio Zamorano	41,304	3.3 %
Eduardo Frei	255,769	20.7 %			

Alessandri had promised Chileans a fiscally conservative regime, but his term of office was beset by earthquakes and a series of bad harvests that left the country in poor economic shape. Inflation wrecked his economic programs and set the scene for the 1964 presidential elections, which marked the beginning of the end for an older Chilean political life style.

Left-wing elements joined to support Allende again under the banner of the *FRAP,* a Popular Front coalition. The center and right backed the Christian Democrats, who nominated Eduardo Frei. Frei won the 1964 election with 1,409,012 votes (56.09%) to 977,902 (38.93%) for Allende. The Christian Democrats, however, had oversold themselves and had promised a revolution without bloodshed. Dramatic programs for social reforms were blocked by both left- and right-wings groups in Congress, although legislation to nationalize Chile's copper mines was passed. But again inflation hurt the regime, and the developments of 1969 point up the problems.

This book chronicles the events in Chile from 1969, the year before Allende became president, through 1973, the year in which Allende was overthrown and in which he met his death. The material of this volume consists principally of the printed record compiled by FACTS ON FILE in its weekly reports on world events. Where changes or additions were made, the purpose was usually to clarify or to provide necessary amplification. A conscientious effort was made to record all events without bias and to make this book a balanced and accurate reference work.

JORDAN M. YOUNG

Princeton, New Jersey
September, 1974

1969: Christian Democratic Decline

Ruling Party Loses Power

The elevation of Salvador Allende Gossens, an avowed Marxist, to the presidency of Chile in 1970 was preceded in 1969 by an erosion of the power of the ruling Christian Democratic Party and a heightening of the polarization between left and right.

Congressional Elections Rebuff Frei. The reform policies of President Eduardo Frei Montalva's Christian Democratic Party were rebuffed March 1, 1969 in congressional elections that showed a move to the right in Chilean national politics. Though the ballots were almost evenly divided between left, right and center parties, the right-wing National Party rose to second place in Congress. The election was viewed as a test of popular support for the Christian Democratic Party and as a forecast of the 1970 presidential election. At stake were all 150 seats in the Chamber of Deputies and 30 of the 50 seats in the Senate.

Final election results, announced by the Interior Ministry March 3, gave the Christian Democrats only 31.1% of the votes cast, compared with 42% in the 1965 general elections; in addition, the party lost its majority in the Chamber of Deputies (including nine seats it had held in the capital, Santiago). The National Party won 20.9% of the votes, compared with 13% in 1965. The Radical Party, a centrist middle class group that had moved to the left, won about 13.4%, down slightly from 1965; however, the Radicals lost to the Nationalists their position as second largest congressional party. The Chilean Communist Party, the largest in Latin America outside of Cuba, rose from 12% of the vote in 1965 to 16.6% in the current election. And the Socialist Party, farther left than the Chilean Communist Party, won 12.8% of the votes, up from 10% in 1965. Other parties accounted for the remaining 5.2% of the vote.

The new composition of Congress was reported as follows (pre-election composition in parentheses):

Christian Democratic Party—55 deputies (82), 23 senators (12); National Party —34 deputies (9), 5 senators (3); Radical Party—24 deputies (19), 9 senators (10); Communist Party—22 deputies (18), 6 senators (5); Socialist Party—15 deputies (15), 4 senators (6); Others—no deputies (4), 3 senators (6).

Of Chile's 3,250,000 registered voters, 29.5% abstained (compared with 19.4% in the 1965 election), even though voting was mandatory and abstention or the casting of blank ballots was legally punished by a fine.

The Christian Democrats had steadily declined in popularity since 1964, when Frei had been swept into power with 56% of the vote; one element in the decline was Chile's middle class, which increas-

15

ingly opposed Frei's economic and social reform programs. Frei could not constitutionally succeed himself, and the party's leading potential candidate was Radomiro Tomic Romero, considered to be the left of Frei. Party leaders had conceded that an absolute minimum of 30% of the popular vote was necessary to show that the party was capable of winning the 1970 presidential election. Within the party the more conservative elements received considerably more support in the election than did their leftwing rivals.

The National Party, a fusion of rightist groups seen as nearly moribund in 1964, apparently reclaimed many conservative voters who supported Frei in 1964. (The right had not run a presidential candidate in 1964.) The party had associated itself with the potential presidential candidacy of former President Jorge Alessandri Rodriguez, 72, an independent conservative. Following the announcement of the election results, hundreds of Nationalist demonstrators marched through the streets of Santiago March 3, waving placards supporting Alessandri.

(Salvador Allende Gossens, who had run in former presidential elections on a joint Communist-Socialist ticket, was re-elected to his Senate seat March 1.)

Puerto Montt Clash Stirs Protest. A clash between squatters and police March 9 in the southern city of Puerto Montt led to repercussions reaching into the leadership of Chile's ruling Christian Democratic Party.

Eight persons were killed and at least 30 were wounded when police fired into a group of about 100 squatter families to dislodge them from privately-owned land on which they had erected huts. Twenty police were reported injured by clubs and rocks thrown by the squatters during the melee.

The clash generated political protests throughout Chile. Police were placed on alert March 11, and the Senate was called into special session March 12.

The Communist-led National Labor Confederation called for mass protests against the killings. The Federation of University Students also condemned the action. Senate President Salvador Allende (the potential presidential candidate of the Socialist Party) and Senator Julieta Campusano (Communist Party) visited the area and asserted that the squatters had been raked by machine-gun fire.

Left-wing rebels within the Christian Democratic Party issued a declaration March 11 in which they charged that the government did not represent the working class but rather the capitalists. Asserting that a party split was inevitable, the rebels expressed hope for a coalition of all leftist political forces in Chile. Le Monde reported March 22 that left-wing party members had called for the resignation of Interior Minister Edmundo Perez Zujovic. Five prominent senior Christian Democrats joined in opposing the government's action: Senators Rafael Agustin Gumucio and Alberto Jerez; Deputies Julio Silva Solar, Vicente Sota and Jacques Chonchol.

The youth section of the Christian Democratic Party issued a declaration denouncing the government's action and called Perez directly responsible for the incident; four of the party's youth leaders March 23 lost their membership rights for two years as a result of their protests. The London publication Latin America reported March 28 that Radomiro Tomic had also joined in the protest.

President Eduardo Frei Montalva rejected the attacks on his administration and on Perez. In an emergency meeting, the Christian Democrats' National Council March 14 had issued a statement of "full support" for Frei's government. Perez asserted March 14 that the violence was "the result of persistent provocation by the opposition who, becoming professional agitators, have been using the needs of the poor people for their own profit." He accused Luis Espinoza, Socialist senator from Puerto Montt, of instigating the affair, Le Monde reported March 15. (Espinoza had reportedly been arrested March 8 and taken to another city.) Attacking his Christian Democratic opponents, Perez publicly called Deputy Silva Solar "a Communist," Latin America reported March 28.

(According to the London publication government spokesmen had implied that the government feared a Socialist-led civil disobedience campaign. Apparently, Socialists had been involved in a number of organized "squat-ins," though the organizers in some cases were said to have been Christian Democratic leaders.

(Perez later resigned as interior minister "for personal reasons," Le Monde of Paris reported July 6. He was succeeded by Patricio Rojas, president of the OAS Inter-American Cultural Council and former undersecretary of education.)

Communists Win Labor Victory. The Washington Post March 16 cited a Los Angeles Times report that the Communist Party recently had won a majority of seats on the governing council of the Chilean Workers' Central (CUTCH), the national labor confederation. With 14 of the council's 27 seats, the Communists became the majority group for the first time.

In another development, CUTCH, a blue-collar union, gained two of Chile's largest white-collar affiliates—the Confederation of Private Employes and the National Association of Government Employes. Thus, with its increased strength, CUTCH represented about 12% of the Chilean working force of 2.5 million persons, the majority of whom were not organized. CUTCH and its affiliates currently controlled workers in such key sectors as transportation, mining, large manufacturing and civil service.

Left rejects Tomic. The Communist and Socialist parties March 23 said they would not back Radomiro Tomic for president in 1970. Tomic had said March 19 that without "the support of the left, there will not be a Tomic candidacy. It is as simple and as clear as that."

Tomic's statement, quoted in an interview with the Washington Post, was considered significant because the Christian Democratic Party had come to power in 1964 as Chile's only alternative to Marxist rule. (The party currently was beset by warring left and right factions.) Tomic added that while he felt the Christian Democrats could win the presidency without the support of the two Marxist parties, he did not think he could govern without them.

The Communists and Socialists charged that Tomic had helped draft President Frei's copper "Chileanization" policy, under which Chile became a partner of U.S. firms operating its copper mines. The two Marxist parties had supported direct expropriation of the mines.

Tomic announced April 9 that he was "irrevocably" out of the campaign. (Four months later, however, he reversed this decision.)

In a letter to party chairman Renan Fuentealba, Tomic declared that "there is no basis for a Christian Democratic strategy of popular unity for 1970 which would be manifest in an agreement of all the political and social forces committed to the substitution of the capitalist system." Tomic asserted that the lack of unity was due to factors "in the control of the government, the party and the forces of the left, including the Marxists."

Crisis Splits Christian Democrats. Tensions within the ruling Christian Democratic Party broke into the open May 4 when the party's national committee rejected demands of its left-wing faction for a "popular union" with Chile's Marxist parties and voted instead to support a Christian Democratic candidate in the 1970 presidential election. Almost immediately, a number of high-level Christian Democrats defected and formed a separate organization.

The national committee, with some 500 delegates from all regions of Chile, voted 233 to 215 against the "popular union" proposal. Its action constituted a victory for President Eduardo Frei Montalva's policy over the party's "rebels" and their allies, the "terceristas" (a third or middle faction between Frei's "official" group and the rebels). Radomiro Tomic, leftwing Christian Democrat who had worked with Frei to form the ruling party, had become one of the main supporters of the "rebel" campaign for a "popular union."

The defeat of the leftist proposal was followed by replacement of the party's board of directors, formerly headed by Senator Renan Fuentealba. The new officers included Justice Minister Jaime Castillo as president and Juan Hamilton, former housing minister, as first vice-president. It was directed to choose the party's candidate for the presidency within 60 days.

The effects of the national committee's vote were illustrated May 6 by the resignation from the party of Senator Rafael Agustin Gumucio, a leader of the rebel faction. Gumucio, who had participated in the founding of the Christian Democratic Party, said in his letter of resignation: "In the course of 35 years of political activity, I never thought, before now, that the moment could arrive when for motives of political honesty I should have to leave the party." Denouncing what he called a change in the party's basic orientation, Gumucio said: "The advanced currents of Christian thought are no longer taken up by us and in fact we are less an instrument for the revolutionary changing of society than one of social status, a force administering the system, guaranteeing the established order."

Gumucio's resignation was followed May 9 by those of Jacques Chonchol, architect of Chile's agrarian reform program, Senator Alberto Jerez and Deputies Vicente Sota and Julio Silva Solar. (President Frei's political counselor, Jorge Cash, who had submitted his resignation May 7, was persuaded May 8 to remain in the party in the interest of party unity.) A number of labor union members and a sizable fraction of the party's youth group also decided to leave the party, Le Monde of Paris reported May 11. Chonchol declared May 9 that the dissenters represented "about 30% of the force of the party." He asserted that they were now going "to work for the union of all the popular forces."

In reaction to the leftist dissent within its ranks, the party's disciplinary commission expelled 19 members from the party and suspended 13 deputies for two months, Le Monde reported May 18.

Disaffected party members, meeting in Santiago May 17–18, formed a new left-wing organization, the Movement of United Popular Action (MAPU). About 450 delegates elected an interim national coordinating commission for MAPU and designated Chonchol as its head. Other commission members included Senators Gumucio and Jerez, Deputy Silva Solar and youth leaders Juan Enrique Vega, Enrique Correa, Rodrigo Ambrosio and Jaime Estevez. The delegates also decided to hold a constituent convention within 60 days in order to establish themselves as an official political party. Chonchol called for "the unity of all those who are in favor of profound change and of sweeping away the capitalist system, because we hope to make revolution in Chile. Popular unity is the revolutionary instrument which will build in Chile a Socialist and communitarian society."

(Salvador Allende, president of the Senate, meanwhile, ended a visit to North Korea May 8.)

U.S. Ambassador Accused. Senator Renan Fuentealba charged that the U.S. ambassador, Edward Korry, had interfered in Chilean political affairs, the Washington Post reported May 18. Fuentealba claimed that Korry had tried to persuade President Frei and other Christian Democratic leaders to reduce the chances of a Marxist victory in the 1970 elections by making way for a right-wing victory by Jorge Alessandri. An Alessandri administration, Korry reportedly had argued, would be transitory and would pave the way for a Christian Democratic return in 1975. Korry denied the charges.

Radical Party Purge. In advance of the 1970 campaign, the centrist Radical Party ousted several former party leaders.

The Radical Party, holding its 24th national convention, expelled a number of right-wing members, the London publication Latin America reported July 11. The purge, described as "a necessary cleansing operation" by the party's new president, Carlos Morales Abarzua, ousted Julio Duran, the party's 1964 presidential candidate, Deputies Rafael Senoret and Julio Mercado and two former presidents of the party, Angel Faivovich and Jaime Tormo.

PDC Names Tomic. The ruling Christian Democratic Party (PDC) officially nominated Radomiro Tomic Romero Aug. 15 as its candidate in the September 1970 presidential elections.

A lawyer and former ambassador to the U.S., Tomic won the nomination on a platform carefully phrased to appeal to both the right and left elements of the factionalized party. Negotiations within the party's national council had continued up until the last moment and resulted in a program that essentially would continue Frei's policies.

Tomic outlined the program of the "second Christian Democratic government" in a statement approved by the party assembly as the political and economic manifesto for the election campaign. On the controversial copper issue, Tomic pledged a new PDC government that would continue "with the process of recovering our basic riches begun in the present period" and would "complete by law, if it is required in the national interest, the nationalization of all the principal copper-producing enterprises, reiterating Chilean dominion over all the mineral rights in our territory." In an apparent appeal to the party's conservatives, however, he stressed that the program would "not seek either the collectivization or the general nationalization of the Chilean economy." (Tomic had criticized as inadequate President Frei's proposal to gradually bring about the full state ownership of two of Anaconda's copper mines in Chile.)

In an appeal to the left, Tomic stressed the importance of maintaining a national struggle against "capitalist and neo-capitalist structures" and added that the party should reject the "values and motivations of the institutions which give expression to bourgeois society and to a capitalist and neo-capitalist economy which degrades the dignity of labor and wastes scarce capital resources and national savings." He added that the minority interests currently controlling the nation "must be replaced by the three million-man labor force of the country and Chileans who constitute its active population."

Tomic called for doubling the national income within 10 years, lowering the voting age to 18, broader agrarian reform and provision for the use of plebiscites, especially in cases of irreconcilable differences between the parliamentary and executive branches of government.

Two other declared candidates were in the presidential race: Sen. Alberto Baltra of the Radical Party and Sen. Rafael Tarud, independent.

(News from Chile reported Sept. 13 that Carlos Figueroa, former undersecretary of agriculture, had been appointed economy minister. He replaced Enrique Krauss, who had resigned to direct Radomiro Tomic's presidential campaign.)

Presidential Candidates. Three more Chilean parties chose candidates for the 1970 presidential elections. Sen. Salvador Allende, a three-time loser in the presidential race, was chosen by the Socialist Party at its weekend meeting Aug. 30–Aug. 31. Jacques Choncol was nominated Sept. 28 by the Movement of United Popular Action (MAPU), and the Chilean Communist Party selected poet Pablo Neruda as its candidate, the Miami Herald reported Oct. 2.

Other declared candidates included Sen. Alberto Baltra of the Radical Party and Sen. Rafael Tarud of the Independents.

Jorge Alessandri, 73, Nov. 2 also officially announced his candidacy for the 1970 presidential elections. The Chilean embassy reported that he had accepted the nomination of some independent groups and would also be supported by the National Party.

Leftist Unity Program. The five political parties of the left adopted a common program in preparation for a unified stand in the 1970 presidential elections. In passages of the platform published Dec. 21, the Socialist, Communist and Radical parties, along with the Popular Independent Alliance and the Unified Movement of Popular Action, pledged to fight imperialism, the bourgeoisie and large landowners. The parties also stressed the importance of nationalizing large mining firms, accelerating agrarian reform policies and expropriating large monopolistic firms.

Brief Military Uprising

Army Rebellion Put Down. In an action that aroused fears of the first military takeover in Chile in more than 35 years, two regiments of the army's Second Division revolted against the government of President Eduardo Frei Montalva Oct. 21, 1969. The regime, responding to what it called an "attempt at military sedition," immediately imposed a state of siege throughout the country. Leaders of the revolt, however, insisted that it was not political but was aimed at low salaries and poor working conditions in the armed forces. The short-lived rebellion, which was over Oct. 22, resulted in the replacement of Frei's defense minister, a military leader, with a civilian and the dismissal of the commander in chief of the army.

The uprising erupted in the Yungay regiment, based in San Felipe, about 50 miles north of Santiago, and the Tacna regiment, based in Santiago. The government reported that the Yungay regiment's revolt had been quickly suppressed Oct. 21 with the arrest of its leaders, who included Major Arturo Marshall, recently ordered into retirement.

The Tacna regiment's revolt was led by Gen. Roberto Viaux Marambio, recently dismissed as head of the First Division in Antofagasta. About 50 high-ranking army officers from the War Academy were reported to have joined the rebels at the Tacna regiment's barracks. In interviews Oct. 21, Gen. Viaux stressed that the rebellion was not intended to overthrow the government but was aimed at "the army high command, which has not controlled nor solved the serious problems within the army." Claiming that 85% of the armed forces supported his position, he stressed that he was still "profoundly loyal to President Frei, and if the chief of state so orders me I will lay down my arms."

In ordering the state of siege Oct. 21, President Frei urged Chileans to support the government and reported that a majority of the armed forces were "maintaining, as always, their discipline and loyalty." He called the revolt an "attempted coup d'etat" and a "crazy adventure."

Government troops surrounded the Tacna barracks Oct. 21, while garbage trucks and earth-moving equipment encircled the Presidential Palace. Congress was suspended, and censorship was imposed on incoming and outgoing re-

ports. In addition, an estimated 3,000 persons massed outside the Presidential Palace to demonstrate their support of Frei, while several national unions called for strikes to support the government.

A brief flurry of gunfire erupted at the Tacna regiment headquarters late Oct. 21, and 14 civilians were reported wounded.

The revolt ended early Oct. 22, when Gen. Viaux turned over the Tacna barracks to Gen. Alfredo Mahn. Viaux issued a communique reaffirming the rebels' "absolute loyalty" to President Frei and to constitutional authority; he claimed later that day that the rebels' demands had been "fully accepted—some immediately, and others to be fulfilled later."

Announcing the end of the revolt, Frei asserted that a "general of the republic and a group of officers tried to change our constitutional status" and would be tried by a special military tribunal. He concluded the incident had proved that Chile's "armed forces do not accept indiscipline. The people do not tolerate coups."

Frei ordered the dismissal of Defense Minister Gen. Tulio Marambio Oct. 22. He was replaced by Sergio Ossa Pretot, until then minister of public works and transportation. Defense Minister Ossa indicated Oct. 23 that President Frei would ask Congress for authorization to increase military salaries. Gen. Sergio Castillo Aranguiz resigned as army commander in chief Oct. 24; he was replaced by Gen. Rene Schneider Chevreau.

President Frei announced Oct. 23 that the state of siege would be lifted the next day and that censorship of news reports would be ended.

Viaux was sentenced Dec. 15 by a military court to 18 months in exile for his role in the October rebellion. Six other officers were also found guilty and were sentenced to 41 days military arrest.

Background developments—Among the events that apparently influenced the uprising:

Gen. Viaux had been retired as commander of the First Division in early October after he had sent a letter to President Frei complaining of low pay scales and morale in the armed services. He pointed out that a beginning copper miner earned $250 a month, more than an army colonel with 25 years' service ($240 a month).

Viaux's dismissal sparked a protest letter by officers in his division demanding his reinstatement. Newspapers then picked up the Viaux story and began to report widespread unrest in the army. This in turn led to a government crackdown on the press. Police Oct. 17 confiscated editions of El Diario Ilustrado and held up editions of El Mercurio, both of Santiago. Editions of La Segunda, a Santiago evening paper, were seized Oct. 17, and the paper's editor, Mario Carneyro Castro, was arrested on charges of internal security violation.

Earlier rumors of an impending revolt in the army had been reported by the Miami Herald Sept. 27 and 29. The Herald cited Chilean news reports of Sept. 25, which stated that Major Marshall had been arrested for arriving late with his battalion for ceremonies held Sept. 18 in celebration of Chile's Independence Day.

Military Unrest Continues. President Eduardo Frei Montalva imposed a state of emergency on Santiago Province Nov. 19, following continued rumors of military plots against the ruling Christian Democratic government. The decree, ordered to counter an "active campaign of rumors designed to create a climate of insecurity and alarm to disturb the institutional order," authorized the government to impose press censorship and to make arrests without a warrant.

Further security measures were ordered within the armed forces and other strategic institutions in Santiago Dec. 7, and some army units were reinforced. In a statement Dec. 9, Army Commander in Chief Rene Schneider explained that seven officers had held secret meetings "related to a supposed movement or coup that was being prepared elsewhere and that had to be anticipated" in order to act first. The meetings also discussed protection of Viaux in light of rumors of kidnaping or other action against him.

The Chilean National Conference of Bishops, in response to the coup rumors

Dec. 13, asserted that the armed forces "institutions are called upon to integrate themselves in the common effort of the nation without defining by themselves what is the common good or becoming organisms of political decision. . . . " "We sincerely believe," the bishops asserted, "that a change of regime, forcefully imposed by minority groups, would only bring new evils to the country."

Economic Developments

Foreign Loans & Trade. Among developments of 1969:

The Chilean Development Corporation (CORFO) reported Jan. 20 that it had completed negotiations with West Germany's Kreditanstalt fur Wiederaufbau for loans totalling $7.5 million. (Chile was reported to have received about $200 million in loans from West Germany since 1962.)

CORFO reported Feb. 19 that Carlos Massad, Chilean Central Bank president, had announced that the 1968 balance of payments had attained a surplus of $135 million, the highest ever recorded in Chile's history. A favorable world copper market and the government's copper marketing policy contributed to the surplus.

The Bank of London and South America Review reported in April that Chilean reserves had reached a record level of $200 million by the end of 1968.

The InterAmerican Development Bank announced April 10 that it had extended a loan of some $20 million to assist a farm development project benefiting 29,700 rural families in central Chile. The project called for development of arable land and investment in machinery, livestock and infrastructure projects. Involving a total outlay of $74.7 million to be administered by the Corporation of Agrarian Reform, the project would provide jobs for more than 17,000 farm laborers. The land was to be devoted to cereals, vegetables, field crops, fruit trees, forage and livestock.

Recent trade negotiations with the Soviet Union resulted in agreements for U.S.S.R. purchase of Chilean agar-agar, iodine and unprocessed wool and Chilean purchase of Soviet olive oil, machinery and possibly railroad equipment, the Chilean Development Corporation newsletter reported Sept. 15.

Rumania and Chile signed an agreement providing for joint exploitation of Chilean deposits of non-ferrous metals, the Chilean embassy bulletin News from Chile reported Oct. 20. The two countries formed a joint company to carry out the agreement.

The Chilean Development Corp. reported in May 1970 that exports in 1969 had risen to $1.1 billion from $904.3 million in 1968, while imports had risen to $911.5 million from $801.6 million in 1968. The Corporation had reported April 13 that Chile's large, small and medium-scale copper mining concerns in 1969 had produced 756,600 tons or 14.3% of the total world production of primary copper.

Effects of Drought. Addressing the nation on the consequences of the 1968 drought, President Frei asserted that more than 90% of the nation's irrigated land had been affected and that the most productive regions had been the hardest hit (Le Monde report April 10). The drought was reported to have been the worst in Chile in 119 years.

Frei said that the drought had also affected electricity production, transportation, mining, and industrial and commercial activities. (The journal Latin America reported April 11 that electricity was available only 13 hours per day.) Frei added that "an additional 30 or 40 million dollars of foodstuffs which the country has been unable to raise, must be imported."

The Washington Post March 16 cited a Los Angeles Times report that rainfall deficits in 1968 had ranged from 100% at the northern edge of the Chilean drought zone to 52% at the southern edge. Santiago Province, the nation's leading agricultural section, reported 2.75 inches of rain in 1968, 81% below normal. The Times of the Americas, published in Miami, reported April 16 that the Chilean Meteorological Agency had predicted "a seriously low water year" for 1969.

The Bank of London and South America Review reported in its March issue that the drought had cut 1968 agricultural production to 10% below the 1967 level. Production of maize fell by 63% and rice by 45%. About 28,000 head of cattle were reported lost. But the area sown to wheat fell only by 6%, and production of rye and lentils actually rose 49% and 180%, respectively.

The New York Times reported May 25 that the drought apparently had ended. Rain was falling in the central valleys, and the Andes mountains were already covered with snow. The drought had caused estimated losses of $68.3 million to livestock and crops, the Bank of London and South America reported in its May review. In addition, it had forced the country to leave 180,000 hectares of land uncultivated and to spend $46.9 million on recovery projects.

'Chileanization' of Copper Firms Set. In his annual state-of-the-nation address to Congress May 21, President Frei said he planned to seek extended Chileanization of the nation's foreign-owned copper firms along with acquisition of a larger share of the firms' earnings.

Nationalization of copper operations was a major political issue in Chile, and Frei had been elected in 1964 on a platform that included increased Chilean participation in copper profits.

Advocating Chileanization—or part ownership—rather than outright nationalization, Frei asserted that the plan "enjoys prestige abroad, and allows for the easy financing of development plans, while conforming to our possibilities." He added that Chileanization also "prevents serious domestic and foreign problems and allows the country to advance, without creating uncalled for tensions and conflicts, through a Chilean formula that might lead to full ownership." (Left-wing Christian Democrats and Chile's Marxist parties had been pressing for outright nationalization of foreign-owned copper mines.)

Frei declared that while the government could achieve Chileanization through existing legislation, an agreement would have to be reached with the companies concerned, "since you cannot compel anybody to become your partner." Referring to the high profits currently earned by copper producers, Frei said he would introduce legislation "to increase the state's participation in the higher prices of copper prevailing in the world market."

Frei praised the contributions of the copper firms to Chile's economic development. Copper currently accounted for more than 65% of the nation's exports; Chile's output, the world's fourth largest, reached about $780 million in 1968.

Anaconda Co. and Kennecott Corp., the two major copper producers in Chile, would be directly affected by the Frei plan. Chuquicamata, the world's largest open-pit copper mine, and the El Salvador mine were both wholly owned by Anaconda subsidiaries, and the Chilean government held a 25% interest in a new Anaconda mine, Exotica, which was to become operative in 1970. In a news conference following Frei's speech, Finance Minister Andres Zaldivar indicated that the government would seek at most a 51% interest in the Chuquicamata and El Salvador mines. The other major mining property in Chile was the El Teniente mine, the world's largest underground copper operation, Chileanized in 1967 through an agreement with its owner, Kennecott. Under the agreement, Chile gained 51% ownership of the mine and Kennecott retained 49%. The government also held a 30% interest in a smaller mine, Rio Blanco, controlled by Cerro Corp.

Anaconda's chief executive official, C. Jay Parkinson, said at the company's annual meeting in Montana May 21 that he had recently informed Frei of the company's preparation "to undertake immediate studies of the matters he has presented to us and to discuss certain procedures to meet at least in part the government's desire for greater participation in the present high price of copper."

The current tax arrangement between Anaconda and the Chilean government had been negotiated in 1967 and was scheduled to run for 20 years. Both Anaconda and Kennecott were currently involved in major expansion programs in Chile. Anaconda obtained more than two thirds of its copper and more than half its total income from its mines in Chile, while Kennecott's operations in Chile accounted for less than one-third of its worldwide copper production and only about one-fifth of its total earnings.

Government officials and Anaconda executives opened negotiations June 2 on Chileanization of the company's operations.

Anaconda pact—President Frei announced June 26 that his government and the Anaconda Co. had agreed on a plan for the "negotiated and progressive" nationalization of the company's major copper mines in the country. The agreement, the biggest undertaking of its kind in Latin America, provided for a gradual government takeover of the Chuquicamata and El Salvador mines and the Potrerillos processing plant, with full Chilean ownership to result before the end of 1981.

Going beyond Frei's "Chileanization" program for copper, the plan provided for the Anaconda Co. to transfer all of the assets and liabilities of Anaconda's two wholly-owned subsidiaries—the Chile Exploration Co., operating the Chuquicamata mine, and the Andes Copper Mining Co., operating the El Salvador mine—to two new mining companies Jan. 1, 1970. The government at this point would purchase 51% of the stock of the two new companies, the purchase price to be calculated from a December 1968 assessment of slightly less than $200 million. The price would be payable, with tax-free interest at 6% per year, in U.S. dollar-bonds in semi-annual installments over a 12-year period to begin Jan. 1, 1970. Chile was to begin participating in the profits of the companies Sept. 1, 1969. The remaining shares of the two new companies (49%) would be purchased after Chile had completed payment on 60% of the first 51% of the shares, with the purchase price calculated from the companies' average net earnings.

In addition, the agreement established a new tax schedule, retroactive to June 1, 1969, whereby the two companies would receive additional and increasing income from the sale of copper as the world copper price went above 40¢ a pound. (The world copper price had risen from 31¢ a pound in 1964 to about 63¢ in 1969.)

President Frei, in a national broadcast June 26, called the agreement "a reality today which has been achieved within a legal framework and by means of a respectable negotiation." He explained that a "nationalization process undertaken unilaterally or in a contentious way would have meant serious restrictions with respect to availability of credits or foreign investments indispensable for the development of the country."

The Anaconda Co. in New York issued a statement June 26 explaining that the board of directors had recommended the plan "in order to avoid expropriation by the government of Chile through legislation." The statement noted that the agreement was "subject to corporate legal requirements and stockholder approval" of the two subsidiary companies involved.

(Chilean Minister of Mining Alejandro Hales set the estimated cost to Chile for the nationalization of the Chuquicamata and El Salvador mines at between $600 million and $650 million over a period of 12 to 24 years, the Wall Street Journal reported July 8. Independent mining sources had placed the total value of the mines, excluding the copper ore, at between $700 million and $1 billion.)

Since negotiations with Anaconda had begun June 2, two bills demanding outright expropriation of the firm's operations had been introduced in Congress. (The Socialist and Communist parties, stressing that the accord was contrary to national interest, maintained that Congressional approval was necessary and announced that they would oppose the plan, Le Monde of Paris reported July 2.)

Kennecott agreement—Mining Minister Alejandro Hales announced an agreement with Kennecott Copper Corp. allowing Chile a larger share of profits from Kennecott's El Teniente mine, the Wall Street Journal reported Oct. 6. Under the plan, Kennecott agreed to grant Chile a larger share of the income from sales of copper at more than 40 cents per pound. Hales explained that

the plan would increase Chile's total receipts from 72.6% to 91.8% of the mine's profits. The price-level agreement was similar to that reached in June with Anaconda Co.

Hales also announced that Chile would complete within a few days payment of $80 million for its 51% interest in El Teniente (under a 1965 agreement allowing Kennecott to keep 49%) as well as its $23.7 million share of the mine's expansion program. After receiving the payments, Kennecott Dec. 12 officially handed over to the Chilean government 51% of its shares in El Teniente.

(About 8,600 El Teniente workers struck Oct. 3, after rejecting a 45% wage increase offer; they were demanding a 70% increase plus other benefits. Following government mediation, the dispute was settled Oct. 7 when the miners accepted the 45% wage increase, fringe benefits and a $150 return-to-work bonus.)

1970 Budget. The government presented a budget of 17.5 billion escudos ($1.6 billion) to the National Congress, the Chilean Development Corporation reported Sept. 15 in its newsletter Chile: Economic Notes. The total, a 30% increase over the 1969 budget, included increased expenditures from wage readjustments, higher service on Chile's external debt and outlays for social benefits. According to the publication Latin America Sept. 5, the 1970 budget decreased the allocations for housing, education, health, agrarian reform and industrialization.

Salary Increases. The government announced a 28% salary increase in the private and public sectors, starting Jan. 1, 1970. The increase was determined by the 28% increase in the cost of living during 1969. (Wage increases ranging from 20–80% for the military had gone into effect Nov. 20.)

(Chile's cost of living had increased by 27.9% in 1968. The Bank of London & South America reported in its September Review that Economy Minister Enrique Krauss recently had announced an anti-inflation program that included a freeze on most prices for the remainder of 1969, a cut in government expenditure, encouragement of exports and restrictions on credits and liquidity.)

Other Developments

Assembly of Bishops. Concluding a plenary assembly in Santiago Aug. 7, Chilean bishops published a document analyzing the role of Roman Catholics in the political and social life of Chile. The declaration affirmed the wish of Catholics for "profound social transformation in order to end injustice, cultural and economic barriers [and] inadequate profits that pull our country from its natural riches." Praising the "sharp sensitivity" of certain radical priests and Catholics, the bishops warned that the evolution of their ideas carried both "a promise and a risk." On birth control, the bishops expressed "their disagreement with the national health service's campaign for contraception" and stressed that they upheld entirely the terms of Pope Paul VI's encyclical Humanae Vitae, which excluded contraceptives.

Student Riots. A wave of student violence spread across the country in early September, Le Monde reported Sept. 7. Many persons were reported wounded and at least one killed in the disorders, which hit Santiago, Valparaiso, Talcahuano and Copiapo. The London publication Latin America reported Sept. 19 that Atacama Province, in which Copiapo is located, was declared an emergency zone by the government. Government officials accused the Revolutionary Movement of the Left (MIR) of fanning the unrest.

Andean Trade Pact Signed. Five South American nations signed a Subregional Andean Pact May 26, formally establishing the Andean Common Market. The treaty was signed in Bogota by Bolivia, Chile, Colombia, Ecuador and Peru. A sixth Andean nation, Venezuela, had taken part in the 33 months of negotiations that preceded the treaty, but withdrew during the last week of discussions; the pact, however, provided an 18-month grace period during which Venezuela could join as a founding member.

The Andean bloc, a subregional group within the Latin American Free Trade Association (LAFTA), agreed in the pact to abolish all internal tariffs among the five states by 1980 and to establish a common tariff scale for the bloc's foreign trade. Three product lists, to be drawn up by 1970, were to set the content of Andean trade. Members were allowed to exclude certain products from those included in the tariff exemption plans—Chile and Colombia each had the right to designate 250 exempt items; Bolivia and Ecuador, 350; and Peru, 419.

Foreign Agreements. Among developments in Chile's foreign relations during 1969:

Chile and Hungary ratified a 1967 agreement on cultural and technical-scientific cooperation Oct. 27.

The Chilean embassy bulletin reported Nov. 3 that Chile had agreed to purchase an atomic reactor from Great Britain.

The Miami Herald reported Nov. 14 that Chile had recently purchased two submarines, two small auxiliary ships and modern army equipment from Great Britain.

Constitutional Reform. A controversial bill reforming Chile's 44-year-old constitution was approved 114–79 by the Chilean Congress Dec. 29. The bill's provisions included an extension of executive powers, particularly in financial matters, and a lowering of the voting age to 18. The reforms were scheduled to go into effect Nov. 4, 1970, when the new president assumed office.

1970: Allende Becomes President

Frei Regime's Final 10 Months

Salvador Allende Gossens became president of Chile in November 1970. He was the first candidate running on a Marxist platform to be elected president of a non-Communist country in a democratically held election.

During the first 10 months of 1970, Chile was ruled by the Frei regime, which had been inaugurated in November 1964.

State of nation address. President Eduardo Frei Montalva delivered his final state of the nation address May 21 and gave an assessment of his six-year administration. Stressing that the nation currently had a choice between democracy or authoritarianism, Frei said: "I am convinced that violence cannot dominate in Chile, but we have to choose between a discipline established by law and the will of all and a state of force."

Outlining the accomplishments of his government, Frei pointed out that education had been given first priority with construction of 3,000 new schools, the increase of compulsory education from six years to eight and a decrease in illiteracy from 16.4% in 1964 to 11% in 1969.

Frei noted that under the land reform program, 1,224 farms with an area of 3.2 million hectares, had been expropriated to benefit 150,000 people. (In a development related to land reform, Herman Mery, the head of the government agrarian reform institute in Linares Province, was killed April 30 in an incident involving proprietors of an estate that had been expropriated. President Frei attended the victim's funeral, and both houses of the National Congress held debates on the incident.)

Frei's speech included reports that the Gross Domestic Product showed an average annual increase of more than 5% from 1965–1969, and that balance of payments for the same five-year period registered an average annual surplus of $101 million, with a $182 million surplus recorded in 1969. In addition, the Central Bank's international monetary reserves increased from $114 million in 1964 to $480 million in 1969.

Strikes & violence. The regime had called in troops and imposed a state of emergency in Nuble Province Jan. 31 in an effort to check a farm workers' strike. Workers in the area, about 250 miles south of Santiago, seized and barricaded nine ranches following a strike by about 6,000 farm laborers from 200 farms. The strikers were protesting "very poor" working conditions and demanded immediate expropriation and redistribution of some of the larger farms and ranches. The laborers returned to work Feb. 2, ending the strike.

27

■The Central Workers Movement (CUT) staged a one-day strike July 8 in an effort to press demands for salary increases and improved working conditions. One student was killed in street violence which erupted in Santiago. The government had declared the strike "illegal" and of "clear political significance" in light of the presidential elections Sept. 4.

Anti-government plots denounced. The army announced April 29 that two officers and 14 enlisted men had been dismissed for participation in "extra-institutional activities" connected with a "clandestine civilian movement." Although the clandestine group was not identified, reports indicated that it concerned the Movement of the Revolutionary Left.

President Frei had revealed an abortive plot against the government by a right-wing group March 25. Eleven men, including a retired general, Horacio Gamboa, were reported arrested in connection with a plan to kidnap high government officials and overthrow the Frei regime. A military court found Gamboa and two other retired officers guilty of conspiracy March 30.

Economic Developments

Anaconda nationalization. The first of two stages in the "negotiated nationalization" of Anaconda Co. subsidiaries in Chile went into effect Jan. 1, 1970.

Substantially all the assets of the two Anaconda subsidiaries that had operated the Chuquicamata and El Salvador mines —the Chile Exploration Co. and the Andes Copper Mining Co.—were transferred to two newly-created Chilean firms—the Compania de Cobre Chuquicamata S.A. and Compania de Cobre Salvador S.A. The Anaconda subsidiaries in turn received 49% of the stock of each of the two new firms, while the government's Copper Corp. of Chile (CODELCO) received the other 51%. CODELCO made a payment of $174.5 million in promissory notes to the Anaconda subsidiaries for its 51% interest.

Anaconda announced Feb. 24 that a "condition of force majeure" had been declared at the Chuquicamata and El Salvador mines, authorizing the violation of sales and delivery contracts due to situations beyond the control or anticipation of the concerned companies.

Pointing out that scheduled copper deliveries would be cut by about 40% during March, Anaconda Chairman C. Jay Parkinson explained that the dislocations in the mines "would have occurred under any ownership" and were "not in any way related" to the company's agreement with the Chilean government.

Parkinson had said Feb. 9 that the mining properties of Anaconda's subsidiary Santiago Mining Co., in operation in Chile since 1916, had been sold in December 1969 to a group of private Chilean investors.

Parkinson also announced Feb. 9 that initial stripping of the Exotica mine (owned 75% by Anaconda and 25% by Chile) was "essentially complete . . . and operations are expected to start in mid-1970 at an annual rate of 225 million pounds (112,500 tons) of copper."

Frei inaugurated the Exotica copper mine July 4.

Mining. Among other mining developments of 1970:

The International Finance Corporation (IFC) announced Feb. 10 that it was joining Chilean, Japanese and U.S. interests in financing a $32.5 million copper mining project in northern Chile. The new venture, to be known as Minera Sagasca S.A. (Sagasca), was sponsored by Continental Copper and Steel Industries, Inc. of New York (the major shareholder with a 58% interest in the venture), the Chilean government copper agency Codelco, and the IFC. IFC's investment in the venture totaled $10.9 million, while Continental was to provide $9 million and Codelco $3.5 million. In addition, Dowa Mining Co. Ltd. of Japan extended a $10 million loan to Sagasca and pledged to purchase at least half of the mine's output for the first six years of operation.

Chile and Rumania announced Feb. 25 that they had agreed to form a mixed commission to formulate plans to explore and exploit Chile's mineral resources.

President Frei inaugurated the Rio Blanco copper mine July 25, 10 months ahead of schedule. The $157 million project was expected to produce concentrates containing 65,000 short tons of copper a year. The Rio Blanco mine was constructed and was to be operated by Compania Minera Andina, S.A., which was owned 30% by the Chilean state copper agency Codelco and 70% by Cerro Corp.

Other events. The government lifted import curbs from all items except luxury goods, electronic equipment and automotive components, the Journal of Commerce reported Jan. 9. The action was designed to increase competition with foreign industries.

The government statistical office reported that the cost of living in Chile had increased 29.3% during 1969, compared with 27.9% in 1968, the Miami Herald reported Jan. 11.

The World Bank announced approval April 29 of a $10.8 million loan for the construction or improvement of four sections of national highways. The four sections, totaling about 103 miles, were scheduled for completion by 1973 at a cost of $23.8 million.

President Frei Aug. 11 authorized the government to buy, for $81.3 million, Boise Cascade Corp.'s share of Chilectra, the nation's largest privately owned electric power company, which supplied 27% of Chile's power needs. Boise Cascade held about 75% of Chilectra's stock through its subsidiary South American Power.

Foreign Affairs

Cuban relations discussed. Foreign Minister Gabriel Valdes confirmed Jan. 27 that Chile was discussing with other hemispheric governments renewal of diplomatic and trade relations with Cuba. "Whether Cuba belongs or does not belong to the Organization of American States is its own affair," he said, "but we believe that the widest possible continental unity is worthwhile." He added that even Venezuela, formerly a strict anti-Cuba adherent, was participating in the discussions. La Nacion, a Santiago newspaper that usually reflected the views of the Chilean government, had published an editorial Jan. 25 calling for a resumption of relations between Chile and Cuba.

Rafael Moreno, vice president of the Chilean Agrarian Reform Corp., announced Feb. 20 that Chile had agreed to sell $11 million worth of foodstuffs to Cuba. Moreno explained that $3 million worth of garlic, beans and onions would be delivered in 1970 and another $8 million worth of foodstuffs in 1971.

The Chilean action presumably ruptured the trade embargo imposed against Cuba by the Organization of American States in 1964. All OAS members except Mexico were reported to have complied with the embargo, which stipulated that "the governments of the American States suspend all their trade whether direct or indirect with Cuba excepting foodstuffs, medicines and medical equipment that may be sent to Cuba for humanitarian reasons."

Chilean and Cuban officials in Havana signed an agreement to exchange TV news programs between the Cuban Broadcasting Institute and the television channel of the Catholic University of Chile, the New York Times reported Aug. 8.

A Cuban trade delegation visited Chile July 10-17; the group was invited by a subdivision of the Chilean agrarian reform organization.

Soviet relations. The Alliance for Progress newsletter reported Feb. 2 that a 1967 Soviet credit of $15 million to Chile for the purchase of machinery and equipment was followed by an exchange of trade delegations, Chilean sale of wool to the U.S.S.R., and plans for Chilean sale of seafood, wines, textiles and footwear.

Chile and the U.S.S.R. signed their first cultural and scientific cooperation accord Feb. 16. Calling the agreement "a bridge across Chilean and Soviet young people," Chilean Education Minister Maximo Pacheco Gomez explained that the pact included Soviet aid in construction of an astral observatory in the northern Andes mountains.

200-mile sea limits. Chile and eight other Latin American nations claiming 200-mile territorial sea limits upheld May 9 the right of all maritime states to "establish the limits of their sovereignty and maritime jurisdiction, in accordance with their geographical and geological characteristics. . . ." Meeting in Montevideo, Uruguay May 4–9, the participants adopted the Declaration of Montevideo on Sea Rights. The statement was signed by Argentina, Brazil, Chile, Ecuador, El Salvador, Nicaragua, Panama, Peru and Uruguay.

In addition to upholding the 200-mile sea limit, the declaration also affirmed "the right of maritime countries to dispose of the natural resources of the sea adjacent to their coast and the floor and sub-floor of the same sea, in order to promote the maximum development of their economies and raise the living standard of their peoples." The statement also asserted the right "to explore, conserve and exploit the living resources" in territorial waters "and to regulate the management of fishing and aquatic hunting."

Fishing meeting inconclusive. Chile, Ecuador, Peru and the U.S. held a 13-day meeting on fishing rights without reaching agreement on outstanding disputes, the Wall Street Journal reported Sept. 25. Delegates to the session, held in Buenos Aires, reported some progress. The four nations agreed to meet again before July 31, 1971.

U.S. delegate Donald L. McKernan noted that while there had been 16 incidents involving U.S. boats which had violated the territorial waters of Chile, Ecuador and Peru in 1969, there had been only four so far in 1970. He added: "None of these three Latin American countries has asked the U.S. to modify its jurisdictional principles, and our country hasn't asked them to do the same, but I still think we will be able to reach an accord."

Trade & transport steps. Trade on 175 items between Chile, Colombia and Peru was freed from tariff and other restrictions in April, the Alliance for Progress Newsletter reported May 25. The three Andean nations took action as the Andean Group pact officially came into force April 15.

Public works and transport ministers of Argentina, Bolivia, Brazil, Chile, Paraguay and Uruguay concluded a two-day meeting in Montevideo June 5 with an agreement to accelerate development of inter-connections of Latin transportation systems. The ministers agreed to meet annually to discuss regional transportation problems.

Presidential Campaign

Allende named presidential candidate. Following several months of debate, the five left parties constituting the Popular Unity Movement chose Sen. Salvador Allende Gossens Jan. 22, 1970 as their presidential candidate.

Allende's nomination had been assured when the other four contenders— Jacques Chonchol of the Movement of Unified Popular Action, Alberto Baltra of the Radical Party, Pablo Neruda of the Communist Party and Rafael Tarud of the Popular Independent Alliance— withdrew.

Pre-election violence. Two students were killed in Puente Alto June 26 as sporadic street violence broke out in major cities. More than 100 students were reported arrested, while about 20 police and several dozen students were injured.

The violence in Puente Alto, 15 miles from Santiago, erupted during a student demonstration in support of a strike by administrative personnel at a trade school in the town.

The government June 26 blamed the violence on the Movement of the Revolutionary Left (MIR) and certain members of the Chilean Socialist Party and claimed that they had been supported in this and other attacks, bank robberies, etc. by outside elements in an attempt to disrupt the electoral process.

∎In pre-election violence Aug. 28, one man was killed and 100 others reported injured in clashes between supporters of presidential candidates Jorge Alessandri and Radomiro Tomic. The clash brought the eight-month campaign total to six dead and more than 200 injured, according to the Miami Herald Aug. 29.

Allende Elected President

Allende wins plurality. Allende won a plurality of votes in the presidential election Sept. 4, 1970.

According to official totals announced Sept. 5, Allende polled 36.3% of the ballots with 1,075,616 votes, while his nearest competitor, former President Jorge Alessandri Rodriguez, the candidate of the right, won 1,036,278 votes or 34.9%. Radomiro Tomic Romero, the candidate of the ruling Christian Democratic party, polled 824,849 votes or 27.8%; he conceded late Sept. 4. Slightly more than 16.3% of the electorate abstained from voting.

Under Chilean law, the choice between the two top contenders in the presidential election was to be thrown to the bicameral Congress if none of the candidates received an absolute majority of votes. Congress—with 80 seats controlled by Allende supporters, 75 by Christian Democrats, and 45 by Alessandri backers—was scheduled to meet in joint session Oct. 24.

Allende, supported by a coalition group including the Socialist and Communist parties, had based his campaign on an "anti-oligarchic" and "anti-imperialist" program, which pledged nationalization of major foreign and private firms in mining, banking and communications. He also advocated the dissolution of the present bicameral Congress in favor of a "people's assembly," a revision of the judiciary system, as well as a strong program of agrarian reform. Allende was among the founders of the Chilean Socialist party in 1933. A medical doctor, he had served as health minister under President Pedro Aguirre Cerda in the early 1940s. He also served

in Congress as a deputy, a senator and then as president of the Senate. He had run unsuccessfully for president in 1952, 1958 and 1964.

Alessandri, 74, officially running as an independent but supported by the right-wing Nationalist party and other rightist groups, was the son of a Chilean president and was himself president of the country from 1958 to 1964. He was the only one of the three candidates to pledge support of the capitalist system of government and favored moderate reforms within the traditional constitutional framework. He based his campaign on an appeal for law and order.

Tomic, who helped found the Christian Democratic party in 1938 (known then as the National Falange), ran a middle-of-the-road campaign, rejecting both capitalism and Marxism as solutions to Chilean development. However, he took a stance that was to the left of President Frei's current program of social reforms.

In a press conference Sept. 5, Allende hailed his victory and pledged to enact the Socialist program adopted by the left-wing coalition supporting him. He asserted that he would "never" favor a one-party system in Chile but reiterated his intention to establish diplomatic and trade relations with all nations, including Cuba, North Vietnam, North Korea, Communist China and East Germany. He added that he favored retention of Chilean membership in the Organization of American States "so as not to renounce an important international tribunal." He also said that he would seek the rescheduling of Chile's $800 million outstanding debt to the U.S.

In a statement issued Sept. 6, Alessandri supporters indicated that they would not accept Allende's victory. The statement, signed by the Nationalist party and other right-wing groups, said: "We appeal to democratic forces, to their representatives and to the free men and women of Chile, who make up the immense majority, to unite to defend the constitutional right to designate the president of the country." Alessandri, who had said during the campaign that he would recognize as president the candidate who polled the most votes in the general election Sept. 4, did not sign the statement.

Alessandri announced Sept. 9 that he would resign if elected president by the Congress Oct. 24. Alessandri said: "In case I am elected by the Congress, I would resign, which would mean a new election. I state now in categorical terms that I would not participate in it for any reason."

The leadership of the Christian Democratic party Sept. 7 rejected a suggestion by Alessandri supporters that they block Allende's election in Congress Oct. 24.

Christian Democratic party President Benjamin Pardo declared Sept. 11 that Allende could count on the support of the Christian Democrats in Congress Oct. 24 if he "grants the necessary [democratic] guarantees in a real and effective manner." Pardo stressed that the governing party was "interested in . . . the survival of a pluralistic society, politically, socially and culturally."

The conservative daily El Mercurio and the lawyers' organization Patria y Libertad published a joint editorial Sept. 11 supporting another election in which the electorate would have a clear choice between a Marxist and a non-Marxist candidate.

Election aftermath. Allende Sept. 9 appealed for calm and confidence in counteracting what he described as a "wave of economic terror" in Chile. He accused right-wing sectors opposed to his election of provoking economic insecurity.

Bank withdrawals, which had been heavy Sept. 7, decreased Sept. 8, and the government moved Sept. 9 to assure Chileans of the continued "normality" of the economy. Finance Minister Andres Zaldivar said Sept. 9 that the government had printed new money to meet any demands and assured depositors "that they will be able to make their withdrawals." The stock market, closed Sept. 7, reopened Sept. 8 to slow trading and depressed prices, but there appeared to be a wait-and-see atmosphere.

Allende charged Sept. 12 that a group was plotting to assassinate him. He said he could name those involved. A Santi-

ago radio station had said Sept. 11 that an attempt had been made against Allende's life, but Juan Achurra, undersecretary of the interior, denied the report.

Speaking at a rally in Santiago Sept. 13, Allende warned that the nation would be paralyzed by resistance if Congress failed to confirm him as president. Although urging calm, Allende said that if he was not the next president the "country will stop." He added: "Workers will occupy factories, peasants will occupy the land and civil servants will occupy their offices."

Among later developments following the Sept. 4 elections:

■ Sporadic bombings rocked Santiago Sept. 26–Oct. 8. Among the targets were two Chilean-owned supermarkets Sept. 26, a bank and the stock exchange Oct. 3, the home of a right-wing congressman and a bank Oct. 4, and the Ford Motor Co. offices Oct. 8. Supporters of the rightist presidential candidate Jorge Alessandri blamed the bombings on left-wing terrorist groups, while Allende supporters blamed the violence on clandestine right-wing groups.

■ Finance Minister Andres Zaldivar said Sept. 23 that Chile had moved from economic expansion to near-recession following the presidential elections. Speaking to a nationwide audience, Zaldivar said that "economic and psychological factors have created an emergency situation in recent weeks" in which sales of durable goods had dropped to between 50% and 80% and other sales were off about 30%. The first evidence of trouble after Sept. 4, Zaldivar explained, was a run on banks and savings associations from which $90 million in deposits had been withdrawn between Sept. 4 and 17. The Central Bank had been forced to use its funds to keep money flowing through the banks and the government had printed an additional 340 million escudos.

The Central Bank Oct. 16 curbed the sale of dollars to Chileans traveling abroad. Central Bank President Carlos Massas explained that about $43 million had been sold to Chileans for foreign travel since the election and that this amount was twice as much as had been sold the previous month.

(The New York Times reported Oct. 18 that the cost of living in Chile had risen another 2.7% in September. The total rise for the first nine months of 1970 was more than 32%.)

■ Senior U.S. officials, briefing Midwest editors in Chicago Sept. 16, expressed fear that a Communist regime in Chile could threaten Argentina, Peru and Bolivia. The briefing, the transcript of which was made available Sept. 19, was the first public statement by the Nixon Administration on the Allende victory.

Allende explains program. Allende pledged Sept. 30 that his new government would be "a multi-party government, a nationalist, popular, democratic and revolutionary government that will move toward socialism." In an interview published by the New York Times Oct. 4, Allende explained that he was not going "to establish a Socialist regime tomorrow. Socialism cannot be imposed by decree. It is a developing social process."

Among the responses Allende made to previously-submitted questions:

". . . we can and we must use the excess that our nation's economy produces, which today leaves the country or stays in the hands of monopolies, to create the state area of the economy that will rule over the rest of national economic development. Our program establishes three areas: a state area, a mixed area for private and state capital and a private area."

". . . we must recover our basic resources that are in the hands of foreign capital, essentially American—copper, iron ore, nitrates, which are in your hands, the hands of American monopolies. Then we must nationalize the monopolies that influence the social and economic development of the country. To this we must add a serious wide-ranging profound agrarian reform, the nationalization of banking and state control over foreign trade."

"We are not going to imitate either the Soviet Union or Cuba or China. We are going to look for our own way, and in accordance with that reality we will take the necessary steps to assure the widest

possible satisfaction of the essential needs of Chilean men and women."

"There will be no predominance of either the Communist party or the Socialist party, which are both Marxist parties. I am a founder of the Socialist party, and I must tell you that I am not totalitarian. On the contrary, I think socialism frees man. The program of Popular Unity is not a Communist program, nor is it a Socialist program. . . ."

"We have said that we are going to expropriate those investments that fundamentally and essentially influence national economic development."

". . . So far as foreign investment is concerned, we will adhere to the proposed agreement within the Andean Pact."

"We do not want to usurp anything from anyone manu militari—that is, by force. Rather we want to nationalize in accordance with Chilean law, examining each case separately and indemnifying in accord with what this examination determines and in accordance with our laws."

"Our aim is not to isolate Chile. On the contrary, our aim is to tie Chile to all the countries in the world, seeking in the commercial field Chile's best interests."

"In the political field, the only thing we really want is our absolute independence. We are supporters of self-determination and nonintervention."

"We want to increase our cultural and commercial relations with the United States, but we want to have the right to open relations with Cuba."

"I believe that the [Roman Catholic] church will not be a factor against the Popular Unity government. On the contrary, they are going to be a factor in our favor, because we are going to try to make a reality out of Christian thought. Furthermore, there will be the widest religious pluralism."

"We have said many times that we have no political agreement or understanding with the M.I.R. [the Revolutionary Movement of the Left]. The tactics that they have set, and do set, for themselves are strictly their own responsibility."

"As for the people of the right, I believe that there is a sector linked to imperialist interests that will be ready to use any means whatever. Among these means are violence, economic chaos or an assassination attempt. We will answer reactionary violence with revolutionary violence, but that will be an answer. If others unleash violence, we will answer with violence, but we are not going to unleash violence. We reject terrorism on principle, by our very ideology, by conviction and also out of a humanitarian spirit."

Party accord assures Allende victory. The Christian Democratic party and the leftist coalition Popular Unity group agreed Oct. 9 on a program of constitutional reforms and thus virtually assured Allende of the necessary vote in Congress to make him president.

Allende, backed by 80 votes in the bicameral Congress, needed the support of the 75 Christian Democratic seats in order to achieve a majority and gain the presidency. The Christian Democrats had agreed Oct. 4 to support Allende if he would agree to certain democratic guarantees and constitutional reforms under his leftist government.

The package of constitutional amendments, sent to Congress Oct. 9, guaranteed the right of free association in political parties, which in turn were granted equal access to state-controlled communications media. The proposals provided for the right of private, nonprofit education supported by state funds, if necessary, and free from political interference in admissions, texts, teacher appointments and curriculum.

The section referring to the armed forces prohibited the formation of private militias or the appointment of police or military officers without education in technical academies. In addition, only Congress would be authorized to change the strength of the armed forces or the national police. (The Christian Democrats had sought unsuccessfully to limit Allende's freedom to choose subordinate armed forces and national police officers.)

The constitutional amendments had to be approved by each house of Congress separately, then wait for 60 days before being submitted to a joint session of Congress for approval. Presidential signature and promulgation would follow. Thus, the reforms would come into effect considerably after the Nov. 4 swearing in of the new president.

Alessandri withdraws. Presidential candidate Jorge Alessandri Rodriguez Oct. 19 requested his supporters in Congress not to vote for him in the runoff election for president.

In a statement released Oct. 19, Alessandri explained that his withdrawal from the congressional election would "contribute to Dr. Salvador Allende's assuming the supreme command in a climate of greater tranquility that will strengthen confidence so that the country's economic activity will recover." Alessandri also extended his "best wishes for success . . . to the next president of Chile, whose long and proven democratic conviction, reflected in attitudes of constant respect for the constitution and the laws, is well known."

Schneider slain. Gen. Rene Schneider Chereau, commander in chief of the Chilean army, was shot Oct. 22, just two days before Allende's election as president was confirmed by Congress, and he died Oct. 25.

Schneider, 57, was shot at least three times by an unknown assailant after three cars halted his limousine as he was being driven to work. President Eduardo Frei Montalva declared a state of emergency in Chile, giving the government control of public order, establishing press and radio censorship and imposing a curfew. Frei also placed on emergency alert all units of the armed forces and the national police. Maj. Gen. Carlos Prats Gonzalez, chairman of the joint chiefs of staff, temporarily assumed Schneider's post.

Schneider had taken a strong stand of political neutrality by the armed forces during the current left-right tensions in Chile and had pledged to honor Congress' choice of president. Speculation in Chile indicated that his assassination may have been part of a right-wing plot to prevent Allende from assuming the presidency.

Police officials said Oct. 26 that they had identified an extreme rightist as the prime suspect in the assassination. Police had arrested about 150 persons for questioning under the state of emergency but had released most of them. Aniceto Rodriguez, secretary general of the Socialist party, one of the units of the left-wing coalition supporting Allende, charged Oct. 25 that Schneider's assailants had all been trained by the Central Intelligence Agency in the U.S. He explained that the Socialist party wanted to "identify the CIA as the moral author of this crime, which is not in the Chilean character; such a crime has never been committed before in Chile."

Ex-Gen. Roberto Viaux was arrested Oct. 28 and booked Nov. 3 in connection with Schneider's assassination.

Viaux, who turned himself in at the home of his lawyer, said in a letter made public Oct. 28 that he had "never given orders to cause physical or moral harm to anybody. I profoundly regret what happened to the commander in chief of the army."

Booked along with Viaux was his father-in-law, retired Col. Raul Igualt. In addition, Viaux's brother-in-law, Julio Eduardo Fontecilla Rojas, was arrested Nov. 3 in Peru. At least eight other persons had been officially booked in the case. Viaux and Igualt were formally accused of co-authoring the plan that resulted in Schneider's death. The state of seige, imposed following the shooting of Gen. Schneider, was lifted Nov. 4.

Congress elects Allende. A joint session of Congress elected Salvador Allende Gossens as president of Chile Oct. 24.

The Chilean Senate and Chamber of Deputies met in joint sesion Oct. 24 to choose the nation's next president from the two top contenders in the Sept. 4 presidential election. Allende, supported by a coalition of left-wing parties, received 153 votes in the secret balloting while runnerup conservative candidate Jorge Alessandri Rodriguez received 35 votes.

Upon hearing of his victory, Allende called for the creation of "a new society, a new conscience, new morals and a new economy." "Now we need a disciplined people capable of sacrifice and work," he said. Planned victory celebrations were canceled because of the shooting of Gen. Schneider.

(Soviet President Nikolai V. Podgorny sent a note of congratulations to Allende following his election, Tass news agency reported Oct. 24.)

Allende inaugurated. Salvador Allende was sworn in as president Nov. 3, 1970. He pledged before a joint session of Congress to "maintain the integrity and independence of the nation and keep and obey the constitution."

Allende's inauguration ceremonies were attended by representatives from more than 60 foreign nations, including an official delegation from the U.S. and unofficial delegations from North Vietnam, Communist China, East Germany and Cuba. In a salute to these unofficial delegations, Allende explained that "even though we do not have official relations with these countries, our peoples are united in the same hope." Charles A. Meyer, assistant secretary for inter-American affairs, represented the U.S., and Carlos Rafael Rodriguez, minister without portfolio, headed the Cuban delegation.

Following the ceremonies, President Allende made a brief speech in which he paid tribute to the armed forces, the national police and slain army commander Rene Schneider. He expressed conviction that Chileans would continue working and producing more, "but this time we will work for Chile and for all the Chileans, not for only a few."

Cabinet sworn in. Allende's 15-man cabinet, named Oct. 30 and sworn in Nov. 3, included three members of the Communist party's Central Committee and four members of the Socialist party. The remaining posts went to the other groups making up the Popular Unity coalition which supported Allende in the presidential election.

The cabinet (parties in parentheses):

Finance—Americo Zorilla Rojas (Communist party); public works—Pascual Barraza (Communist); labor—Jose Oyarce Jara (Communist); economy—Pedro Vuskovic Bravo (independent); agriculture—Jacques Chonchol Chait (Popular Action Unity Movement or MAPU); housing—Carlos Cortes Diaz (Socialist party); interior—Jose Toha Gonzalez (Socialist); foreign relations—Clodomiro Almeyda Medina (Socialist); education—Mario Astorga Gutierrez (Radical party); national defense—Alejandro Rios Valdivia (Radical); justice—Lisandro Cruz Ponce (Independent Popular Action Movement); land and colonization—Humberto Martinez Morales (Social Democratic party); public health—Oscar Jimenez Pinochet (Social Democratic); mining—Orlando Cantuarias Zepeda (Radical); secretary of the presidency—Jaime Suarez Bastidas (Socialist).

In actions Nov. 4, Allende named Gen. Jose Maria Sepulveda Galindo commander of the nation's national police and confirmed the appointment of Gen. Carlos Prats as commander in chief of the army. (Prats had been named temporary army commander following the shooting of Gen. Schneider.) Raul Montero and Gen. Cesar Ruiz had been named navy and air force commanders respectively, it was reported Nov. 5.

Allende's Foreign Policies

Cuban ties re-established. President Salvador Allende Gossens announced Nov. 12 that he had "decided to re-establish diplomatic, consular, commercial and cultural relations with the Republic of Cuba."

In a six-minute nationwide speech, Allende explained that the action would contribute "to ending a situation which we consider unjust towards a sister nation that is struggling to shape its own destiny according to the sovereign will of its people." Allende added that documents resuming relations between the two countries had already been signed by Chilean Foreign Minister Clodomiro Almeyda and Cuban Minister without Portfolio Carlos Rafael Rodriguez, who had headed the Cuban delegation to Allende's inauguration Nov. 3.

Allende asserted that the 1964 Organization of American Staes resolution that called on hemispheric nations to sever ties with Cuba lacked "juridical and moral basis" and that the measures adopted by the OAS did not "serve the interests of peace and friendship between the countries in the way stipulated by the charter of the United Nations."

The U.S. State Department Nov. 13 strongly criticized Chile's decision to resume relations with Cuba. State Department spokesman Robert J. McCloskey said "we deplore the fact that Chile has acted outside the consultative framework decided in 1964 by OAS foreign ministers for collective consideration of the question of Cuba by OAS member states." He added that the U.S. planned "to continue to support the existing OAS decision and recommendations on Cuba and we hope other OAS members will continue to do likewise."

U.S. diplomats said Dec. 19 that State Secretary William P. Rogers had sent a 25-page telegram to all U.S. hemispheric ambassadors urging them to warn Latin American foreign ministers against resuming relations with Cuba.

Rogers' message, apparently sent on White House orders, included detailed information on the U.S.' conviction that Soviet and Cuban subversive activities existed in Latin America. The telegram was reported to have concluded that the new Chilean government was playing into Cuban and Soviet hands in its resumption of diplomatic ties with Havana.

North Korean step taken. The Chilean Foreign Ministry announced Nov. 16 that it had signed an agreement with North Korea for the establishment of a North Korean commercial office in Chile. In a related development Nov. 17, Chile withdrew from the United Nations Commission on the Unification and Rehabilitation of Korea. In a letter to the U.N., the Chilean government explained that it wanted "to be in a position to explore other possibilities for actions" to promote peace in Northeast Asia.

U.S. closing stations. U.S. officials announced Nov. 3 that the closure of three U.S. Air Force scientific observation stations in Chile had been speeded up for political reasons, although the move had been planned since early 1970 for economic reasons.

The officials added that the stations, described as meteorological and ionospheric observation centers, were not covered by any formal agreement with the Chilean government. Brig. Gen. Thomas P. Coleman, deputy director of public information for the Air Force, confirmed in Washington Nov. 2 that the U.S. was closing the three stations but denied that the closure had been accelerated. He claimed that the Air Force would "be out by the end of the year and that has been our timetable all along." The three stations were located at Easter Island, Punta Arenas, on the

Magellan Strait, and Quintero, near the port of Valparaiso.

The Chilean government announced Nov. 22 that it planned to send an investigation team to Easter Island to study the sudden U.S. withdrawal, but later reports indicated that an understanding had been reached between the governments. Chilean Foreign Minister Clodomiro Almeyda told a press conference Nov. 27 that "the problem of Easter Island has been solved" and that Chilean interests had been protected.

The Economy

Economic goals outlined. Treasury Minister Americo Zorrilla outlined to Congress Nov. 27 the government's economic goals for 1971. He stressed that the objective of Allende's administration was to "replace the present economic structure, putting an end to the power of monopolistic capital, both Chilean and foreign, and also to big landholdings, so as to begin the construction of socialism."

Zorrilla said that a salary increase equal to the increase in the cost of living during 1970—about 35%—would be authorized in January. (Some reports indicated that certain workers would receive an increase of 66%.) The government also planned to increase employment and to forbid layoffs.

With a long-term emphasis on socialism, Zorrilla said, the government in 1971 would completely nationalize the 26 private banks in Chile and the U.S.-owned portions of the nation's copper industry. Monopolistic textile and cement firms would also be nationalized. Agrarian reform would be stepped up and cooperatives and state farms would be established.

Zorrilla reported that the government also planned to extend its control over foreign trade, through creation of a state enterprise to handle food imports and an agency to handle imports of raw material and manufactured goods.

Zorrilla said the Chilean escudo would not be periodically devalued as it was during the previous administration.

The government had announced an emergency housing plan Nov. 9 to provide 120,000 new homes for poor families during the next 14 months.

3 firms taken over. The government took over the administration of two firms controlled by U.S. interests Nov. 20 and acted Dec. 1 to expropriate a Chilean privately-owned firm.

Undersecretary of Economy Oscar Garreton announced Nov. 20 that President Salvador Allende had ordered the takeover of Nibsa, a plumbing and heating fittings manufacturer, and Alimentos Purina de Chile, S.A., an animal feed and chicken-raising firm. In both cases the action was based on a 1945 Chilean labor law that provided for federal intervention to protect the interests of Chilean workers. Garreton charged that actions of the two firms had deprived Chileans of work.

Nibsa was officially taken over "to normalize the labor situation and so that the company would continue giving work and production to Chileans." Alimentos Purina was taken over "to renew work within the firm and to solve the problems of the company's workers and of all peasants or farmers who depend on the firm." (Nibsa was owned 50% by Northern Indiana Brass Co. of Elkhart, Ind., 25% by the European consortium Adela and 25% Chilean-owned. Alimentos Purina was owned 80% by Ralston Purina de Panama, a subsidiary of Ralston Purina Co. of St. Louis, and 20% by Chilean Agustin Edwards.)

The government Dec. 1 nationalized Bellavista Tome, the country's largest fabric manufacturer. The firm, controlled by Teofilo Yarur, a Lebanese immigrant of a family prominent in Chile's textile industry, was reportedly on the verge of bankruptcy. Its 1,350 workers had struck three weeks previously for unpaid wages. Bellavista Tome's Santiago manager, Antonio Pi, explained that the firm had been unable to get credits from the state bank during the past few months.

Mining nationalization set. President Salvador Allende submitted a constitutional amendment Dec. 21 authorizing the government to immediately nationalize the copper mining industry. The action would affect the investments of three U.S. firms—Anaconda Co., Kennecott Corp. and the Cerro Corp. (The Wall Street Journal estimated Dec. 23 that Anaconda and Kennecott had invested $600 million–$650 million in their Chilean mines.)

Stressing that the nationalization was designed to allow Chile to "be the owner of its basic wealth," Allende explained that compensation to the firms would be made in cash over a 30-year period at 3% annual interest. The amount of compensation was to be established by the government comptroller's office, and the government would be authorized to deduct "excessive profits" between 1955 and 1970 from the government's payments. In addition, an appeals court would be set up to allow the firms to challenge the government's decision on the amount of compensation.

Under Chilean law, the proposed constitutional amendment had to be approved separately by both houses of Congress, then by a majority of a joint session in a procedure which required at least 60 days. Following approval of the amendment, Allende's government would be authorized to submit specific nationalization proposals to Congress.

(The previous government under Eduardo Frei Montalva had already begun a system of "Chileanization" of the U.S.-owned copper interests, whereby Chile would eventually have full ownership of most of the important mining properties.

(The Chilean state-owned copper agency charged Dec. 24 that Anaconda and Kennecott owed the government $40 million in dividend payments for the first nine months of 1970. Anaconda representatives called the accusation erroneous.)

Bank plans. President Allende announced Dec. 30 that his regime would nationalize Chilean commercial banks in order "to give more credits to small- and medium-size entrepreneurs and to block the monopolies from hoarding

available credits." Allende also said that the legislation, to be submitted to Congress in January, would exclude foreign banks operating in Chile, but he added that the government would work with the foreign banks to "look for direct understanding based on the interests of the country and giving consideration to their rights."

Workers' role assured. Benefits for workers and a voice for workers in economic policy were guaranteed Dec. 7 in an agreement signed by Allende with the Central Workers Union.

The agreement provided for participation of workers in government action through representation in planning organizations, as well as in the administration of state-owned and mixed enterprises, reduction of unemployment through provision of 180,000 jobs in the next 14 months, and creation of a Central Committee on Wages and Salaries to formulate a new wage and salary policy.

Andeans limit foreign investment. The Andean Common Market agreed to limit foreign ownership of firms in the five member states to 49%, it was reported by the Wall Street Journal Dec. 28. Peru, Chile and Colombia were to have 15 years to institute the agreement, while Bolivia and Ecuador were to have 20 years.

In addition, foreign firms in Andean states were to be allowed to send home only 14% of their profits from mid-1971 on.

The Andean members also reportedly passed resolutions to bar foreign investment in banks, insurance firms, electrical energy firms and telecommunications firms. Foreign investment in broadcasting and newspapers was also to be prohibited, with foreign firms said to be given one year to sell their interests.

Other developments. The government's Industrial Development Corp. Dec. 11 announced a plan to restructure the nation's automotive industry and eliminate most foreign car assembly plants.

Under the plan, the government would call for bids by international auto firms to form no more than three partnerships with the government for assembly plants. The government was to hold 51% interest in each firm. The plan also stipulated that "the firms currently installed in Chile that don't win bidding will cease their activities in the country entirely by 1972."

■ The government Dec. 16 ordered a total housing rent freeze during 1971.

■ President Allende launched a program to provide each child in Chile with one-half liter of milk a day, it was reported Dec. 18.

■ President Allende announced Dec. 31 that the government had purchased 51% of the Lota-Schwager coal mine, the nation's largest coal complex, from a Chilean consortium.

Other Events

Skyjacking foiled. Two men had failed in an attempt to commandeer a Chilean airliner.

One would-be hijacker was killed and another wounded Feb. 6 in a 10-minute gun battle with two detectives aboard a Chilean National Airlines (LAN) jet in Santiago; the two detectives and a stewardess were also wounded in the melee. The two hijackers—identified as Pedro Lenin Valenzuela Bravo, 19, who was killed, and Oscar Marcelo Vasquez —had seized the plane on a flight from Puerto Montt in southern Chile to Santiago. There were 35 passengers aboard during the shooting.

Ground and air LAN employes staged a 12-hour protest strike Feb. 7 over the shooting, demanding "guarantees that nothing of this sort is going to happen again." The plane's pilot and co-pilot protested the shooting and the LAN staff chief in Santiago called the order to shoot a "criminal" one. He explained: "The aircraft's petrol tanks could have exploded, causing an incalculable catastrophe." The Chilean government defended the police action and ordered an investigation into the situation.

Pollution panel. In July, then-President Eduardo Frei set up an emergency national commission on pollution. According to a New York Times report July 25, Santiago—situated in a valley just west of the Andes—had a constant air pollution problem due to an air-inversion system.

Riot police, rebels. The government announced Nov. 11 that the special riot police force was to be absorbed into the nation's regular national police units.

Sedition charges against imprisoned leftist revolutionaries were lifted Nov. 11, although reports indicated that some terrorists still faced criminal charges for robbery.

Press. Augustin Edwards, his mother and his brother were reported Nov. 11 to have quit the board of directors of the El Mercurio publishing firm, Chile's largest newspaper chain. The papers, which supported Jorge Alessandri Rodriguez in the presidential campaign, had been threatened with nationalization by Allende. Sonia Edwards remained on the board of directors as vice chairman, while Agustin Edwards was replaced as board chairman by Fernando Leniz, general manger.

■ The right-wing weekly periodical PEC (Politics, Economy and Culture) was suspended Nov. 17 for two weeks on charges that it interfered with the nation's internal security law.

Red leads students. Communist party member Alejandro Rojas was re-elected president of the Federation of Chilean Students Nov. 24. Rojas, who represented the left-wing Popular Unity coalition of President Allende, was opposed by Christian Democratic candidate Jorge Rodriguez. The election, which was originally held Nov. 19, had been repeated Nov. 24 after Rodriguez withdrew charging fraud.

University clash. Classes at the University of Concepcion were suspended Dec. 3 following the fatal shooting the previous day of a student in a clash between two factions of leftist student groups.

The student battle had begun Dec. 2 when members of the extremist Revolutionary Leftist Movement (MIR) attacked Communist party members during a student election campaign. Arnoldo Rios, the victim, died from gunshot wounds in the head.

President Salvador Allende called on the students Dec. 3 to "re-establish a climate of democratic coexistence, discarding all forms of aggression."

The two groups reportedly resolved their differences later that day when the candidate of the Popular Unity group (which includes the Communist party) stepped down in support of the MIR candidate in the student elections.

1971: First Year Under Allende

Policy, Politics, Extremist Violence & the Press

Neighborhood court plan fails. The government of President Salvador Allende Jan. 7, 1971 announced plans for establishment of neighborhood "people's tribunals" to try minor crimes and offenses. The tribunals, to hear cases such as drunkenness, child neglect and disturbance of the peace, would be authorized to set punishment ranging from public admonition to fines to sentences of forced labor.

A bill to create the "people's" courts was sent to Congress by Allende Jan. 22, but it ran into immediate opposition, and the Allende government withdrew the bill March 4. The Christian Democratic Party had announced Jan. 25 that it opposed the plan. Some elements of Allende's Popular Unity coalition also opposed it, as did Supreme Court President Ramiro Mendez.

The plan had been announced by Oscar Alvarez, architect of Allende's judicial reform project. Alvarez explained that the tribunals would "answer the need of the people for solution of domestic cases that fall outside the area of organized justice."

(President Allende was reported Jan. 7 to have pardoned 43 imprisoned members of the Revolutionary Left Movement.

(In a public declaration June 4, the Christian Democrats demanded the dissolution of the president's personal armed bodyguard, consisting of leftist youths, as unconstitutional. The statement said that the "state's interior security law considers the substitution of the public force by a private militia a crime.")

Altamirano heads Socialists. Sen. Carlos Altamirano was elected secretary general of the Socialist party Feb. 1 at the party's national congress in La Serena. Altamirano was considered a representative of the more radical members of the party, one of the major components of the Popular Unity government of President Salvador Allende Gossens. Altamirano had been jailed in 1969 following a public speech in which he reportedly supported armed revolution.

President Allende was reported to have supported Altamirano as head of the party over the more traditional Sen. Aniceto Rodriguez; Rodriguez withdrew his candidacy before the balloting.

The Socialist party's new central committee included Foreign Minister Clodomiro Almeyda Medina, Secretary General of the Presidency Jaime Bastida Suarez and Deputy Laura Allende de Pascal, President Allende's sister.

41

As head of the party, one of Altamirano's first tasks was to direct the Socialist campaign for the municipal elections in April.

(In a news conference reported Feb. 6, President Allende asserted that he would not yield to pressure from Socialist party radicals to increase the pace of change in Chile. "We have said that the transformation and the changes are going to be within the bourgeois democracy," Allende said. "And if Comrade Altamirano thinks we should go faster, I will tell him why we are not going to go faster.")

Municipal elections. President Salvador Allende and his Popular Unity Front government received a strong mandate April 4 in 280 municipal elections. In the first popular test of Allende's administration, candidates of the leftist parties making up the Popular Unity Coalition received 49.73% of the 2,823,784 votes cast; the four opposition parties received a total of 48.05% of the vote. Interior Minister Jose Toha described the vote April 4 as a "majority backing for the popular program of change which we have initiated."

Allende's Socialist party had the biggest gains since the September 1970 elections. Its candidates received 22.38% of the vote. Nevertheless, the Christian Democratic party, with 25.62% of the vote, was still the largest single party in Chile. Narciso Irureta, president of the Christian Democratic party, said the vote showed that "the people want changes, but . . . want them democratically and without violence." The two right-wing parties, the National party and the Democratic Radical party, jointly polled just under 22% of the vote, while the Communist party, a major unit in Allende's coalition, won 16.96% of the vote.

The April 4 elections included 210,000 voters 18–21 years old, who voted for the first time.

■ Former President Eduardo Frei April 12 confirmed his confidence in the Allende government. In a press conference in Madrid, Frei stressed that democracy in Chile was not in danger because it "was stronger than govern-

ments." "This is not only a conviction shared by the majority of Chileans, it is a manner of living," he added.

Terrorists seized. The government announced Oct. 5 that it had arrested the leaders of an ultra-leftist terrorist band, the Revolutionary Armed Forces (FAR). Ten people were reportedly arrested in police raids.

Sea ministry. The creation of a Ministry of the Sea was reported in March. Humberto Martones, land and colonization minister, was to add the new post to his portfolio.

Ex-minister assassinated. Edmundo Perez Zujovic, 59, former Interior minister and head of the rightist wing of the Christian Democrat party, was assassinated June 8. He died of five bullet wounds in a car ambush outside his home by three men firing submachine guns.

The government of President Salvador Allende immediately placed the province of Santiago under a state of emergency, suspending some constitutional rights, and imposed a five-hour night curfew. Military units were placed on alert throughout the country.

Police announced June 8 that they had implicated Roland Rivera Calderon, 24, in connection with the slaying. Rivera Calderon was identified by Perez Zujovic's daughter, Maria Angelica Perez, who was with her father at the time of the attack.

In an address June 8, Allende declared that the murder was a "deliberate provocation intended to alter the institutional life of the country." He said the crime was "an offense against Chile, the people and their government."

The opposition Christian Democrats said the assassination was the result of a "climate of hate, defamation and of violence," and demanded the immediate dissolution of armed groups that act outside the law. The party asked Allende to turn over the investigation of the assassination to army intelligence because it "lacked confidence" in the Chilean detective force, headed by leftists. Eduardo

Frei, former president and a leader of the Christian Democrats, said in Brussels, according to a June 9 report, that the slaying was an "atrocious crime" which was the result of a long campaign of lies "which have spread hatred in the life of Chile."

The ruling Popular Unity coalition repudiated the killing and declared that "we are confronting a plan against the security of Chile and the life of the Chileans."

The Communist and Socialist parties, the Popular Unity coalition's powerful groups, charged in official statements June 10 that the U.S. Central Intelligence Agency was behind the assassination of Perez Zujovic. Miguel Enriquez, leader of the extreme leftist Revolutionary Left Movement (MIR), which had seceded from the ruling coalition, charged that the assassination was the work of the "extreme right and the CIA."

Suspects killed—Two brothers, both left-wing extremists accused of slaying Perez Zujovic, were killed in a gunfire exchange with police in Santiago June 13.

Roland, 24, and Arturo Rivera Calderon, 20, armed with machine guns and grenades on their belts, died as police converged on a private garage which was apparently a munitions armory for the leftist organization the Organized Peoples' Vanguard (VOP). Six other persons, three men and three women, were arrested in the garage. A third suspect, Heriberto Salazar Bello, also identified as a VOP member, burst into police headquarters June 16, killed two detectives and pulled a grenade, killing himself.

Coalition loses vote tests. In what was regarded as a test of popular support for Allende's Popular Unity (UP) coalition, a candidate of a united anti-Marxist opposition defeated the government candidate in an election in Valparaiso province July 18 for a vacant seat in the Chamber of Deputies (lower house). The election took place nine days after a severe earthquake struck the province.

Dr. Oscar Marin, a 62-year-old physician, received united support from the opposition Christian Democratic, National and Democratic Radical parties

to win the seat. He narrowly defeated Hernan del Canto, 31, a Socialist labor leader, who ran as the government's candidate.

Senator Narciso Irureta, president of the Christian Democratic party, said that "the defeat of Mr. del Canto is a clear warning that the electorate does not want Marxism."

In another political development, the Popular Unity coalition lost control of both houses of Congress, according to a July 23 report in the French newspaper Le Monde. Fernando Sanhueza, Christian Democrat deputy, was elected president of the Chamber of Deputies July 20. The two other members of the Chamber's ruling bureau were Christian Democrats. Christian Democrats already controlled Senate leadership.

The coalition had been defeated in the election June 11 of the University of Chile rector. Edgardo Boeninger, the incumbent rector and independent Christian Democrat, defeated Eduardo Novoa Monreal, a key legal adviser to President Allende, who had the support of the Communist and Socialist parties and the Communist-led University Student Federation.

Deputies quit Christian Democrats. Six parliamentary deputies announced their resignations July 31 from the Christian Democratic Party (PDC).

Explaining in a letter to the party's president, Sen. Narciso Irureta, the deputies said the party had renounced its "leftist Christian policy" by creating an alliance with the rightist National and Democratic Radical parties in the Valparaiso election.

In the letter, the deputies said they would join a new "Christian Left" movement formed earlier in the week when the leadership of the youth wing of the Christian Democrats resigned July 28 to protest the recent election tactics.

The national council of the PDC met July 31 and released a statement saying that their "understanding" with the rightist parties during the election was "accidental."

Cabinet crisis. President Salvador Allende suffered his first Cabinet crisis when four ministers, members of the ruling Popular Unity (UP) coalition, submitted their resignations Aug. 7. The resignations were a result of divisions within both the Radical party and the Unified Popular Action Movement (MAPU).

The four Cabinet members were Orlando Cantuarias (mines), Mario Astorga (education) and Alejandro Valdivia (defense) of the Radical party and Jacques Chonchol (agriculture) of MAPU.

The Radical party had split Aug. 3 when Radical Sen. Americo Acuna announced that he and 10 other senators and deputies had made an "irrevocable" decision to abandon the Radical party after a party congress declared the party to be "Socialist" and a "workers' party." Acuna said his faction would continue to work within the Popular Unity coalition, adding that they considered themselves "democratic Socialists and not Marxists." He said his group would support "the fulfillment of the Popular Unity program within a democratic framework in which it was conceived, respecting all legality." The defectors said they would form a new Independent Radical party pledged to support the interests of the Chilean middle class.

MAPU minister Jacques Chonchol and three MAPU representatives left the movement after deciding to affiliate themselves with the new "Christian Left" movement recently formed by Christian Democratic Party dissidents. Chonchol and his followers criticized MAPU for converting itself into a party "of strong Marxist content" and of adopting "as its fundamental basis a category of Marxist-Leninist thought."

On the day the resignations were submitted, Allende held a Cabinet meeting in which the Radical party members told him that he must either "refuse or accept totally" the resignations. This reportedly placed Allende in a difficult position if he wanted to accept only some of the resignations while refusing others.

Offers by ranking government officials to resign were traditional when their party suffered an internal crisis. The crisis was resolved Aug. 11 when Allende refused the four resignations, while accepting a fifth, that of Oscar Jimenez Pinochet, health minister from the Socialist party. He resigned Aug. 10 to permit Allende to give the ministry to a MAPU representative, since Chonchol would now be representing the "Christian Left."

Political leaders accused. The rightist National party Sept. 8 submitted to the Chamber of Deputies a constitutional accusation against Economy Minister Pedro Vuskovic. The call for censure involved the National party's claim that Vuskovic had been involved in illegal government takeovers, or "requisitions," of several large private textile plants.

It was announced Sept. 11 that the government had presented a formal complaint to the appellate court against the president of the rightist National party, Sergio Onofre Jarpa, accused of violating a state internal security law.

The lawsuit was based on statements by Jarpa reported in the newspaper, Tribuna, in which he accused the government of "slowly transforming Chile into a totalitarian Communist state, opening the way to Soviet penetration in Latin America."

Christian Democrats drop support. The New York Times reported Sept. 26 that the Christian Democrats, the principal opposition party, had ended its working compact with the Popular Unity government Sept. 24.

The break reportedly resulted from a prolonged campaign against Christian Democrat leaders in the leftist Santiago press. Included in the campaign was a series of personal attacks on former President Eduardo Frei Montalva, a Christian Democrat, in newspapers controlled by the Communist and Socialist parties, the major members of the ruling coalition.

Members of the Christian Democratic Youth Wing fought with young supporters of the Allende government Sept. 24 outside Christian Democrat party headquarters.

The Miami Herald had reported Sept. 17 that an agreement had been reached between Allende and leaders of the Christian Democrats. Allende reportedly promised to moderate his leftist policies in return for more cooperation from the Christian Democrats who pledged not to join with the opposition National party in an attempt to impeach Economy Minister Pedro Vuskovic.

Under the agreement, Allende would define his nationalization plans by sending to Congress a bill that would state which businesses and industries his government planned to nationalize and which would remain in private hands. The president also promised the Christian Democrats a bill that would safeguard job security for workers in nationalized industries that did not sympathize with the governing Popular Unity coalition.

Unicameral assembly bill rejected. A bill offered by Allende Nov. 11 to replace the two-house Congress with a unicameral Assembly of the People was rejected Nov. 27 by the Constitutional Committee of the Chamber of Deputies. The vote was 8–4 with one abstention.

The committee, dominated by opponents of Allende's Popular Unity government, also moved to block any attempt by the president to dissolve parliament by introducing a bill that dissolution could be approved only by a national referendum.

Camilo Salvo, a radical deputy, called the proposed bill "much more in keeping with our presidential system" and said it "would be a step forward in easing legislative procedures."

In the proposed Congressional reform, the initiation of legislation would be permitted by petitioners who collected 5,-000 signatures. The Communist-led Central Confederation of Labor would also be permitted to initiate legislation.

A decision by the Popular Unity coalition's Marxist and leftist parties to press for the unicameral legislature had been reported by La Prensa of Buenos Aires June 28.

The coalition's objective would be to replace the present legislative power, composed of a senate and chamber, by a powerful unicameral assembly that would be able to designate supreme and appellate court judges. The purpose of the plan would be to create "only one modern, democratic and popular chamber" which would "express nationally the popular sovereignty." The plan was vehemently opposed by opposition parties in the congress.

Allende's decision to hold a plebiscite on the assembly plan had been announced by the government Sept. 9.

The idea of a unicameral legislature was rejected by the opposition Christian Democrats.

Sen. Narciso Irureta, the Christian Democrats' president, said Nov. 21: "What the proposed measures seek is, simply, to obtain total control over the legislative and judicial power in a new move reflecting the well-known Marxist tactics of seeking total power at any cost."

Press problems. The executive committee and advisory council of the Inter-American Press Association met in Rio de Janeiro Jan. 25 and Jan. 26. The chairman of IAPA's Freedom of the Press Committee, Julio de Mesquita Neto of Brazil's O Estado de Sao Paulo, asserted that Chile "still had press freedom," but he denounced an "atmosphere of fear" which he said prevailed in the nation. He added that IAPA's principal concern in Chile was the fate of El Mercurio, the conservative newspaper formerly operated by the Edwards family.

Allende telegraphed Neto Feb. 8 to deny that his government was restricting press freedom. Allende told Neto that "even though this may disappoint you, in Chile there is absolute respect for the mediums of distribution of thought and opinion."

Publication of the leftist paper Puro Chile had been suspended Jan. 29 for four days. The paper was charged with libel against three senators. In place of Puro Chile, an almost identical paper called Dulce Patria with the same address appeared on the stands.

The government announced Feb. 12 that it had bought the Zig-Zag publishing firm.

The items bought included Zig-Zag's equipment and plant and the copyrights of some of its magazines. Zig-Zag, the largest magazine publishing enterprise in Chile, was reported close to bankruptcy, with debts exceeding $1 million. In arbitration over a wage dispute in January, the government had granted Zig-Zag workers wage increases of up to 45%. President Allende said Zig-Zag would continue to publish, under its own editorial control, Ercilla, Vez, Eva and Rosita, while the government would publish Hechos Mundiales, Estadio, Saber Comer and Confidencias.

El Mercurio charged Aug. 8 that press freedom in Chile appeared threatened by government actions taken to nationalize Chile's principal producer of paper. El Mercurio warned that there was a "certain danger" that the government could intervene when it opposed the editorial policy of a newspaper.

(The government said Oct. 9 that it would soon nationalize the country's four private paper mills. The decision was made after Allende met with ex-President Jorge Allesandri, who owned Chile's largest paper firm.)

El Mercurio Sept. 12 denounced what it described as "the attacks and the pressures that were growing against it" from government sources. In an editorial, it asked public opinion "to recognize the fact that the attacks on El Mercurio have exceeded all limits and that the responsibility must inevitably fall on the authorities . . ."

Allende announced Sept. 15, at a meeting of the National Labor Union, that his government had decided to close the United Press International (UPI) offices in Chile. (But this decision was reversed before the month had ended.) Allende said the government was acting against UPI because of a UPI report printed Sept. 14 in the Colombian newspaper El Tiempo. The report referred to a small Chilean aircraft carrying some Allende bodyguards from a trip Allende had made to Colombia. The plane had been reported lost.

The UPI report quoted El Tiempo as stating that Colombia was investigating the possibility that the plane had landed in a part of Colombia where it had allegedly been carrying arms and subversive literature to guerrillas. UPI also carried a denial of the story by Chilean Interior Minister Jose Toha, stating that the plane had arrived in Santiago as scheduled.

Allende also accused the UPI of distributing false and partial news printed by foreign newspapers which presented a false image of his government. The president referred specifically to United Press reports that he had met with Colombian Sen. Nacho Vives while visiting in Bogota and with the recently overthrown Bolivian President Juan Jose Torres while in Lima.

Interior Minister Toha reportedly told the director of the Foreign Correspondents Association in Santiago Sept. 16 that the government's action was aimed at UPI as an enterprise, not at any of its correspondents, who would not be expelled. He said UPI would no longer be able to distribute international news in Chile nor send news from Chile outside the country. Toha said the action would not affect UPI's national service, which employed 10 Chilean journalists.

The official government and Socialist party newspaper, La Nacion, published an editorial Sept. 17 saying that the government's decision "should be greeted with patriotic rejoicing and national pride." It added that UPI had a dual role in Chile: "to inform and misinform."

The Interior Ministry announced Sept. 26 that Allende had reversed his decision and would permit UPI to continue operations.

The ministry said, however, that the conduct of the UPI bureau chief in Santiago, Martin P. Houseman, was "unacceptable" and that he would have to be removed.

It was reported that Allende had reversed his decision following a series of talks with UPI's Latin American manager, William McCall. The ministry said McCall had agreed that UPI "transmitted false news stories which affected Chile internationally."

At the 27th annual IAPA meeting, held in Chicago, Chile was the subject of a resolution condemning actions against press freedom. The association voted Oct. 29 to call on Chile to lift restrictions against publications critical of the Allende administration.

Rene Silva Espejo of El Mercurio, the conservative Santiago daily, had predicted in an earlier session Oct. 28 that the Chilean economy would in time be totally controlled by the state, "leading to monopoly in the production and distribution of newsprint, which can end with extortion of that portion of the press which disagrees with the administration."

Francisco Galdames, editor of Santiago's Ultima Hora, took exception to the description by his colleagues of Chile's government as "Marxist-Leninist" or "Allende's socialism."

"I disagree with both terms," said Galdames, adding that IAPA must view the changes in Latin America, particularly Chile, in the "broader concept of what is happening today in the world. We in Chile are not living through socialism, but through a popular social movement."

The Allende government announced Nov. 15 that it would take over the last privately-owned pulp and paper manufacturing company in Chile, Compania Manufactura de Papeles y Cartones.

This paper company was the sole independent source of newsprint for Chilean newspapers and magazines. Opposition critics voiced fears that the government would refuse to provide opposition newspapers with newsprint if it gained controlling interest in the company.

The right-wing newspaper Tribuna was suspended Dec. 6 for 24 hours by Gen. Augusto Pinochet, the Santiago army garrison commander, for allegedly violating state of emergency regulations (imposed Dec. 2 and lifted Dec. 9) that forbade the media to publish anything that would disturb public order. Tribuna had criticized the armed forces for continuing to support the Popular Unity government.

The Allende government closed down Radio Balmaceda Dec. 10 for 48 hours "for serious offenses against the president and the armed forces." The offenses were not specified. The station, which was owned by the opposition Christian Democratic party, had been highly critical of the Allende administration. It was the second suspension in a month for the station.

It was reported Dec. 10 that the government's Popular Unity party had lost control of the Chilean Natonal Association of Journalists in elections Dec. 6–9.

The Allende government Dec. 21 sent to Congress a bill to establish a National Newsprint Institute to assure adequate supervision of newsprint distribution.

In charge of administering the institute would be three representatives of the National Press Association, two members of congress, three representatives of the College of Journalism, two members of the Central Workers Union (CUT) and two representatives appointed by President Salvador Allende.

Allende opposes extremists. In a speech Nov. 4, 1971, marking the first anniversary of his Socialist coalition government, President Salvador Allende told 70,000 workers and students in Santiago's national stadium that the goals of his government included "changing Chile's institutions" to meet modern needs.

Reviewing his first year in office, Allende condemned both left-wing and right-wing extremism and especially those on the far left who criticized his government for "infantile revolutionary ideas" and who wanted to force a faster rate of revolutionary change.

Allende also criticized party functionaries who had shown "sectarianism" or laziness in their government jobs. He said that "public posts are not sinecures for party comrades" and indicated that incompetent officials would be dismissed.

The president defended his decision not to pay compensation to U.S. copper companies for nationalized properties because of their illegally earned "excess profits," adding that Chile's willingness to assume the firms' debts to foreign creditors was a form of compensation. Allende insisted his government did not intend to destroy the institution of private property. He promised that the country, while following the "Chilean road to socialism," would remain a pluralistic, democratic and free society.

University clashes, rector accused. President Allende Nov. 19 ordered the criminal prosecution of University of Chile rector Edgardo Boeninger and a group of opposition legislators that opposed Marxist control of the university.

The charges against the rector, a member of the opposition Christian Democratic Party, resulted from fighting that had broken out Nov. 17 between

Marxist and non-Marxist members of the student body. Two of the university's faculties were occupied and 50% of the classes suspended in a campaign by non-Marxist members of the student body and faculty to obtain a university plebescite to determine the university's sentiment about Marxist plans to restructure the 12 professional schools and faculties.

(The non-Marxists, including Boeninger, claimed that the Marxist majority on the University Council wanted to bring the institution under the political control of the Popular Unity government.)

Students of the leftist Chilean Students Federation occupied the headquarters building of the university Nov. 17 and detained Boeninger for several hours. Accompanied by 15 congressmen, Boeninger then led 200 students and professors to the presidential palace to protest the takeover of the headquarters building. Before they were able to request an interview with Interior Minister Jose Toha, the group was intercepted by national police, who used tear gas to prevent the group from entering the palace.

The Communist party, which formed part of the governing coalition, Nov. 18 described the march on the palace as a "fascist maneuver" and called on workers, students and all "democratic forces" to mobilize in defense of the government.

Allende ordered the prosecution of Boeninger, opposition parliament members and students for "violent entry" and "assault" against the palace guard.

After Allende ordered criminal proceedings against Boeninger and the 15 legislators, the presidents of the Senate and Chamber of Deputies sent a message warning Allende that his action threatened "Chile's democracy and international prestige."

Clashes continued at the university Nov. 22 and 26.

The Nov. 22 clash involving more than 2,000 students erupted in the center of Santiago as anti-Marxist students from the private Catholic University staged a march to show solidarity with University of Chile students who were demanding a plebiscite.

(Boeninger said in a report Nov. 27 that his supporters had collected enough signatures to call a plebiscite without the approval of the governing board.)

The Marxist majority on the university governing board had refused to approve the plebiscite and Nov. 26 challenged Boeninger and the council to resign so that new elections of university officers could be held, a move approved by the Allende government.

The Nov. 26 clash erupted as 1,000 anti-Marxist students marched from the University of Chile law school, where students had occupied the building for a month, to the Congress.

The university crisis spread to Valparaiso Nov. 25 where more than a dozen students were injured. It was also reported that shots were fired in Concepcion Nov. 27 in another related clash.

Riots bring on state of emergency. A state of emergency was declared in Santiago Dec. 2 after more than 150 persons were injured in violence set off by a Dec. 1 march by 5,000 women protesting food shortages and a visit to Chile by Premier Fidel Castro of Cuba.

The "March of the Empty Pots," organized by opposition Christian Democratic and National parties, was the largest and most violent demonstration since Allende took office.

What started out as a peaceful march of women beating pots and pans turned violent when bands of youths from the extremist left-wing Revolutionary Left Movement (MIR) and the Communist party's Ramona Parra Youth Brigade threw rocks at the women and 80 club-carrying youths escorting them. Riot police fired tear-gas grenades among the demonstrators but a group of 200 women regrouped and were intercepted by Communist youths.

More than 100 rock-throwing youths were arrested by the national police, acting under orders of Gen. Augusto Pinochet, commander of the Santiago army garrison.

Street skirmishes between Marxist and anti-Marxist youths (who had also been involved in recent clashes over control of the University of Chile) continued through the night.

Shortly after daybreak Dec. 2, Allende declared a state of emergency, which banned street demonstrations, allowed arrests without warrants and invoked news censorship. Later in the day anti-Marxist youths defied the state of emergency and demonstrated in a new outburst against the government. A 1 a.m.–6 a.m. curfew was imposed by Gen. Pinochet Dec. 3.

Interior Minister Jose Toha charged Dec. 2 in a televised statement that the violence was part of an "orchestrated, seditious plan" to destroy the government, and ordered the shutdown of two opposition radio stations, Radio Balmaceda and Radio Agricultura, which had broadcast repeated calls Dec. 1 for women to take part in the march.

(The Christian Democratic party voted Dec. 3 to begin impeachment proceedings against Toha on charges of tolerating armed extremist groups in Chile. Leftist Christian Democrats opposed the motion, which could lead to the resignation of a minister who was widely believed to be a moderating influence on the government.)

President Allende said Dec. 2 at a farewell rally for Premier Castro that "the germs of fascism" were at work in Chile. "I respect the opposition as long as it remains within the law, but I know very well how to distinguish between opposition and sedition," he told a crowd of 40,000.

Allende added that it was a "strange coincidence" that street demonstrations had broken out at the same time that U.S. newspapers published reports that aides of President Nixon believed "the days of the popular government of Chile were numbered."

(Gen. Carlos Prats, the chief of the Chilean army, declared Dec. 12 that the armed forces were "professional institutions which have not intervened, are not intervening, and will not intervene in politics." His statement was in reply to a charge Dec. 11 by Defense Minister Alejandro Rios that there was a well-prepared extreme right-wing campaign to invoke sedition among army units.)

Allende, opposition hold rallies. Fewer than 20,000 people turned out Dec. 20 for a rally called by the left-wing Chilean government as a demonstration of support for President Salvador Allende.

(The use of such rallies had been advised Dec. 2 by Cuban Premier Fidel Castro, who criticized Allende's lack of emphasis on "mass mobilization" during his Chilean visit.)

Allende told the crowd that the opposition, which had started impeachment proceedings against two of his ministers, had "begun a political process that is aimed against you."

The government rally was clearly smaller than a rally Dec. 16 sponsored by the Christian Democrats, which drew about 60,000 people to the National Stadium.

At the opposition rally, Sen. Renan Fuentealba, president of the Christian Democratic party, announced that his party would initiate impeachment proceedings against Interior Minister Jose Toha as a warning to the Allende government against permitting acts of violence by extremist left-wing groups.

Fuentealba, who had played a large part in negotiations by which Allende obtained Christian Democrat votes for his election in 1970, said the Christian Democrats were ready to collaborate in the construction of "a Socialist society, Chilean style, with democracy and political pluralism," but would oppose a "Cuban style socialism that Chileans cannot accept." He added that Castro's three-week visit had "intervened blatantly in Chile's internal affairs."

Economic Policy & Business Developments

Problems, goals & reforms. The Alliance for Progress newsletter April 5, 1971 summarized Chile's presentation to the subcommittee of the Inter-American Committee on the Alliance for Progress (CIAP). Chilean Economy Minister Pedro Vuskovic Bravo had headed the delegation to the Washington meeting Feb. 22–24 in Chile's first economic presentation before an international panel since Allende's government came to power in November 1970.

Highlights of the Chilean presentation, according to the Alliance for Progress newsletter, included: the Chilean government had set the following problems to be overcome: unemployment, economic stagnation, insufficient internal saving, inequitable distribution of the national income and wealth, foreign dependence, monopolistic exploitation and a deeply rooted "psychology of inflation."

New goals set by the Allende government included definition of new development standards aimed at effecting substantive change in the relations of economic power and the flow of the productive system. Basic structural reforms planned included state ownership of the large-scale mining, banking and other productive or distributive corporations; expediting and deepening agrarian reform; and working towards a state-controlled foreign trade.

Land redistribution. Agriculture Minister Jacques Chonchol had announced Jan. 1 that the government planned to expropriate all farms of more than 80 hectares.

In an effort to halt illegal seizures of farms by peasants dissatisfied with the government's land redistribution rate, President Allende sent a bill to Congress calling for the imprisonment of the ringleaders of the land seizures, it was reported Feb. 6. Reports indicated that some of the seizures, particularly numerous in Cautin Province and Colchagua Province, had been led by leftist university students and members of the Movement of the Revolutionary Left (MIR), as well as some local officials of Allende's government.

Allende called on local and party officials and union leaders Feb. 16 to "prevent isolated, indiscriminate" seizures of farms. Government officials had announced the previous day that all farms that could be legally expropriated would be taken over by the end of 1971. The National Society of Agriculture, however, had earlier claimed farmers were being harassed and that many small and medium-sized farms smaller than the legal minimum acreage for expropriation had been taken over, it was reported Jan. 26.

The government warned July 31 that it would no longer tolerate the takeover of farms and private property by squatters and ordered police to evict any land

invaders. Interior Minister Undersecretary Daniel Vergara said the full force of the law would be used to insure that private property was respected.

Marcelo Maturana, editor of the right-wing magazine PEC, was jailed by a military judge on charges of violation of Chile's internal security law, it was reported March 4. The magazine had recently warned Allende to use police force to stop the illegal seizure of farmlands in southern Chile.

The Paris newspaper Le Monde reported Sept. 14 that the Chilean government had ordered Sept. 12 the arrest of the directors of an illegal campaign of land seizures in the southern part of the country. It was the first time the Popular Unity government had decided to take action against MIR, the radical leftist group that organized the land occupations.

The minister of agriculture, Chonchol, gave deeds to houses and small parcels of land to 1,330 farmers in Cochagua province Dec. 19.

In a similar move, property had been given to 1,500 peasants at Limache, north of Santiago, Nov. 24.

Warning. The National Confederation of Production & Commerce, at an emergency meeting attended by 200 delegates, warned Jan. 19 that the economic policies of President Salvador Allende were leading the private sector to early bankruptcy. Confederation President Jorge Fontaine explained that the organization was referring to the government's price freezes, wage increases and higher taxes.

Banking developments. Control of the O'Higgins Bank passed to the state following the central bank's purchase of a majority of the bank's stock, it was reported Jan. 23. The Israeli Bank had already passed to control of the state through the same method.

The government had assumed the administration of the Bank of Credit and Investments, the nation's third largest bank, it was reported Jan. 17. The bank was charged with repeated violations of reserve regulations.

The central bank took control of the Panamerican Bank Jan. 29, charging it with carrying on "irregular" operations, the exercise of "illegitimate" pressures on debtors and infraction of central bank rules. Other banks that had been taken over for infringment of state regulations included the Edwards Bank and the Hipotecario Credito bank, according to a Feb. 7 report in La Prensa of Buenos Aires.

The state's development corporation, Corfo, decided to withdraw its deposits held in private banks and place them in the central bank and the O'Higgins Bank it was reported Feb. 7.

Hugo Fazio, Chilean central bank vice president, in an article in the newspaper El Siglo cited by the Journal of Commerce Feb. 18, said the banks that had come under state control would retain their present structures and names but that credit, deposit and personnel policies would be altered. Fazio explained that the state's banking policy was designed to rationalize and democratize credit, to allow for more participation of workers and depositors in the banks' operations, to pass to the banks some of the credit functions then exercised by semistate institutions, to create new banks for different sectors of the economy, to establish regional banks and block the concentration of banking activity in Santiago, and to eliminate the influence of the private sector in the central bank.

Three foreign banks, the French & Italian Bank for South America, the Bank of America and the Bank of London decided, according to a June 9 Le Monde report, to sell their shares to the government. The Central Bank announced July 15 that it had reached agreement with the latter two banks on nationalizing their Chilean branches.

The acquisition of foreign banks was in line with the Allende government's aim of establishing a state banking monopoly. Since November 1970, 60% of Chile's private banking system had been nationalized.

Central Bank President Alfonso Inostroza announced Sept. 20 that a preliminary agreement had been reached between the Chilean government and the First National City Bank of New York (Citibank) on the sale of the bank's Chilean branches.

Inostroza said Chile had agreed to pay Citibank about 30% more than the $3.5 million book value of the bank's eight Chilean offices. Payment would be made over a five-year period.

Day of work donated. More than two million Chileans donated one day of work without pay Sunday, May 16. The day was officially declared the "National Day of Voluntary Work" by the government. President Allende took part by assisting in a house-raising in a suburb of Santiago. Most members of the government, including the Christian Democrats, also took part.

Bethlehem Mines sale set. President Allende confirmed March 27 that Chile had signed a contract with Bethlehem Iron Mines Co. of Pennsylvania to purchase its iron mines in Chile. The sale, the first major takeover in Chile's policy of nationalizing all mining resources, would reportedly bring Bethlehem about $30 million, although Allende declined to reveal a specific price. Allende said payments, based on an audit of the book value at the end of March, would be made over 17 years with interest at 5.5%. The first instalment would be paid in July 1973.

(Armco Steel Corp. announced that it had agreed on the sale to the Chilean government of more than half of its 70% interest in Armco-Chile for $1 million, it was reported March 28 in the Miami Herald. Armco would sell 35.7% of its interest in the firm and retain a 34.3% interest.)

7 arrested in 'copper plot.' Seven persons were arrested in Santiago March 7 in connection with an alleged "copper plot" designed to affect the national interests of Chile. The seven—two Chileans and five foreigners, including a U.S. citizen—were accused by Mining Minister Orlando Cantuarias of plotting to drive down the price of copper on the international market by offering nonexistent Chilean copper for sale in Europe through a Swiss-based brokerage firm. The accused were charged with violating Chile's Internal Security Act and were held in prison.

The "plot" was further complicated March 10 when Social Democratic Sen. Narciso Irureta charged that government officials had been involved in order to get a "payoff" on copper sales. The dispute between government and opposition legislators reached a peak in the Chamber of Deputies March 23 when several deputies engaged in fist fights.

The seven persons arrested in the plot were Howard Edwards, currently under indictment for perjury in Fort Lauderdale, Fla., Alfred Koening of Switzerland; Miguel Alberto Aspee Bouza of Argentina, Miguel Sanz Frankel of Uruguay, Eduardo Dehers of Argentina, Aldo Orezolli of Chile, and Zvonimir Medovic of Chile.

Other copper developments—Chile Feb. 25 had announced plans to sell copper directly to Communist China, bypassing the usual practice of dealing through the London Metals Exchange. Chile and Communist China had established diplomatic relations in January.

The government Feb. 25 announced cancellation of a contract with the Anaconda Co. subsidiary Anaconda Sales Co., which handled a considerable amount of Chile's overseas copper sales.

(Anaconda Co. announced in New York Feb. 25 that "contraction of business activity" in general and Chile's nationalization plans had caused it to cut its quarterly dividend from 47.5¢ a share to 25¢ a share.)

Chile's State Copper Corp. (Codelco) April 2 officially took over the sales operations of the Anaconda Co. mines. Codelco set up a central sales agency in Santiago and was to operate with local branch agencies abroad.

The regime had acted March 17 to strengthen its supervisory control of Anaconda and Kennecott Copper Corp. mines by sending Codelco directors to Anaconda's Chuquicamata mine and Kennecott's El Teniente mine to supervise the operations of the mines and to oversee the naming of Chilean workers to posts being vacated. Foreign management had been leaving the jobs in the mines ever since President Allende announced his nationalization plans; the New York Times reported March 18 that about 300 foreign and Chilean techni-

cians and officials had left since Allende's government took over in November 1970. In addition, the Allende government had recently announced that salaries to foreign management personnel at Anaconda and Kennecott mines would be paid in Chilean currency rather than dollars. Anaconda had promised to relocate staffers who wanted to leave Chile.

The Allende regime had admitted that production problems in the mines would prevent it from producing enough copper to meet all its sales contract obligations on the world market, the Wall Street Journal reported March 15.

El Teniente mine takeover. The government announced May 20 it had taken over financial and operational control of El Teniente Mining Co., one of the three largest copper enterprises in Chile.

El Teniente had been administered by the Kennecott Corp., which owned 49% of the operation. The government's Codelco owned 51%.

Mining Minister Orlando Cantuarias said the move was made because "irregularities in production" were found in four of the eight giant converter ovens in the mine, and this caused a drop in copper production. The company was also reported to be operating with a $5.5 million deficit.

The Chilean government appointed eight administrators to control both the finances and operations of the company.

The Kennecott firm had retained a contract to manage the mine after selling 51% interest to Codelco in 1967.

Chile nationalizes copper. The Chilean Congress unanimously approved July 11 a constitutional amendment authorizing the president to nationalize the copper properties of the American-owned Kennecott, Anaconda and Cerro corporations. All 158 senators and deputies present, representing every major Chilean party, voted in favor of the reform. The vote constituted final ratification of the constitutional amendment.

The congressional vote was preceded by a massive propaganda campaign. July 11 was officially designated "National Dignity Day" by the Popular

Unity government and thousands of posters and newspaper ads proclaimed that Chile was about to "reclaim her riches."

Allende signed the bill July 15.

Allende denounces U.S. firms—The day congress approved the bill, Allende spoke at Kennecott's El Teniente mine in Rancagua, 50 miles south of Santiago. The president denounced Anaconda and Kennecott for taking excessive profits and poor planning.

In his accusations, Allende referred to studies made recently by the French Mining Society and by a Soviet economic mission. The president had called in the foreign experts to help determine the actual state of the mines to be taken over. According to the French report, Anaconda failed to remove rubble creating a barrier to production and costing $20 million to remove; inadequate equipment found in poor repair would cost $30 million; the recent exploitation of the mines, removing only the best ore and leaving great amounts of slag, would result in lower profits for the Chileans; conditions at El Teniente were described as ruinous.

Allende's attack on the mines' management presumably was part of a campaign to build up public opinion against the payment of substantial compensation for the expropriated properties. According to the new law, indemnification would be determined by Chile's comptroller general, basing the amount on the companies' book value as of December 31, 1970, discounting taxes, fines and depreciation of machines. No indemnification would be given for the copper deposits themselves.

The law gave the president a key role in determining compensation by permitting him to deduct "excessive profits" from the book value.

In his speech at El Teniente, Allende called on copper workers to "defend the revolution through more production." He conceded that a large expected income from the nationalizations would not be realized immediately and that the mines would have trouble financing their own development programs.

(In a speech to miners Feb. 7, Allende had said that he would attempt to avoid reprisals from the U.S. when he nationalized U.S. mining interests in Chile "so that they [the U.S.] do not doors of credit to us." "We d[e] to take the route of provoking those who invested their money in Chile long ago," he said. "We do not want to take the route of undue confiscation or usurpation." However, Allende warned that he would "not pay the price of indignity.")

■ Carlos Altimirano, secretary-general of the Socialist party, the largest party in the ruling Popular Unity coalition, July 27 told an assembly of Socialist union leaders, attended by diplomatic representatives of several Communist nations, that the Chilean government should not compensate U.S. investors for nationalization of copper mines.

Altimirano reviewed the profits realized by the U.S. companies and the state in which they left the mines. He also referred to the advantages they had gained during the previous administration of President Eduardo Frei. He said the U.S. firms did not deserve compensation "because the profits they took out of our country are a thousand times more than they have invested."

In August, the Socialist party asserted that Chile "should not pay any compensation whatsoever" to U.S. private interests for the nationalized copper enterprises.

Socialist Congressman Carlos Gonzales said the "stand not to compensate the companies was unanimously and formally adopted" by the party's central committee meeting.

Soviet aid reported. An official of Codelco had disclosed June 1 that Chile had arranged with the Soviet Union for technical aid in the extraction of raw materials, especially the copper mined by formerly U.S.-owned companies.

The announcement coincided with the arrival May 29 of a Soviet mission headed by Vladimir Nikovich Kostin, deputy minister of non-ferrous metals. Kostin was reported to have offered to advise a pilot project at the recently expropriated El Teniente Mining Co.

The Soviet mission estimated Chile's copper production for 1971 to be 825,000 metric tons, about 18% lower than the planned output, according to a July 25 report. Codelco had estimated that copper production would be 990,000 tons. The mission attributed the fall in production to engineering deficiencies and mismanagement of U.S.-owned mines before their nationalization.

State mine strike. The first strike in an important nationalized industry ended July 6 after a 24-hour stoppage by 10,000 workers of the Lota-Schwager Co. coal mines. The unions, controlled by the Communists, accepted 40% pay raises.

12-day copper strike. The government of President Salvador Allende faced its first strike in the nationalized copper industry Aug. 1 when 5,000 workers of the El Salvador mine refused a formula arrangement for a 38% pay increase offered by the company and asked for a salary raise of 45%. The strike ended Aug. 12 with a settlement reported at 43%, including automatic cost-of-living adjustments.

It was the first strike in the copper industry since Congress passed the nationalization law. The workers' position was considered a direct challenge to the leftist Popular Unity government. Officials of the Labor Ministry had withheld comment.

(A five-day wildcat strike of 400 supervisors at the country's three largest copper mines had ended Aug. 19. The government arrested 15 strike leaders and fired nine other supervisors.

(The strike was started at the Chuquicamata mine by supervisors protesting the appointment of outsiders to high supervisory positions. The supervisors' union said these had been "political appointments" that had violated seniority agreements.)

Mining research center. The United Nations Development Program (UNDP) approved a five-year project costing $2 million to assist the Chilean government in setting up a national Mineral and Metallurgical Research Center, according to a U.N. bulletin released Aug. 5.

The main objectives of the Center would be to contribute to the extractive capabilities of copper and other metals and non-metallic elements; to introduce better technology and reduce production costs in the smelting and refining process; and to study specific metallurgical problems.

2 Anaconda firms seized. It was reported Sept. 1 that two subsidiaries of the Anaconda Copper Co. had been seized by the Chilean government for alleged failure to pay $8 million owed to Chile since 1958. A judge ordered the physical property and bank accounts of the Andes Mining Co. and the Chile Exploration Co. impounded.

Allende deducts 'excess profits' on copper. President Salvador Allende announced Sept. 28 that he would deduct $774 million in "excess profits" from the book value compensations paid to the U.S. copper companies Anaconda Co. and Kennecott Copper Corp. for nationalized copper properties.

Since the net worth of U.S. copper interests in Chile was estimated at only $550 million, the deductions—if upheld by a five-man indemnification tribunal as expected—would mean that the copper companies would receive no compensation.

Another U.S. company, the Cerro Corp., was not mentioned by Allende since production at its mine began in 1970 and no profit had yet been realized.

Under the legislation nationalizing Chile's copper mines, the comptroller general would determine the "book" value of the companies' investments. "Excess profits" would then be determined by the president and deducted from the book value to determine compensation.

In his televised speech Sept. 28, Allende justified the deductions by contending that the companies had made profits of more than 10% on their holdings since 1955, the beginning date in the legislation for determining "excess profits."

Allende said "the people of Chile have accumulated rightful claims [on the copper companies], which they exercise today, rationally and legitimately, by deducting excess profits that the nationalized companies had obtained."

Chilean Foreign Minister Clodomiro Almeyda Medina told the U.N. General Assembly Oct. 1 that Chile's nationalization of copper mines was in keeping with U.N. principles. Almeyda cited several U.N. resolutions and declarations, including one asserting the right of nations to freely exercise sovereignty over their own resources.

Almeyda said the compensation issue involved U.S. private interests and should not alter Chile's traditional friendship with the U.S., which he referred to as "that great nation."

An Anaconda statement Sept. 29 said "Allende's accounting theory is nothing more than a thin pretext for confiscation. The fact is he's now contrived to grab the world's biggest open-pit copper mine plus a second major underground mine and not pay a dime."

Kennecott President Frank R. Milliken said Sept. 29 that Kennecott "will get nothing for its 49% equity interest in the expropriated El Teniente mine." He added that "Allende has somehow computed Kennecott's alleged excess profits over the past 15 years to be more than our total earnings from Chile in that period and more than the entire net worth of El Teniente."

Comptroller rules on compensation. Chilean Comptroller General Hector Humeres announced Oct. 11 that the Anaconda Company and the Kennecott Corp. should receive no compensation for their nationalized properties. A third U.S. company, the Cerro Corporation, which owned 70% of a new mine, was held to have a claim of $14 million.

(Under Chilean law, the comptroller general would determine indemnification, based on the companies' book value as of Dec. 31, 1970.)

Humeres set a book value of $242 million on Anaconda's Chiquicamata mine, but Allende's recent deduction of $300 million in "excess profits" plus $18 million for other charges left a claim of $76 million against the company.

The Kennecott El Teniente mine was given a book value of $319 million. Allende's deduction of $410 million in excess profits plus other deductions left a claim of $310 million against the firm.

Humeres said the nationalization law provided only for indemnification, not for the collection of a net deficit.

The comptroller general's announcement came after a week of discussions between Chilean Foreign Minister Clodomiro Almeyda and U.S. officials in Washington.

Speaking at a news conference Oct. 7, Almeyda had hinted that his government might reduce substantially the amount of "excess profits" that President Allende had ordered deducted from compensation. He said the two companies involved would be charged only 49% of the excess profits—between $300 and $400 million rather than the $774 million previously announced. Almeyda said he hoped "friendly" relations with the U.S. would not be damaged because of a matter involving $300 million. He also insisted that Chile welcomed private foreign investment but stressed that foreign firms must operate in Chile as "joint ventures" with Chilean entrepreneurs.

Almeyda had met U.S. Secretary of State William P. Rogers Oct. 4 for discussions concerning strained U.S.-Chilean relations over the compensation issue. No progress was reported except an agreement to continue discussions.

The Chilean foreign minister met Oct. 6 with U.S. presidential adviser Henry Kissinger. The New York Times reported a pledge by Kissinger that the U.S. would not attempt to deny Chile access to investment capital in the U.S.

Rogers said Oct. 13 that the decision not to compensate nationalized U.S. copper investments was a "serious departure from accepted standards of international law."

In a formal statement read by State Department spokesman Robert J. McCloskey, Rogers said the U.S. government was "deeply disappointed and disturbed" over the Chilean decision. He said that "the excess profits deductions punish the companies today for acts that were legal and approved by the government of Chile at the time," adding that "no claim is being made that these excess profits deductions are based on violations of Chilean law. This retroactive determination has serious implications for the rule of law."

Rogers warned that the Chilean action might jeopardize the flow of private investment funds to Chile and erode the base of support for foreign aid for Chile and other developing countries.

Replying to Rogers' statement, Almeyda Oct. 14 rejected the U.S.' "veiled pressure" in hinting at financial consequences.

Almeyda accused the U.S. of seeking to "alarm unjustifiably" friendly nations with whom Chile had many interests in common.

Eduardo Novoa, chief legal adviser to President Allende, told a news conference Oct. 14 that the constitutional amendment that permitted nationalization of U.S. copper interests was an act of "historical revision" after years of "exploitation" by foreign companies. He said that "when Lincoln freed the slaves in the U.S., there was no compensation paid to the planters."

Novoa, president of the State Defense Council, limited the hopes of the Anaconda Co. and the Kennecott Corp. of receiving a settlement when he stated that the constitutional clause that gave the president discretionary power to determine excess profits was not open to appeal to a special tribunal that was reviewing the compensation issue.

The day after Rogers' statement, pro-government newspapers in Chile began a campaign to rally the nation behind the government in its confrontation with the U.S. The opposition Christian Democratic and National parties publicly gave Allende their full support.

Sen. Volodia Teitelboim, Communist party spokesman, Oct. 14 accused the Nixon Administration of dropping all pretenses and reverting to the "big stick" era of former President Theodore Roosevelt in U.S. policy towards Latin America.

U.S. Assistant Secretary of State Charles A. Meyer told the House Foreign Affairs subcommittee Oct. 15 that the U.S. was not seeking a confrontation with Chile and would reserve "final judgement" until Chile had finished determining what compensation would be paid to nationalized U.S. interests.

Meyer told the subcommittee that Chile's plans, as they stand now, "do not

provide for just compensation." He attacked the "retroactive" application of excess profits as a disturbing "departure from legal norms."

In response to Congressional criticism regarding the lack of forceful retaliatory measures, Meyer emphasized that "the entire thrust of our policy in the past year has been to try our level best to minimize the chances of a confrontation with Chile."

The New York Times Oct. 14 cited Latin American diplomatic sources as saying that the Chilean government had decided to assume the foreign debts of the nationalized U.S. companies. These debts were said to total $550 million plus an additional $220 million in interest.

Auto industry. It was reported May 28 that the government had "requisitioned" the Ford Motor Co., which had not been in production since December 1970. Requisition signified a temporary government takeover of factories. (Fiat agents expressed interest June 2 in entering into a joint company with the Chilean government to operate the Ford Motor Co.)

The Overseas Private Investment Corp., which insures private U.S. foreign investments, made a $910,000 payment to Ford because its Chilean plant was taken over by the Allende government.

This was the first federal "political risk" insurance payment growing out of Chilean expropriation of U.S. businesses, the Wall Street Journal reported Oct. 15.

General Motors Corp. announced Sept. 27 that it would stop the assembly of commercial vehicles in Chile by Dec. 31. GM said it was forced to close its plant in Arica, which employed 586 workers, "because of the limitations which would be placed on the company under the terms of the government's new automotive industry program." This program called for Chilean government majority participation in plants to assemble specified and approved classes of vehicles only.

Government takes over ITT operations. The government decided to take over operation of the U.S.-owned Chilean Telephone Co. in order to prevent interruption in service, it was reported Sept. 24. The International Telephone & Telegraph Corp. (ITT) owned 70% of the operation.

Interior Minister Jose Toha said that the government had decided to act because the current "precariousness of service . . . could harm national security." He added that the intervention "does not mean that the company will change owners . . . nor a breakdown in negotiations with ITT to reach a definitive nationalization."

In a related development, it was reported Sept. 26 that the general manager of the Chilean Telephone Co. and three others were arrested in connection with alleged fraud in a subsidiary firm that publishes telephone directories.

Other government takeovers. Among other events involving government control of private businesses:

■ The government development firm, Corfo, took control of RCA Victor Electronic Enterprises after acquiring 51% of the firm's stock, it was reported Feb. 25. RCA was to continue advising the firm.

According to a May 28 announcement, the government planned to nationalize the country's nitrate industry. The state-owned Development and Production Corp. would buy a $19.6 million share in the Chilean Mining and Chemical Co. as well as $24.6 million in shares from the Anglo-Lautaro Nitrate Co. Ltd.

The Paris newspaper Le Monde reported Aug. 11 that five principal fishing industries had been brought under state control following a 15 day conflict between workers and industry managers.

Plants seized by workers. Chilean workers Aug. 30 seized two important industrial plants—Cervecerias Unidas, the country's largest brewery, and the Insa Automobile Tire Co., in which the General Tire Co. of Akron, Ohio, was a major shareholder.

The two takeovers reportedly followed a pattern of worker seizures followed by state intervention through appointed administrators. It had been used extensively by the government of President Salvador Allende to extend "public ownership" to important plants.

Drop in foreign investments. Charles Meyer, U.S. assistant secretary of state for inter-American affairs, said there have been few private foreign investments in Chile since President Allende was elected in 1970, the Miami Herald reported Sept. 10.

Meyer reportedly told a closed hearing of the U.S. House of Representatives in June that the decline could be attributed to the nationalization of foreign industries, which had primarily affected American-owned companies.

It was also reported Sept. 10 that a report prepared by private American companies being circulated in Washington had portrayed a grave view of the "declining economic situation" in Chile under Allende's government. The report predicted that within the next six months, there would be "an economic crisis of the first magnitude" in Chile.

The document blamed "poor assessment" of the economic situation by Allende's officials and the president's "own ignorance on economic matters."

Nationalization bill sent to Congress. President Salvador Allende sent to Congress Oct. 19 a bill listing 150 Chilean firms, regarded by the government as playing a key role in the economy, to be nationalized.

The bill divided the economy into three areas. The 150 firms, after compensation, would enter the "social area," becoming the property of the state. There would also be a mixed area of both state and private capital and a totally private sector.

The bill left most of the nation's industries and businesses unaffected by nationalization. Allende stressed that "the road we have chosen does not imply the collectivization of the means of production, but only the fundamentals for national economic development."

The London Times reported Oct. 21 that opposition to the legislation was already intense and that the Christian Democrats had already introduced a rival bill which would give power to nationalize to the legislature rather than to the executive.

Living costs rise. The National Statistics Institute July 8 reported an 11.1% increase in the cost of living for the first six months of 1971. This compared with a 23.9% increase in the same period of 1970.

■ The Miami Herald reported July 28 that black marketeering in some food and consumer goods had begun due to severe shortages and increasing demands. While the government reportedly imported 1,600 tons of beef and 800 tons of chicken for distribution, the shipments were not sufficient to meet the demands of consumers and distributors were selling food at prices above those decreed by DIRINCO, the government pricing agency.

■ Minister of Economy Pedro Vuskovic said, according to an Aug. 1 report, that food shortages and price speculation required more state control of marketing to "knock out the middlemen."

Vuskovic told an assembly of housewives that recent shortages were mainly the result of a large expansion in consumer demand stemming from income distribution policies favoring the lower income sectors. He called on the housewives to organize neighborhood vigilance committees to help the government control price speculation.

Allende imposes state food control. In an address before a national congress of the Communist-controlled Central Labor Union Dec. 8, President Salvador Allende announced that the government would take over full control of food distribution as part of an "offensive against fascist sedition."

He also called for the organization of "neighborhood vigilance committees" to fight food hoarders and black marketers.

The government had assumed control of three major wholesale distributors and ordered 22 cattle auction markets under state management Dec. 7.

Important sectors of wholesale food distribution were already under government control, particularly all marketing of beef, wheat, sugar and other basic products. The government had announced it would also extend state control and open state stores in populous low-income neighborhoods.

In his Dec. 8 address, Allende charged that economic problems in the country were being exploited by political sectors, inside and outside of Chile, whose interests had been hurt by the government's policy of nationalizing foreign-owned properties as well as large domestic industries.

The "campaign against Chile" he said, included the reduction of foreign lines of credit and such things as a comment by Herbert G. Klein, President Nixon's director of communications, that Chile's government would not last long.

Allende said: "To those who say the days of Chile's popular government are numbered, I say that they can swallow their tongues, that this is not a no-man's land, and that the [U.S.] Marines are not going to impose their will here."

Imports restricted. President Allende had ordered imports restricted to essentials in an attempt to avert a crisis in the country's foreign currency reserves, it was reported Nov. 3.

The Chilean Central Bank imposed a 10,000% prior deposit charge on more than 75% of all capital and consumer goods imported from abroad. Under the restriction, a company that wanted to import $100 worth of goods would be required to deposit $10,000 in the central bank.

The Wall Street Journal Nov. 3 cited sources that estimated the central bank's foreign currency reserves dropped from about $400 million to $175 million in the year Allende's leftist coalition has held power.

In another economic development, it was reported Nov. 15 that production of consumer goods for September increased by 30.9% compared with September 1970. The monthly average of the first nine months of 1971 showed an increase of 10.2% in comparison with the same period in 1970.

Currency devaluations. The Chilean Central Bank July 26 had devalued the escudo by nearly 100% on the brokers' market. The rate went from 14.23 to 28 escudos to the U.S. dollar. The bankers' rate remained the same.

In a fresh currency action, Central Bank President Alfonso Inostroza announced Dec. 10 that the government had selectively devalued the escudo about 30% in a move to spur exports, provide aid for low income groups in Chile, and to stem Chile's dwindling dollar reserves.

His announcement came after a week beginning Dec. 6 during which all foreign exchange operations had been suspended.

New rates, effective Dec. 13 with the reopening of foreign exchange operations, devalued the escudo, breaking it down into five different rates for purchase of imports. Only basic foodstuffs and petroleum products were exempted from the devaluation. These would continue to be imported at the former level of 12.21 escudos to the dollar for all imports in an attempt to reduce the impact on the cost of living. The rate for the bulk of industrial imports would be 15.80 escudos to the dollar.

These lower rates would be subsidized by a luxury import rate of 19 escudos to the dollar for automotive parts, cosmetics and home appliances while a rate of 25 escudos to the dollar would hold for items such as whisky, caviar and cigars. The rate for foreign travel was maintained at 28 escudos, although with the special taxes Chileans had to pay the effective rate was 43 to the dollar.

Inostroza said these provisions, differentiating between imports for the "popular sectors" and the wealthy, made the devaluation consistent with the government's policy of distributing income in favor of poorer sectors of the population.

He denied that the exchange reform was due to a "crisis" in Chile's exchange reserve position, saying that the Central Bank had active foreign exchange reserves of about $200 million. However, Inostroza conceded a decline in reserves from $400 million a year ago, which he attributed to the need to meet short-term notes from international creditors, the closing of lines of credit totaling about $200 million by U.S. banks, and a decline in the world price of copper. (Chile's potential export earnings drop $15 million each time the world market copper prices falls 1¢.)

The Washington Post reported Dec. 11 that disrupted production at the recently nationalized mines and increased buying power among the lower classes because of government pay raises had also drained Chile's dollar reserves.

(The International Monetary Fund announced Dec. 10 in Washington that it had granted Chile a credit of $39.5 million to compensate for declining income from copper, and to help alleviate its balance of payments program.)

The Post also reported Dec. 11 that the most influential businessmen's group in Chile, the Industrial Development Society, had criticized the government for its economic policies leading up to the devaluation. "The country knows that the government found itself with the greatest reserves ever in the Central Bank, more than $400 million, so it is difficult to understand how these could have been exhausted in only 12 months," it charged.

Study predicts economic woes. An economic report released Dec. 20 by World Wide Information Services, a private business information agency operating in 138 countries, reported that Chile faced severe credit problems in March 1972 and economic chaos by the following year.

The report claimed that many of Chile's economic troubles resulted from the redistribution of income and socialization of the economy, both supported by President Allende.

"To pay for all this . . . Allende counted on the expected large export earnings of the copper industry," the report said, "but even the most optimistic estimates demonstrate that copper production will be much less than projected, and as the international price of copper is expected to remain low, a 1971 drop of earnings of at least $90 million from 1970 is likely to occur."

The report added that the government was "beginning to admit that Chile has serious economic problems, but it still does not appear to take the politically risky measures needed to bring the economy into adjustment."

Broadcasters strike. Broadcasting workers at all of Santiago's 23 radio stations struck Dec. 24 when union negotiations failed to meet their demands for 45% pay raises.

However, 14 stations supporting the government, accepted a government arbitrator's ruling Dec. 25 in favor of a 25% pay raise and went back to work.

Opposition politicians claimed that the 14 stations had received promises from the government that enough official advertising would be placed with them to pay for the salary increase.

The remaining nine stations, all aligned with the opposition, remained on strike until Dec. 30 when they agreed to concessions made by the government.

Relations With the U.S.

Nixon's views. U.S. President Richard M. Nixon, early in 1971, made clear his dissatisfaction with the new Allende regime.

Nixon said in a TV interview Jan. 4 that Allende's election as Chile's president "is not something that we welcomed, although . . . we were very careful to point out that that was the decision of the people of Chile, and that, therefore, we accepted that decision and that our programs with Chile . . . would continue so long as Chile's foreign policy was not antagonistic to our interests."

Nixon amplified his position Feb. 25 in his State-of-the-World message to Congress. "We are prepared to have the kind of relationship with the Chilean government that it is prepared to have with us. . . . We do not seek confrontations with any government," Nixon said. But those governments which "display unremitting hostility cannot expect our assistance," and those intervening in their neighbor's affairs or facilitating intervention by non-hemispheric powers also should not expect to share in the benefits of the inter-American system.

Allende for 'best' relations with U.S. President Allende stressed in an interview March 23 that Chile wanted "the best— the very best" relations with the U.S. "The United States should recognize that our democracy here is authentic democracy, and that we will never do anything against the United States or contribute to injuring its sovereignty," he said. "For example," he added, "we will never provide a military base that might be used against the United States. Chile will never permit her territory to be used for a military base by any foreign power—by anybody."

U.S. carrier visit canceled. The U.S. Department of Defense announced Feb. 27 that a planned courtesy call by the U.S. aircraft carrier Enterprise to the Chilean port of Valparaiso had been called off. "The operating schedule does not permit the ship to make this port of call and still make her scheduled commitments," the Defense Department said.

In response to the cancellation, Chilean President Salvador Allende, who had invited the ship to make a visit, said Feb. 27: "I have been informed that for operational reasons the ship Enterprise will not dock off our coast. I regret this, but our attitude remains unchanged—the attitude of a people without borders."

Allende had announced the planned visit to the Chilean people in a national broadcast Feb. 25. Allende reportedly extended the invitation for the ship's visit during a meeting with U.S. Chief of Naval Operations Adm. Elmo Zumwalt Feb. 19. Zumwalt was on a courtesy tour with visits in Argentina, Brazil and Chile.

Cancellation of the ship's visit reportedly came after bureaucratic in-fighting between the Defense and State Departments. According to the New York Times Feb. 28, the State Department had recommended cancellation of the visit and had been quickly supported by the White House.

■ The U.S. sent an Air Force delegation to Chile to attend the 40th anniversary celebrations of the Chilean Air Force beginning March 21. The delegation arrived in Chile March 19.

The U.S. Air Force had permanently closed its ionospheric research center on Easter Island Jan. 8. The Air Force reportedly turned over $3 million in equipment to Chile as a gift, while other materiel on the island was sold to the Chilean air force.

U.S. grants arms credits. The U.S. State Department announced June 30 the granting of $5 million in credits to Chile for the purchase of American military materiel. It was the first grant to Chile since Allende's election.

According to the announcement, Chile would use the credits to buy a new transport plane and paratroopers' equipment.

The State Department also confirmed that the U.S. Navy would lease to Chile July 1 the 1,235-ton armed tug Arikara.

U.S. refuses jet purchase loan. The U.S. Export-Import Bank (Eximbank) Aug. 11 rejected a Chilean request for $21 million in loans and loan guarantees for the purchase of three Boeing jetliners because of the unresolved issue of Chilean compensation for recently expropriated American copper companies.

The loan rejection was made at a meeting in Washington by Eximbank President Harry Kearns to Chilean Ambassador Orlando Letelier. Kearns said the loan request was denied because Chile had failed to give proper assurances on compensation for the copper firms. Kearns said "we must have some meaningful guidance on what [the Chileans'] intentions are and the way they will approach a settlement on the copper issue." He indicated that the loan and loan guarantees might be approved at a later date when Chile "offers guarantees of payment."

The New York Times reported Aug. 11 that the Chilean government had been negotiating with the State Department, Eximbank and the Boeing Co. for six months, offering to pay $5 million toward the $26 million price for the three jets, provided that Eximbank agreed to underwrite 40% of the cost in guarantees to five U.S. private banks plus another 40% as a direct loan to Boeing.

It was also reported Aug. 12 that the U.S. would make no commercial loans to Chile while the compensation issue remained unresolved. The Associated Press (AP) said Aug. 11 that Chile had been phased out of the U.S. foreign assistance program. State Department sources were quoted as saying that Chile's exclusion was the result of economic considerations and not as retaliation to Chile's Marxist government. The AP said Chile's exclusion from the development loan program was disclosed in an AID report on projected outlays for Latin America for 1972. The State Department categorically denied the AP report.

(The Eximbank decision and policy was seen as a victory for the U.S. Treasury Department. The State Department had opposed credit restrictions on the grounds that it could complicate political relations and impede efforts to negotiate compensation claims, according to an Aug. 15 report.)

Chilean reaction—Immediately following the loan refusal, Ambassador Letelier said "we cannot consider this a friendly attitude toward Chile." He added that the government of President Salvador Allende was in the process of calculating the compensation to be paid to the copper companies. He added that "the question of compensation . . . has nothing to do with normal commercial operations of the Eximbank."

Chilean Minister of Foreign Affairs Clodomiro Almeyda Medina Aug. 13 criticized the U.S. action as an "attempt at pressure and an illicit and unacceptable interference." Almeyda expressed the hope, however, that the action did not signify a negative change in the U.S. government's attitude in its relations with Chile. He added that "if it becomes necessary, our state airline will explore all other channels which lead to the acquisition of the aircraft it needs for its operations."

Naval exercise. President Allende, who had previously opposed joint military maneuvers with the U.S., approved Chilean participation in Operation Unitas XII, a multi-national naval exercise that began Sept. 10 off the Chilean coast near the northern port of Arica.

Asked about the Chilean government's reversal of opinion, a Chilean spokesman said "the government of Chile wants its navy to have professional relations with all navies of the world which want to make mixed operations."

U.S. threatens aid cut. U.S. Secretary of State William P. Rogers Oct. 21 told representatives of six major U.S. corporations affected by recent expropriations in Chile that the U.S. government would take steps to cut off all aid to Chile unless its government provided adequate compensation.

Represented at the secret meeting with Rogers were the Anaconda Co., the Ford Motor Co., International Telephone & Telegraph, Ralston-Purina, the First National City Bank of New York and the Bank of America.

Rogers reportedly told the representatives that the U.S. intended to invoke the Hickenlooper Amendment, requiring suspension of aid to any country failing to provide for adequate compensation for expropriated American properties. U.S. officials said the discussion covered options available to Washington in dealing with Chilean expropriations.

Invocation of the Hickenlooper Amendment would not significantly affect Chile since bilateral aid to that country has been minimal.

Socialists urge default in U.S. debt—The Socialist party, the largest in the governing left-wing coalition, declared Dec. 18 that Chile had the right to refuse to pay debts of more than $2 billion to the U.S. "if North American imperialism continues economic and diplomatic aggression" against Chile.

The statement also called for rapid takeovers by the state of industries, wholesale distributors and export-import concerns, as well as for a stepped-up campaign to bring more agriculture under state control.

Chile scores speculation on overthrow of Allende. A six-nation Latin American tour by U.S. Presidential Counselor Robert H. Finch Nov. 11–25 led to Chilean complaints about White House speculation that Allende might be deposed soon.

Although the journey did not include a visit to Chile, Herbert G. Klein, White House director of communications, told reporters in Washington Nov. 30 that he and Finch had reported to President Nixon a "feeling" they gained in conversations during their Latin trip that the Allende government "won't last long."

Klein said that, although their mission had "no direct knowledge of the Chilean situation," its members' impressions concerning the fate of Allende "will be part of the report" they would make to Nixon.

It was unusual for senior Administration officials to discuss publicly the possibility of the overthrow of a foreign regime with which the U.S. maintained correct relations, even though strains existed.

Chilean Foreign Minister Clodomiro Almeyda delivered a formal note in Santiago Dec. 1 to U.S. Ambassador Nathaniel Davis protesting Klein's statement.

Relations With Communist Countries

Ties with Communist China set. Chile established diplomatic relations with Peking Jan. 5, 1971, joining Cuba as the only Latin American nations recognizing the Communist Chinese government. Immediately following the announcement by Chilean Foreign Minister Clodomiro Almeyda, Nationalist China cut its ties with Chile, calling the Chilean action "a very unfriendly act."

The agreement to establish ties had been negotiated in Paris by the ambassadors to France from Chile and Communist China and had been concluded Dec. 15, 1970. A joint communique dated Dec. 15, 1970 and issued in Paris Jan. 5 asserted Peking's contention that Taiwan was "an inalienable part of the territory of the People's Republic of China" and that "the Chilean government takes note of this statement." The communique also said: "The Chilean government recognizes the government of the People's Republic of China as the sole legal government of China."

The Chilean Foreign Ministry said the establishment of relations with Communist China "fulfilled one of the basic points of the government's platform and will help to correct the injustice of the alienation of China from the orbit of the United Nations."

Nationalist Chinese Ambassador to Chile Ti-Tsun Li closed the embassy in Santiago and left the country Jan. 5.

China to buy copper—It was reported Dec. 16 that Communist China would buy 65,000 tons of copper annually from Chile over the next four years. The sales would represent an annual income of about $70 million for Chile.

North Vietnamese commercial visit. Chilean Foreign Minister Clodomiro Almeyda announced March 25 the formal recognition by Chile of a North Vietnamese commercial mission.

Relations with East Germany. Chile announced April 6 that it had agreed to establish diplomatic relations and exchange ambassadors with East Germany. The agreement, concluded in East Berlin March 16, was signed by East German Foreign Minister Otto Winzer and Alcides Leal Osorio, Chilean secretary of state for foreign affairs.

Soviet bloc trip. A Chilean economic mission, led by Foreign Minister Clodomiro Almeyda, left Santiago May 14 for a trip to seven eastern European countries and the Soviet Union. The mission was regarded as a major move on the part of President Allende to increase trade with the Communist bloc countries and to obtain economic trade for Chile's "construction of socialism."

In Hungary May 20, Almeyda emphasized the "common political aims" of the governments of Chile and Hungary. Bilateral trade between the two countries, according to the foreign minister, would be accelerated within the year to reach about $1 million annually.

At a news conference after a meeting in Moscow with Soviet Premier Aleksei Kosygin May 28, Almeyda discussed his desire to develop contacts with the Council for Mutual Economic Assistance (COMECON) and "to study the possibilities of cooperating with the organization." Almeyda also said he had signed agreements with the Soviet Union for the expansion of trade and for Soviet technical aid.

In Yugoslavia, Almeyda conferred with Marshal Tito June 1 after talks with Yugoslav officials on possible co-production of aluminum. In Prague June 8, Almeyda and Czech Foreign Trade Minister Andrej Barcak signed a protocol on economic and technical cooperation between the two countries.

After Almeyda's return, a Foreign Ministry official announced Aug. 6 that Chile had obtained $300 million in credits from the Soviet Union and other eastern European countries. The credits would be used to promote industrial development.

It was announced Dec. 9 that the Soviet Union and Chile had signed a "program of cooperation for 1972" that would provide Russian aid for Chile's fishing industry. It would include the use of Soviet fishing boats and construction of new fishing harbors in Chile with Soviet technical aid.

Report of Soviet arms credit denied. A report in the New York Times Oct. 13 which cited U.S. military sources as stating that the Soviet Union had granted $50 million in arms credits to Chile was denied by the Chilean Foreign Ministry as "absolutely false," the Times reported Oct. 22.

Chilean Ambassador to the U.S. Orlando Letelier said "there have been no negotiations nor any offer related to such type of credit between Chile and the Soviet Union," the Miami Herald reported Oct. 21.

Relations with Albania. Chile and Albania decided to establish diplomatic relations, according to Sept. 12 reports. A communique on establishing relations was signed by the two countries' ambassadors to Italy.

Castro visits Chile. Premier Fidel Castro of Cuba visited Chile Nov. 10–Dec. 4. He called his 25-day visit to Chile, which included airport stopovers Dec. 4 for meetings with the presidents of Peru and Ecuador, a "triumphant success" and "proof that we are not as alone as we once were."

It was the Cuban leader's first trip to Latin America since 1959, and signified a breach in the united policy of diplomatic and economic boycott of Cuba begun when the Organization of American States (OAS) expelled Cuba in 1962.

From his arrival in Chile Nov. 10, Castro received an enthusiastic reception, mainly among organized students and workers. Despite a heavy cold, he made two or three speeches a day the length of the country. Castro made appearances in the cities of Santiago and Concepcion and in fishing towns and mining camps from Antofagasta in the extreme north to Punta Arenas, Chile's southernmost city.

The only denunciation of his visit came from right-wing nationalists. According to a Nov. 17 report, the opposition Santiago newspaper Tribuna called Castro's visit—which had been extended from 10 to 24 days—"marathonic." Right-wing congressmen introduced a motion Nov. 29 that the visiting Cuban premier end his trip "as soon as possible."

In Santiago Nov. 11, Castro indicated an end to the Cuban dogma that guerrilla violence was the only means to revolution. Asked if he believed that armed struggle was the only way to achieve power, Castro said Cuba had never excluded elections as a means of attaining that goal. His comments were seen by observers as a veiled criticism of the Chilean terrorist group Revolutionary Left Movement (MIR), which had criticized Allende for not being radical enough.

Castro's low-key approach during his appearances was interpreted as an effort not to make unnecessary domestic difficulties for President Allende or interfere in Chile's internal affairs. However, a Dec. 1 demonstration of 5,000 women protesting Castro's visit and food shortages raised antagonisms between the Allende government and its anti-Marxist opposition to a new level of violence.

Castro Dec. 4 called these clashes "an escalation of fascist sedition" and said that "perhaps our visit has served as a stimulus for those who want to create difficulties for the popular government."

Castro had touched on Chilean internal politics for the first time Nov. 14 at Chuquicamata, the world's largest open-pit copper mine, which had been nationalized in July. His visit coincided with a dispute between militant mineworkers and the government over pay. Castro told the workers that they should put the state's interest before their own.

In appearances before peasants, workers and students, Castro often repeated his call for the people to work harder under socialism. He said that the Allende government would bring socialism to Chile if the left-wing parties were united and if the workers increased production, two of the Allende government's most persistent problems.

Earlier Cuban-Chilean events—Cuba and Chile Feb. 12 signed a commercial agreement providing for about $20 million worth of trade. The terms included sale of Cuban sugar to Chile and Cuban purchase of Chilean agricultural products, cellulose, wood, copper and steel.

■ Cuba and Chile signed a communications agreement Feb. 15 in Santiago. The pact included establishment of a Santiago-Havana radio network which could later be transformed into a telex system.

■ Juan Enrique Vega, the first Chilean ambassador to Cuba since 1964, arrived in Havana, according to a report May 23.

■ The Soviet news agency Tass reported Aug. 2 that the Cubans and Chileans had signed a five-year agreement on scientific and technical cooperation. The agreement provided for the mutual exchange of specialists, data, scientific and technical documentation and experience. A standing mixed inter-governmental commission would implement the agreement, according to the report.

■ It was reported Aug. 4 that Chile and Cuba had signed a joint declaration attacking agreements of the Organization of American States (OAS) through which Latin American nations had broken diplomatic relations with Cuba.

The joint declaration said "both parties believe that the OAS agreements that brought the rupture of diplomatic, consular and commercial relations between the countries of Latin America and Cuba are without juridical and moral value." It added that both countries "believe that the policy of economic isolation constitutes a violation of the right of self-determination of the Cuban people on the pretext of damaging their course of economic development."

■ The Miami Herald said Oct. 8 that Cuban and Chilean women had signed a public document calling on the women of Latin America to "join the liberation battles of their people." A Cuban women's delegation had been in Santiago to attend the Women's Political Committee of President Allende's Popular Unity government.

Latin American Relations

Chile vs. kidnaping convention. Chile joined the 22 other Organization of American States (OAS) in a special foreign ministers' meeting that opened Jan. 25 and closed Feb. 2 with only Chile opposing the adoption of a convention condemning diplomatic kidnaping.

The kidnaping convention, adopted 13–1 with two abstentions, labeled as a "common crime, whatever the motives" kidnaping, murder and other acts of terror against diplomatic and other foreign officials. The text also provided for denial of the right of political asylum to the kidnapers and terrorists and authorized their extradition and/or trial. However, the final text of the convention, considered to be a mild document, authorized any country to refuse extradition if it considered the accused person guilty of a political rather than a criminal act.

Chile voted against the convention, stressing that it violated the sovereignty of Latin American nations.

'Ideological pluralism.' An agreement was signed in Bogota May 8 by Alfredo Vasquez, Colombian foreign minister, and Clodomiro Almeyda, his Chilean counterpart, which called for "ideological pluralism" between states in the United Nations and within the inter-American system, and for the self-determination of nations.

The declaration was significant as a step in bridging a widening gap between conflicting ideologies in Latin America. Observers said it could also impede efforts by the U.S. to continue the policy of "ostracism" of Cuba by the Organization of American States.

The agreement also called for a 50% increase in commercial trade between Chile and Colombia. The ministers also called for further financial, industrial, cultural and educational agreements.

Chilean President Allende, however, apparently was involved in the release by Uruguay's Tupamaro guerrillas Sept. 9 of British Ambassador Geoffrey Jackson, who had been kidnaped and held in a "people's prison" for eight months.

In Washington, D.C., a member of the British Parliament, Judith Hart, said Sept. 10 that Allende had told her recently that Jackson would be freed soon. British officials confirmed the report of Allende's role in the ambassador's release.

Historic Argentine-Chilean meeting. Chilean President Salvador Allende and Argentine President Alejandro Agustin Lanusse held a two-day "summit" meeting July 23–24 in the northern Argentine city of Salta. The meeting marked the first time the Chilean president had left his country since taking office in 1970.

The meeting, called to ratify an agreement for arbitration of the Beagle Channel border dispute, was regarded as historic mainly because the leaders represented different ideological political positions. Allende, a Marxist theoretician, had said he would lead Chile down the "road to socialism." Lanusse was the third Argentine military president since the military deposed President Arturo Illia in June 1966, and the military regime had taken a strong anti-Communist position on inter-American affairs, although Lanusse had softened the government's stance.

Accord on Beagle Channel—One day before the meeting began, an announcement was made in London that Chile and Argentina had agreed to a formula for ratification of the Beagle Channel dispute. The agreement, negotiated by the foreign ministers of both countries, consisted of three parts: a list of 18 articles providing for the border to be established by Britain's Queen Elizabeth on the basis of a technical decision by a five-man arbitration court composed of judges from the World Court; a modus vivendi to be applied while the court was deliberating; and a joint Chilean-Argentine declaration approving the eventual decision which would be binding on both sides. Both presidents subscribed to the formula during their meeting in Salta.

Friendship stressed—Lanusse welcomed Allende at the airport July 23, stating that the meeting was "a testimony of the firm friendship that unites Argentina and Chile." Allende replied that the countries shared common hopes and a common future which made possible a "juridical solution to the only difference existing between our common native lands."

During the meeting, the two heads of state reinforced the spirit of friendship in ceremonies in which each president decorated the other with his country's highest distinction.

Allende explained during the conference that, while his plans and objectives adhered to Marxist principles, they would be implemented to conform to the specific circumstances and characteristics of Chile. He added that "by means of the popular government over which I preside, Chile is building a humane and independent economy, inspired by Socialist ideals."

Lanusse replied by stating that "Argentina prefers to promote its development on the basis of all its people and the defense of free initiative in the private sector, reconciling this with the overall national interests."

The issue of terrorism and violence was also discussed by the two. Allende repudiated terrorist tactics and the use of "institutionalized crime" as a political weapon.

Declaration signed—The conference concluded with both presidents signing the "Declaration of Salta," which ratified the arbitration agreement on the border dispute and expressed a "firm will to continue strengthening the bonds of amity" between the two nations. It stated that the friendship had its bases in the "respect for the principles of non-intervention in the internal and external affairs of each country and in the will to resolve their problems in a peaceful and juridical manner." The declaration also referred to the desire of both countries to maintain sovereignty over a 200-mile territorial coastal limit.

The statement also called for joint efforts to expand trade, transport, tourism and exchange of technology while de-

claring that the "human factor" would remain of "fundamental importance in the relations beween the two states."

Lanusse visits Chile. Argentine President Lanusse visited Chile Oct. 16–17. During his 28-hour stay, Lanusse conferred with Allende and backed the Chilean government in its nationalization of U.S. copper interests.

Lanusse said Oct. 17 that he did not expect or want the U.S.to impose sanctions against Chile as a result of the nationalization of U.S. copper properties. In that event, he said, Argentina would intervene to look for a solution as a friend of both Chile and the U.S.

Allende on 3-nation trip. President Allende made an 11-day trip to Ecuador, Colombia and Peru Aug. 24–Sept. 4.

Allende arrived in Quito, Ecuador, Aug. 24 on his first stop of the tour. The announced purpose of his visit with President Jose Maria Velasco Ibarra was to show that governments with totally different ideologies could co-exist harmoniously. Allende and Velasco Ibarra signed a joint declaration Aug. 26 calling for unilateral recognition and diplomatic and commercial relations with Cuba by those Latin nations who wished to do so "when it is deemed convenient."

The text was considered a setback for the OAS, whose secretary general, Galo Plaza, had wanted the organization to act as a group in re-evaluating relationships with Cuba. The declaration emphasized that the U.N. was the principal organism of international relations. The two presidents said that the "universality of the United Nations does not admit any limitation." This assertion was taken as implicit support of the admission of Communist China to the U.N.

The joint statement also rejected any illicit interference with the sovereign decisions of those nations that wanted to preserve their natural resources. This was a reference to the dispute with the U.S. over Ecuador's 200-mile territorial water limit and Chile's dispute over compensation for nationalized U.S. copper firms. The two presidents called for the "solidarity of peoples that fight for their autonomy and independence."

Allende was welcomed enthusiastically in Bogota, Colombia, Aug. 28 in what was considered his most important stop. In a brief airport ceremony when he was met by Colombian President Misael Pastrana Borrero, Allende said he had come "as the Chilean president" and not "as a representative of a political movement." (Leaders of Pastrana's Conservative party had protested Allende's visit, describing it as "inopportune and unnecessary," and accused Allende "of all types of crimes against the Colombian right." Liberals and the opposition ANAPO party had welcomed Allende's visit.)

Allende's Colombian visit contained few formal appearances, but he made informal speeches, and the trip took on the atmosphere of a political campaign. In a joint declaration signed Aug. 31, Pastrana and Allende "solemnly reaffirmed their conviction that only the respect for self-determination and non-intervention in the international affairs of other states make possible the fruitful cooperation among nations." This statement was seen as a diplomatic victory for Allende in his effort to gain support for his nationalist posture in the dispute with the U.S. over copper compensation.

The two presidents hailed the apparent breakdown of ideological barriers between countries and called for Latin American unity to confront industrialized countries on economic issues. The statement affirmed the inherent right of Latin American countries to exploit their own natural resources, including seabed and subsoil rights, while calling for the limitation of military expenditures in Latin America.

At an Aug. 31 press conference, Allende reasserted his government's determination to pay "just compensation" for nationalized properties, even though it might provoke continued dispute with the U.S.

Allende also held a brief meeting with ANAPO leader Gustavo Rojas Pinilla, after which Rojas noted that Allende's Popular Unity platform and that of ANAPO were similar.

Allende arrived Sept. 1 in Lima, Peru, where he received his third pledge of moral support for "ideological pluralism" from the head of the Peruvian military government, Juan Velasco Alvarado. Allende concluded his largely ceremonial three-day Peruvian visit Sept. 3 with another joint statement, criticizing the recent economic measures adopted by the U.S. Both presidents indicated "their preoccupation with the protectionist tendencies that were fixed by the U.S." and protested the measures taken to combat American monetary problems.

In an apparent reference to the recent refusal to grant Chile credits for the purchase of commercial jets, Allende and Velasco said "economic cooperation and authorization of international credits should not be used as instruments to force the will of one state" on another.

Foreign Loans & Aid

Loans negotiated. Among foreign loans negotiated by Chile during 1971:

■ The Inter-American Development Bank Jan. 14 approved two loans totaling $11.6 million to help improve and expand two private universities in Chile. The loans, extended from the bank's Fund for Special Operations, provided $7 million for the Catholic University in Santiago and $4.6 million for the Austral University in Valdivia, Chile.

■ The Inter-American Development Bank was reported Aug. 1 to have extended a $15 million loan to Chile to help repair damage caused by an earthquake July 8. The loan would be repaid over 25 years at 3.5% interest.

■ Six European nations agreed to begin construction in 1972 of a $15 million observatory north of Santiago, it was reported March 5. The countries were France, West Germany, Belgium, Denmark, the Netherlands and Sweden.

■ The Buenos Aires newspaper La Prensa reported Dec. 22 that a group of Argentine banks had approved a loan of more than $20 million to Chile for the purchase of foodstuffs, principally Argentine beef.

Renegotiation of foreign debt planned. President Salvador Allende announced Nov. 9 that the Chilean government would seek to renegotiate its foreign debt,which totaled more than $3 billion.

In a television speech, Allende said his government would fulfill its promise to assume all obligations contracted by previous Chilean governments. He added that the renegotiation was planned "to satisfy adequately the interests of both the country and its creditors." Allende said the debt payment schedule was incompatible with sustaining a sufficient rate of development in the new Socialist structure of investment in Chile.

The current schedule called for payment of $300 million in 1971, with $400 million to be paid in both 1972 and 1973.

In his speech, Allende cited the closing of credit lines of $190 million by U.S. banks and the decline of international copper prices as causes for the debt renegotiation.

At a press conference the same day, Allende said the proposed renegotiation would not include the $736 million debts that the government took over from the nationalized U.S. copper companies. He asserted that Chile's foreign debt problems were aggravated by such "unilateral U.S. actions" as the 10% import surcharge and the "suspension of foreign aid."

Earthquake

Earthquake shakes Chile. A severe earthquake, felt for 1,400 miles along the spine of the Andes, struck the populous north-central region of Chile July 9, causing widespread damage in the provinces of Santiago, Valparaiso and Aconcagua. The Interior Ministry reported at least 90 persons dead and 250 injured. The estimates of persons left homeless ranged from 15,000 to 100,000. President Salvador Allende, who toured the region by helicopter July 10, declared a state of emergency in the three provinces and said that 60% of the homes in the area were uninhabitable. Landslides isolated some communities,and many regions were without electricity or communications. Relief efforts were hampered by rain that fell for some 48 hours.

1972: Mounting Opposition

Political & Economic Reverses

Opposition to the Allende regime continued to grow during 1972 in the face of deepening economic problems. Chile was beset by increasingly serious strikes, demonstrations and civil disruptions.

Government set back in by-elections. The government of President Salvador Allende suffered a political setback Jan. 16 with the election of two opposition candidates in Congressional by-elections for a senator from O'Higgins and Colchagua Provinces and a federal deputy from Linares Province.

The elections had been presented by the opposition as an opportunity for more than 200,000 voters to take a stand against the government's program to "construct socialism" in Chile.

Final returns for the senatorial race gave Christian Democrat Rafael Moreno 7,614 votes to 68,338 for Hector Olivares, a Socialist representative of the Popular Unity government.

In Linares Province, Sergio Diez, a candidate of the conservative National party with Christian Democratic backing, received 29,990 votes, while his Leftist Democratic opponent, Maria Elena Mery, received 21,165.

In an attempt to gain government support in the election districts, Minister of Agriculture Jacques Chonchol was reported Jan. 16 as announcing expropriations of 200 large farms under the government's agrarian reform program in Linares and Colchagua.

Thousands of pro-government activists were also reported attempting to gain support in the regions, with one fracas resulting in a shoot-out with police in which six persons were wounded.

The results strengthened the anti-government majority in Congress, which had come into increasing conflict with Allende over the government's socialization program and the large federal budget for 1972, from which the opposition had cut more than $100 million, according to a Jan. 17 report.

(In developments following the two by-elections, Rafael Moreno, the Christian Democrat elected Senator Jan. 16, was stoned Jan. 20 at Rancagua by persons shouting progovernment slogans. In Linares Province, members of the Revolutionary Left Movement were accused Jan. 22 of kidnaping the son of a leader of the National party, whose candidate had been elected federal deputy for the area.)

Leftists concede failings. The governing Popular Unity coalition acknowledged Feb. 9 that it had failed to involve a majority of Chileans in the country's "process of revolutionary transformation."

After a week-long meeting called in the wake of the opposition victories in the Jan. 16 by-elections, leaders of the aligned parties admitted bureaucratic ineptitude, administrative dishonesty and sectarian political attitudes, and scored the tactics of the Revolutionary Left Movement (MIR).

Criticism of the MIR represented a victory for Chilean Communists, who had attributed the recent electoral losses to the MIR's "sectarian extremism." In a document leaked to the newspaper El Mercurio Feb. 3, Communist leaders had said the MIR's extremist rhetoric and its promotion of farm seizures and urban violence had alienated "middle sectors" of the population that might have voted for Popular Unity candidates.

The MIR in turn had accused the Communists of debilitating the "revolutionary mobilization of the masses" and of keeping MIR members out of government jobs. They had been joined in criticizing the Communist party by the Socialist Popular Union, a splinter group of the Socialist party.

The Popular Unity declaration pledged to obtain the active participation of workers, peasants, consumers and the general public in all aspects of the "construction of socialism," and stressed the need to involve women.

Toha named defense minister. President Salvador Allende had shifted his top aide, Jose Toha Gonzalez, to the post of minister of defense Jan. 7. He thus defied the House of Deputies, which, by 80–59 vote Jan. 6, had suspended Toha as interior minister. Alejandro Rios Valdivia, who had held the defense portfolio, was then sworn in as interior minister.

The opposition Christian Democratic party had begun impeachment proceedings against Toha in December 1971 on grounds he had permitted armed groups of radicals to operate and had violated the right of Chileans to protest peacefully.

In swearing Toha to his new post, Allende said the proceedings against Toha had been promoted "solely for politi-cal purposes." He said he would work to reform Chile's constitution "to implant a new and revolutionary constitution that would prevent such impeachment actions."

Allende said, "It must be clearly understood that this is a presidential regime and we will do everything possible to prevent this kind of thing, which is a throwback to an outdated parliamentary system."

Following the government defeat in the Jan. 16 by-elections, Allende's Cabinet resigned Jan. 20, and he named a new Cabinet Jan. 28.

Toha, meanwhile, was impeached by the Senate Jan. 22 for failing to oppose left-wing extremist groups. The vote was 26–0, with 23 senators who supported the government walking out.

The new interior minister was Hernan del Canto, secretary general of the Central Labor Union. Del Canto remarked: "Those sectors that seek to continue on the road of sedition, that want to destroy the popular government and its revolutionary program, will suffer the full rigors of the law from this minister of the interior, who represents the workers." Orlando Cantuarias moved from the Ministry of Mining to the Ministry of Housing, and Rios, defense minister before his interim appointment to the Interior Ministry, became minister of education.

The other new appointments, both from the Radical party, were Manuel Sanhueza as justice minister and Mauricio Yungk Stahl as minister of mining.

Copper output down, payments held up. The New York Times had reported Jan. 5 that production failures in Chile's nationalized copper mines had contributed heavily to partial suspension of foreign payments by the government.

Although production for 1971 was estimated to be 6% higher than 1970, the total for 1971 included the production of two mines, Exotica and Andina, that were not in production in 1970.

In the three largest nationalized mines, Chuquicamata, El Salvador and El Teniente, the production was 9% lower than 1970.

The state-owned Copper Corporation attributed the declines to a variety of factors ranging from sabotage to poor performance by the American managers. However, industry sources attributed the failure to the new Chilean management.

Mine sabotage charged—The government had said Jan. 3 that an attempt had been made over the New Year's weekend to sabotage the El Teniente copper mines. Two men and two women were arrested on charges of having set off a bomb in a pump that supplied water to the mine.

Copper miners win pay raise—Workers at the Chuquicamata copper mine were reported Jan. 3 to have accepted a government contract offering a 30% pay increase, thus avoiding a strike scheduled for Jan. 1. The miners, seeking a 50% increase, had rejected the government's first offer of 20%. The government had projected a 21.8% rise in the cost of living for 1972.

The avoidance of a strike was interpreted by the Wall Street Journal Jan. 3 as a victory for President Salvador Allende.

In addition to the raises, the government promised to spend $3.7 million during 1972 on "social benefits" for the town of Chuquicamata.

Kennecott gets payment. The Kennecott Copper Corp. was reported Jan. 4 to have requested the government to pay a $5.8 million first installment due Dec. 31, 1971 on $92.9 million in notes held by Kennecott for the El Teniente mine.

The request followed suspension of the payment by President Allende Dec. 30, 1971, pending his decision on whether the proceeds of the notes had been "usefully invested" as provided by the constitutional reform that expropriated El Teniente.

In claiming its payment, Kennecott noted that the $92.9 million had been unconditionally guaranteed by Chile and that $84.6 million had been guaranteed with the Overseas Private Invest-

ment Corporation (OPIC), a U.S. government agency.

OPIC said Jan. 4 that if Chile repudiated the debt, it would pay the $84.6 million.

Kennecott announced Feb. 4 that its subsidiary Braden Copper Co. had filed two federal suits against Chile in New York for payment of the first installment.

The New York Times reported Feb. 5 that Kennecott was also appealing, before a special copper tribunal in Chile, massive deductions that the company claimed would wipe out any compensation for its equity interest in El Teniente.

Acting on the suits, a federal court in New York Feb. 18 blocked the bank accounts of nine Chilean agencies. But diplomatic sources estimated that the blocked funds did not exceed $250,000.

The Chilean government then announced Feb. 25 that it would pay $84,618 to the Braden company.

In announcing payment of the debt, Allende said $8,125,000 had been deducted because that much of the original sum had not been "usefully" invested.

The Chilean government paid the first installment March 31, and the federal court attachment on the Chilean accounts was vacated. (Kennecott announced July 6 that it had received a second installment of $5.7 million.)

More funds blocked in U.S. The New York State Supreme Court blocked the New York bank accounts of the Chilean State Copper Corp. (CODELCO) and the State Development Corp. (CORFO) Feb. 29 in response to a suit against the agencies by the Anaconda Co. Anaconda demanded $11.8 million in unpaid interest on promissory notes issued by Chile in 1969 as security for the purchase of 51% of Anaconda's major Chilean copper properties.

In response, Chile suspended a shipment of copper consigned to Anaconda March 1 and announced that it would not honor the $203 million in Chilean notes held by the company. The government further retaliated March 9 by blocking the remaining Chilean real estate and bank accounts of both Anaconda and the Kennecott Copper Corp. According to La Prensa of Buenos Aires March 10,

Kennecott had also obtained a court embargo on official Chilean funds in New York early in March.

Anaconda spokesmen quoted in La Prensa March 10 said company holdings embargoed by Chile amounted only to "a handful" of Santiago properties and very little money.

Chilean copper experts quoted in the Miami Herald March 11 said the U.S. embargos, on the other hand, could seriously affect production at the Chuquicamata mine.

(It was reported July 7 that the Chilean Copper Tribunal had approved a government request to suspend payment of $5.85 million in promissory notes to Anaconda on grounds that Anaconda had made "excess profits" in the country. Chile had paid a first installment after the Chilean bank accounts in the U.S. were blocked.)

Cerro ends role. CODELCO and Cerro Mining Co. agreed to end Cerro's role as purchasing agent for Chile's expropriated copper mines after a five-month run, it was announced Jan. 12.

Under the arrangement, Cerro purchased equipment in the U.S. for use in the Chilean mines formerly owned by itself and two other companies—Kennecott Copper Corp. and Anaconda Co.

Chile asks moratorium on debt payments. With foreign exchange reserves critically low, Chile had asked foreign banks and governments for permission to forgo for three years payment on foreign debts totaling about $3 billion.

A delegation of officials, headed by Chile's ambassador to the U.S., Orlando Letelier, exchanged proposals Jan. 10 with representatives of 44 U.S. banks to which Chile owed payments of more than $200 million.

A drop in copper prices and the failure of expected production increases to materialize had depleted foreign exchange reserves during a time when Chile faced its toughest payments schedule in years.

■ Chile reached a tentative agreement with a group of private U.S. banks Feb. 9 for refinancing $300 million of its total foreign debt. The accord established the basis for loans of $250 million and $50 million, to be used to cover public-sector debts for 1972–74 and the obligations of the Chilean Copper Corp. through 1976.

Default on U.S. loans—Chile defaulted on payments to the Export-Import Bank, U.S. officials reported Feb. 17. Chile was said to be $20 million in arrears to the bank, and $1 million to the Agency for International Development (AID) and the Department of Agriculture.

U.S. State Department spokesman Charles W. Bray 3rd said Chile had warned the U.S. Nov. 12, 1971 that it would suspend payment of debt servicing while it renegotiated its entire foreign debt with creditors in Paris.

The Washington Post reported Feb. 19 that the U.S. had refused several Chilean requests for 90-day extensions on debt repayment. According to a State Department official, the refusal was "a normal banking decision," not intended as "a harsh act."

Travel restrictions imposed. The government announced that it would take control of all airline ticket sales and put new restrictions on foreign travel for Chileans Jan. 15 in order to save dwindling foreign currency reserves.

Under the new regulations a Chilean would first clear his travel plans with the central bank and pay the bank for the air fare. The airline could collect the fare in foreign currency only if it could prove the passenger left the country within two weeks after the central bank issued a travel permit.

Under existing regulations a person could not leave Chile unless another solvent Chilean stood bond for him with the income tax bureau. Travelers could take only limited amounts of foreign currency.

Price increases. In a sharp reversal of economic policy, the government decided Feb. 1 to end its subsidy of basic foodstuffs and to raise prices by percentages that exceeded 1971's cost of living adjustments.

Affected were costs of such items as bread, milk, sugar, oil and tea, which rose by an average of 25–30%, and public transportation, which rose by 60%. In 1971, according to the government, the cost of living rose by 22% over 1970. Opposition Christian Democratic sources, however, claimed the figure was actually as high as 30%.

Minister of Economy Pedro Vuskovic explained that although the previous policy of redistribution of national income had led to a strong expansion of the economy during 1971, it would have to be cut back in order to regain satisfactory levels of investment.

To offset the price increases, Vuskovic announced plans to order employers to pay a differential of 120 escudos (about $4.10) per month to each family, varying with the number of children. The Miami Herald noted Feb. 2, however, that many Chileans felt the bonus would barely cover the increase in bus fare for a family of four.

Food rationing possible. President Allende said Feb. 28 that he would not hesitate to order food rationing if it became necessary "to ensure the future of the people and the progress of Chile."

Speaking in the northern port city of Antofagasta, Allende said food imports cost the country more than $190 million a year, equivalent to 18% of Chile's export earnings. He stressed the special problem of beef, noting that while the population had doubled since 1936, livestock had increased by only 100,000 head.

Allende added that "if we were truly a revolutionary people conscious of this problem, perhaps we could agree if the government said 'for one year nobody will eat beef.' "

Radio subsidy requested. Chile's 140 radio stations appealed to the government March 9 to help them avert a total collapse of the broadcasting industry by granting a subsidy for the salaries of their 6,000 employes. The money would presumably come from a new tax on electric energy consumption which had been introduced in Congress by the opposition Christian Democratic party and was said to have the support of the ruling Popular Unity coalition. The tax would raise about $200,000 monthly.

Daniel Ramirez, president of the National Radio Association and director of the station Radio Chilena, said that since the inauguration of President Salvador Allende, 16 months before, wages for radio employes had risen by 75% while income from publicity had fallen by 42%.

Police clash with handicapped. In an embarrassing incident for the Popular Unity government, police tried to break up a demonstration March 22 by about 300 disabled persons protesting restrictions on imports of wheel chairs, braces and glass eyes, which had been placed on a list of virtually prohibited "luxury items."

Handicapped demonstrators marching on the presidential palace in Santiago were set upon by police officers, who damaged two wheel chairs and left several disabled persons lying in the street. After a crowd gathered to boo the police and two government workers who charged the demonstration was organized by "fascists," the protesters were allowed into the courtyard of the palace, where President Allende apologized and acknowledged the justice of their cause.

Shortly after the incident, Santiago Provincial Gov. Jaime Concha tendered his resignation, which was accepted by Allende.

Suspicions of U.S. Voiced

Neruda charges U.S. plot. It was reported Jan. 1 that Pablo Neruda, Chile's ambassador to France, had accused the U.S. of trying to overthrow Allende through economic pressure and encouragement of subversion.

In a letter to the French newspaper Le Monde, Neruda said former President Eduardo Frei Montalva was "the pivot of the conspiracy," which rested on rightist demonstrations as well as attacks on radical party officers and the homes of Allende and two cabinet ministers.

Herrera attacks U.S. in OAS. Chilean Ambassador Luis Herrera assumed the rotating chairmanship of the Organization of American States (OAS) Permanent Council Jan. 3 and declared that the concept of "juridical equality" among OAS members clashed with the "profound inequality in development" between the U.S. and the countries of Latin America.

Herrera, a member of Chile's Socialist party, described the relationship between the U.S. and Latin America as "serfdom in the economic, political, social, and even cultural realms."

U.S. Ambassador John Jova replied Jan. 3 that the U.S. "disagreed strongly" with Herrera's view. He said one of the most distinctive characteristics of the OAS was that the 23 member countries had equal voting power.

Chile-U.S. trade down in 1971. A U.S. Commerce Department report noted that U.S. exports to Chile had dropped 26.8% in the first 11 months of 1971 as compared with the same period in 1970.

Chilean exports to the U.S. dropped 37.8% for the same period, according to the Jan. 9 report.

Request for more Peace Corps help. The U.S. Peace Corps announced plans to increase its manpower in Chile from 44 to 90 by March in response to Chilean government requests.

Donald M. Boucher, director of the Corps' Chilean operations, said in a Jan. 10 report that 70 requests for aid had been received from Chile since July 1971 and that the country specified that it needed skilled specialists rather than "young people with liberal arts degrees and little practical experience."

The major Peace Corps effort in Chile had been in aiding the growth of the forestry industry so that timber could become a major export product.

Citing requests by 22 current volunteers to extend their two-year terms in Chile to a third year, Boucher said, "That shows that any bitterness between the U.S. and Chilean governments is certainly not felt on an individual level."

Tougher U.S. stand on expropriations. President Richard M. Nixon of the U.S. asserted publicly Jan. 19 that the U.S. would follow a tougher policy against nations that expropriated U.S. property without paying adequate and swift compensation.

He said that in most cases, except in overriding interests of national policy, the U.S. would grant no new economic aid and would oppose loan grants to those countries by international lending agencies. The new policy, which would not be retroactive, would not apply to aid for "humanitarian assistance," such as earthquake and famine relief.

In his statement, Nixon voiced strong belief in the value of foreign aid, especially to less developed nations. But he suggested that the chief victim of expropriation was not the U.S. but the country that stood to lose American investment. He said "the wisdom of any expropriation is questionable," but he did not deny the right of a nation to take such an action.

The key passages in the statement, issued by the White House, declared:

Under international law, the United Sates has a right to expect that the taking of American property will be nondiscriminatory; that it will be for a public purpose; and that its citizens will receive prompt, adequate, and effective compensation from the expropriating country.

Thus when a country expropriates a significant United States interest without making reasonable provision for such compensation to the United States citizens, we will presume that the United States will not extend new bilateral economic benefits to the expropriating country unless and until it is determined that the country is taking reasonable steps to provide adequate compensation or that there are major factors affecting United States interests which require continuance of all or part of these benefits.

Nixon's policy statement appeared to be directed largely at Chile and several other Latin American countries.

Allende scores Nixon statement—Chilean President Salvador Allende Jan. 19 criticized Nixon's statement, Allende said "small dependent countries such as ours . . . have the right to be respected. Our laws are within the framework of our constitution, written by a congress more than 150 years old."

ITT & U.S. policy. A controversey involving the International Telephone & Telegraph Corp. (ITT) and the funding of the 1972 Republican Party National Convention took on international significance March 20. Syndicated columnist Jack Anderson made public March 20–22 material purporting an effort by ITT to influence U.S. policy in Chile, where the conglomerate had six affiliates with 7,900 employes.

Utilizing allegedly ITT documents. Anderson made the charges in his column March 20–21 and released the material to news media March 22. Among its highlights:

March 21 column (made public March 20)—William R. Merriam, head of ITT's Washington office, in a memo to John A. McCone, an ITT director and former CIA director, said that a CIA source he had met with was "very pessimistic about defeating Allende," that "approaches continue to be made to select members of the armed forces in an attempt to have them lead some sort of uprising" and that "practically no progress has been made in trying to get American business to cooperate in some way so as to bring on economic chaos."

March 22 column—J. D. Neal, ITT's director of international relations, telephoned an aide to Henry A. Kissinger, President Nixon's adviser on national security affairs, talked of ITT President Harold S. Geneen's "deep concern about the Chile situation" and asked the aide to tell Kissinger that Geneen was ready to discuss ITT's interest and ITT was "prepared to assist financially in sums up to seven figures."

Anderson said his material revealed ITT efforts and "fervent hopes for a military coup" in Chile and the "generally polite but cool reception" it got from the White House and the State Department. A "more friendly" reception was attributed to the CIA's William V. Broe, who was reported to have visited ITT Vice President E. J. Gerrity Jr. to "urge ITT to join in a scheme to plunge the Chilean economy into chaos and thus bring about a military uprising that would keep Allende out of power."

In the material released March 22:

■ Neal wrote Merriam "we should hope the Nixon Administration will be prepared to move quickly to exert pressure on Allende" but that "because of our weak policy in the hemisphere during the last two years, we cannot count on such immediate and effective action."

■ Merriam wrote Kissinger about ITT's concern over the "serious exposure" of foreign private enterprise in Latin America and the need to "reappraise and strengthen U.S. policy in Latin America." He enclosed ITT's proposals for reaction to expropriation of private U.S. holdings. One of the proposals was to inform Allende that if compensation was not forthcoming "there will be immediate repercussions in official and private circles" and "this could mean a stoppage of all loans by international banks and U.S. private banks." An apparent reply from Kissinger said it was "helpful to have your thoughts and recommendations, and we shall certainly take them into account." Merriam considered the reply "more than perfunctory."

■ Neal reported having been told by U.S. Ambassador to Chile Edward M. Korry that if Geneen "had any ideas about U.S. policy toward Allende's government he hoped this would be relayed to the White House immediately."

ITT received a report from its representatives in Santiago that the State Department had given a "green light" to Korry "for maximum authority to do all possible, short of a Dominican Republic-type action" (a reference to U.S. military intervention) to "keep Allende from taking power."

Administration denial—State Department press officer Charles W. Bray 3rd said March 23 that the Nixon Administration had "firmly rejected" any ideas of "thwarting the Chilean constitutional processes following the elections of 1970." Bray added that the disclaimer applied to the period before the elections as well, and to actions attributed by the documents to the CIA.

Bray refused, however, to formally deny the assertion that instructions were sent to Korry to prevent Allende's inaugural.

Anderson disclosures investigated— The Chilean Congress voted March 28 to appoint a 13-member commission to investigate activities by ITT aimed at keeping Allende from taking office in 1970.

According to the magazine Business Week April 1, John McCone, a director of ITT and former director of the U.S. Central Intelligence Agency (CIA), admitted in an interview that the Anderson documents were authentic. McCone said the company had let the CIA know that it would help with any plan to prevent Allende's inauguration, but denied that ITT had proposed measures of "economic repression" in Chile.

The Chilean government April 4 put on sale a book called "The Secret documents of the ITT," containing English- and Spanish-language versions of the Anderson documents.

Opposition implicated— The heated debate in Chile over the Anderson disclosures was fueled by government attempts to implicate opposition forces in an alleged CIA-directed plot to bring down the Allende government through economic crisis, scare tactics influencing consumers to hoard scarce supplies, and exaggerated accounts of rural violence over land disputes, the New York Times reported April 1.

According to the Times, the government campaign was directed against the Fatherland and Liberty party, the right-wing National party and Christian Democratic ex-President Eduardo Frei Montalva.

Opposition leaders, who angrily denied any dealings with the CIA, demanded that a commission also investigate recent allegations by Anderson that the Cuban embassy in Santiago was a center for fomenting armed revolution in South America, Le Monde reported April 1.

According to Le Monde March 31, the conservative Santiago newspaper El Mercurio, which opposed Allende, had said of the ITT papers that Anderson had been "manipulated" by the Chilean embassy in Washington. Ambassador Orlando Letelier denied the charge.

Purchase talks break down— The Washington Post disclosed April 10 that ITT had rejected a series of proposals by the Chilean government for purchase of its local interests, stalemating negotiations which began in early 1971.

Chilean officials reportedly felt that ITT preferred to wait for its U.S. government expropriation insurance to come due, bringing the company more prompt and possibly greater compensation for its property than it could obtain through a long-term payment agreement with Chile.

(ITT's annual report, cited in the Post April 13, reassured stockholders that the company would collect $89.6 million from the Overseas Private Investment Corp. [OPIC], the U.S. government insurance agency, as a claim for the phone company "taken" from ITT by the Chilean government.)

According to the Post April 10, ITT was taking the position that Chile, by appointing a local "intervenor" to run the Chilean Telephone Co. (Chitelco), had effectively expropriated ITT's interests. It was on this basis that the company made its claim to OPIC.

The Chilean government, on the other hand, insisted that the appointment of an intervenor did not constitute a denial of ITT's ownership of Chitelco, and that it had persistently sought to purchase ITT's 70% interest in the company. The Post said the record of negotiations between Chile and ITT seemed to substantiate Chilean claims that ITT was stalling progress in the talks on the assumption that OPIC payments would bail it out.

ITT reportedly valued its investment in Chitelco at $153 million, about two-thirds of which—$108.5 million—was insured by OPIC. However, Chilean officials maintained the company's interest was closer to $25 million and that ITT had overstated the value of its investment to receive a higher return.

ITT 'confiscation' proposed—The small United Popular Action Movement (MAPU), a party in the ruling Popular Unity coalition, proposed to President Allende the "confiscation" of all ITT property in Chile, the New York Times reported March 30.

MAPU Secretary General Jaime Gazmuri said Allende had accepted the proposal "in principle."

Washington embassy ransacked. Unknown persons invaded the Chilean embassy in Washington over the May 12-14 weekend, rifling the files and stealing official documents, books and radios. The U.S. State Department expressed regret over the robbery May 15.

2nd ITT plot revealed. The International Telephone & Telegraph Corp. (ITT) had submitted to the Nixon Administration in October 1971 an 18-point plan to assure that the Allende government would not "get through the crucial next six months," the New York Times reported July 3.

The ITT suggestions, proposed in a letter and "action" memorandum from William R. Merriam, ITT's vice president for Washington relations, to Peter G. Peterson, then assistant to President Nixon for international economic affairs and currently secretary of commerce, was submitted to the White House Oct. 1, 1971, two days after Chile placed the ITT-controlled Chilean Telephone Co. under provisional state administration.

In the documents, Merriam called for extensive economic warfare against Chile to be directed by a special White House task force, assisted by the Central Intelligence Agency (CIA). ITT further recommended subversion of the Chilean

armed forces, consultations with foreign governments on ways to put pressure on Allende, and diplomatic sabotage.

Merriam proposed putting an "economic squeeze" on Chile through denial of international credit, a ban on imports of copper and other Chilean products, and a similar ban on vital exports to Chile. The measures, Merriam said, should cause sufficient "economic chaos" to convince the armed forces to "step in and restore order."

Merriam suggested that the CIA could help in the squeeze, and urged a deliberate interruption of fuel supplies to the Chilean air force and navy to precipitate the crisis. He also urged that other potential anti-Allende forces, including "the judiciary, civil service, crippled news media [and a] fragment of the legislative branch," be "utilized to every advantage" during "the crucial period."

Merriam further wrote that Allende himself was "personally vulnerable. He is a vain man.... If his projects bog down, he hurts. If his credit is cut, he is embarrassed." Among ways of embarrassing Allende, Merriam suggested disruption of the United Nations Conference on Trade and Development, to which Chile was host in April and May.

Peterson said July 1 that he had received Mirriam's letter but had not read the memo suggesting specific moves against Allende, which he said was not in his files. Peterson said he had not answered the letter because he did not consider it necessary.

ITT seizure bill—The Chilean Senate July 7 approved a bill for the expropriation of the Chilean Telephone Co., largely owned by ITT. The bill had been sent to Congress by Allende May 12. The measure did not provide for the expropriation of ITT's other properties in the country.

The government had announced May 9 that it would expropriate the International Telephone & Telegraph Mining Co. of Chile, an ITT subsidiary created in 1966 for copper explorations, but an ITT spokesman had said the company had gone out of business in 1969.

Struggle Over Socialization

Socialist program. Allende, speaking in Concepcion Feb. 7, pledged to intensify Chile's process of socialization during the next year by nationalizing another 120 industries, expropriating 2,000 farms, completing state takeover of banking and foreign trade, and concentrating generally on improving living standards.

Allende emphasized the need for new investment, implying that he expected help from Chile's foreign creditors, who were meeting in Paris to renegotiate the country's foreign debt. Allende said Chile would repay its debts, but not at a pace that would threaten its development programs.

Election plan—In his speech, Allende also proposed that the Popular Unity parties present a single national list of candidates in the crucial May 1973 Congressional elections, in which all 150 deputies' seats and 25 of the 50 senators' seats would be at stake. Candidates, he explained, would resign from their parties and run on a united Democratic Federation of Popular Unity ticket, preventing the scattering of votes and gaining a simple majority in Congress for the remaining three years of Allende's administration.

The proposal seemed likely to drive the opposition Christian Democrats, who controlled Congress, into an alliance with the right-wing National party and the Social Democratic party. The British newsletter Latin America reported Feb. 18, however, that the Christian Democrats would resist any union with the right and would pin their hopes on an amendment they had just submitted to Congress.

The measure would extend from six months to a year the minimum membership period of a candidate in the party for which he could run for election. This would make it very difficult for Popular Unity candidates to qualify under a single federation, since the elections were only 13 months away.

To make the amendment doubly effective, the Christian Democrats included in the measure a clause prohibiting the retention of a Congressional seat by an incumbent who resigned from his party.

Anti-Socialist bill passed. Congress Feb. 19 passed a series of constitutional amendments that would restrict Allende's efforts to socialize Chile's economy.

The measures, passed by a vote of 100–33 (out of 200 congressmen), prohibited the government from fully or partially expropriating any enterprise without specific authorization by Congress, retroactive to Oct. 14, 1971.

Allende announced Feb. 21 that he would veto the bill, and if Congress overruled the veto, he would appeal to the Chilean Constitutional Court. The London newsletter Latin America said Feb. 25 that such an appeal would claim that to enact the legislation retroactively would establish a precedent which could undermine the constitution. By the time the court announced its decision, the newsletter noted, the President could have pushed through the remainder of his nationalization program.

Chile's three opposition parties challenged Allende Feb. 21 to hold a plebiscite on whether the nation should have a Socialist economy. Sen. Renan Fuentealba, a co-sponsor of the anti-expropriation bill, told the Miami Herald Feb. 21 that Congress would overrule Allende's veto of the bill and that the President's only recourse to overturn it would be a referendum "which he will be certain to lose."

Small private firms encouraged. President Allende had said Jan. 14 that the principal goal of the government in 1972 would be expansion of production by small companies, especially those producing for export, and an increase in public investment. He stressed that small private industries had a major role in Chile even as it moved toward socialism.

Only plants with capital of more than $1 million could expect expropriation, and then only if they were monopolies or deemed to be underproductive.

A government list cited 53 firms subject to nationalization and 38 for a combination of government and private capital. The remainder of more than 30,000 companies were eligible to remain in private hands. The 91 companies to be taken over by the government produced most of Chile's goods, but Allende said the rest could produce a bigger share.

91 enterprises to be nationalized—In a related development, the government Development Corporation (CORFO) announced Feb. 14 that it would buy shares in 91 enterprises which, in its judgment, should pass under state control.

Economy Undersecretary Oscar Garreton said the enterprises had been selected from among 253 companies, and were judged to be fundamental to the nation's economy.

General Motors plant takeover. The General Motors (GM) assembly plant in Arica had been taken over by CORFO Jan. 2 under an agreement reached between the company and the government in 1971.

GM had shut down its assembly lines Dec. 31, 1971, ending assembling operations of all U.S. companies in Chile.

Plant employes were to begin new jobs for CORFO in a company called Corarico Limitada, which was using the assembly plant purchased from GM.

U.S. bank purchased. The First National City Bank of New York and the Allende government signed an agreement Jan. 28 turning over the bank's Chilean operations to the state-owned Banco de Talca.

It was the fifth privately owned foreign bank to be purchased by the government, which now claimed to control more than 50% of Chile's banking.

Factories, goods 'requisitioned.' Economy Minister Pedro Vuscovic announced March 8 that the government had "requisitioned" two enterprises, 47,000 pairs of shoes and hundreds of domestic appliances. The enterprises—a paint factory and a textile concern—were among the 91 that CORFO had decided to nationalize.

Vuscovic charged that the paint factory had been cutting its paints with edible oil and that the textile business had been selling its products at prices above the official limits. The shoes and domestic appliances, Vuscovic said, had been kept off the market by retailers who were waiting for an increase in prices.

According to La Prensa of Buenos Aires March 9, "requisitioning" was a legal measure designed to regulate industrial production or the supply of articles and introduced to fight speculators and monopolists.

The French newspaper Le Monde reported March 11 that the government also claimed to have found more than 200 metric tons of products such as sugar, coffee, beans and table oil "in reserve" at various stores.

Chemical industry purchased—In a related development March 29, the government bought control of the Chilean chemical plants owned by the DuPont Co., paying $1 million cash for 400,000 company shares. The army would assume control of the three DuPont plants in northern Chile, which supplied 75% of the explosives for the country's copper mining industries.

Red infiltration charged. The independent newspaper El Mercurio claimed March 1 that the Chilean Communist party was carrying out a vast plan of infiltration into the nation's armed forces through young Marxists of military service age.

El Mercurio said documents revealing part of the infiltration plan were found in the possession of a law student in Santiago who was a member of the youth section of the Communist party.

Sergio Onofre Jarpa, leader of the opposition Nationalist party, said in a broadcast over Radio Agricultura March 7 that international communism and its allies had begun a struggle for power in Chile. He said that in spite of election defeats that repudiated the Popular Unity government, the government was trying to impose a dictatorship and avoid a plebiscite on its plans.

Breakaway Radical vote. The Washington Post reported March 9 that all seven deputies from the Radical Left party (PIR), which normally supported President Salvador Allende, had joined opposition Christian Democrats and Nationalists to override a presidential veto of a bill which would permit Santiago's university-run television stations to extend their broadcasting throughout the country. The veto was rejected by a 68–26 vote.

At present, the Post said, only the state-controlled Channel 7 broadcast nationwide, and opponents of the government charged it had turned the station into a "Marxist propaganda medium."

Parties merge. Le Monde reported March 14 that two Popular Unity parties, the Independent Action party (API) and the Radical Left party (PIR), had decided to merge.

Elections pact. The London newsletter Latin America reported March 24 that the ruling Popular Unity coalition (UP) and the opposition Christian Democratic party (DC) had agreed on a formula for the 1973 Congressional elections, making certain that the elections would be polarized between the right and the left.

According to the agreement, each party would run its own candidates, but under the umbrella of a coalition. Thus, if the DC made an electoral pact with the right-wing parties, its votes would be added to those of its partners, while the votes of the UP parties would also be added together. The candidate with the highest vote in each coalition would have the rest of the coalition's votes added to his to determine who won a seat. However, a party's votes would not be counted unless they amounted to at least 3% of the total vote.

Parties criticize administration. Separate documents by the Socialist and Communist parties, which formed the backbone of the ruling Popular Unity coalition (UP), severely criticized the Allende administration and its failure to mobilize Chile behind its Socialist programs, the New York Times reported March 17.

A report by Communist leader Orlando Millas to the party's central committee said it was "a matter of life and death" to prevent a further increase in the cost of living, which rose by 10% during the first two months of 1972, as compared

with an increase of 22% for all of 1971. Millas noted that inflation had been fed by a 110% increase in currency issuances during the first year of the Allende administration.

Chile's central problem, Millas said, was to make nationalized enterprises operate "with the same immense profits that they used to give the capitalists." According to the New York Times March 17, nationalized copper mines, cement plants, breweries, textile mills and other industries had shown large increases in costs, declines in productivity and either reduced profits or losses, and the losses had been covered by Central Bank currency issuances, contributing to inflation.

The document by the Socialist party's central committee said the economic base of anti-Marxist forces in private enterprise "must be destroyed" by encouraging workers to seize factories whose expropriation had been blocked by Congress. The document also called on Allende to force a plebiscite on dissolving the opposition-controlled Congress.

Both party documents criticized administrative ineptitude, such as the lack of planning by the state textile committee which produced a shortage of uniforms for schoolchildren, and bureaucrats who received large salaries and drove around in company cars "just like the capitalists."

Congress suspended. President Salvador Allende suspended sessions of the Senate and Chamber of Deputies for a week March 21 to gain time for further negotiations with the opposition Christian Democratic party (DC) regarding Allende's proposed partial vetoes on the recently passed antiexpropriation bill. The move effectively postponed the deadline of March 22, the date by which Allende would have been forced to submit the vetoes.

Pro-government marches. Four marches organized by the Central Labor Confederation (CUT) converged on the center of Santiago March 23 to express massive support for the Popular Unity government in its struggle with the opposition-dominated Congress.

According to the Washington Post March 24, U.S. columnist Jack Anderson's recent report on the International Telephone and Telegraph (ITT) Corp.'s encouragement of a 1970 plot against Allende was a major issue at the rally. In his speech to the marchers, Luis Figueroa, a Communist and secretary general of the CUT, quoted extensively from ITT documents released by Anderson.

(The New York Times reported March 24 that the government press and television system were devoting most of their space and time to the documents, asserting that they not only confirmed left-wing charges of an anti-Allende plot in 1970, but also showed there was a present campaign, backed by the U.S. Central Intelligence Agency, to overthrow Allende.)

Women's march barred. The government canceled a permit March 22 for a demonstration to have been led March 24 by Feminine Power, the women's committee of a group of workers in a private paper industry who sought to prevent government takeover of their company.

Interior Minister Hernan del Canto said the permit had been withdrawn because propaganda supporting the march indicated it had been taken over by issues larger than the one first presented. After receiving the permit, Feminine Power had invited participation of any group which opposed the government, charging that President Allende had created "dearth and misery while [placing] Chile under foreign rule," and billing the demonstration as a second "march of the empty pots."

Rightists arrested—Del Canto announced March 24 that police had raided offices of the right-wing Fatherland and Liberty organization, arresting 12 alleged members of the party for plotting to turn the women's march into a violent confrontation. Among those arrested was Pablo Rodriguez, leader of Fatherland and Liberty.

Del Canto said the raid had netted pamphlets, Molotov cocktails, firearms, clubs, gas masks, fire extinguishers and vials of sulphuric acid. Calling Fatherland and Liberty members "a group of crazy fascists," Del Canto said "it is an evident fact that they intended and still intend to act against the security of the country."

The Washington Post reported March 27 that a Santiago judge had formally charged Rodriguez and another leader of Fatherland and Liberty with violating Chile's internal state security.

Del Canto further charged March 28 that right-wing conspirators had planned to assassinate President Allende, free Gen. Roberto Viaux (who awaited trial on charges of complicity in the 1970 kidnaping and murder of Army Commander in Chief Rene Schneider) and seize power March 24–26.

Del Canto said the main instigator of the plot was retired army Major Arturo Marshall Marchesse, whom he claimed had close links with Fatherland and Liberty. A warrant was issued for Marshall's arrest. Retired Gen. Alberto Green Baquedano, also accused of participating in the plot, was detained March 27.

Land seizures investigated. President Allende sent Interior Minister Hernan del Canto to the southern province of Nuble to investigate a series of land seizures allegedly being carried out by members of the Revolutionary Left Movement (MIR), the New York Times reported March 23. Allende had been under pressure to use force against MIR militants since the Supreme Court's recent charge that they had created anarchy in Nuble and the right-wing National party's claim that they were selling arms in the province.

Del Canto denied the Supreme Court and National party charges March 26 but noted that 80–90 farms in Nuble were "paralyzed." Del Canto said most of these farms figured in government agrarian reform plans, and their owners could be expected to try to subdivide them through notarial procedures so that the farms would fall under the government's official 80-hectare limit.

Del Canto added that the council of the Agrarian Reform Corporation, under the leadership of Agriculture Minister Jacques Chonchol, would meet in Chillan March 27 to begin the expropriation of 140–150 Nuble farms.

(It was reported in July that Chonchol had said that 3,500 large farms had been expropriated during the Allende administration.)

Expropriation curb vetoed. Allende April 6 vetoed the controversial constitutional amendment that would prevent the government from expropriating any enterprise without legislative approval.

According to the London Times April 8, the action represented the failure of efforts initially backed by Allende to reach a compromise with the opposition Christian Democratic party (DC) and avoid a constitutional confrontation.

In an angry message to Congress April 6, Allende said that if the legislature persisted in "an obstructionist attitude towards the executive," he would introduce a bill to dissolve it, and if this failed, he would call a plebiscite on the future of Chile's economy. Opposition leaders had repeatedly challenged Allende to submit his programs to a plebiscite.

PIR leaves government—In a protest against certain ideas expressed in Allende's veto, the moderate Radical Left party (PIR) withdrew from the ruling Popular Unity coalition (UP) April 6. The move was a blow to the UP, since the PIR was important among Chile's influential middle classes, which Allende sought to attract to his programs.

The PIR's two Cabinet officials, Justice Minister Manuel Sanhueza (who had been in charge of government negotiations with the DC over the vetoed amendment) and Mining Minister Mauricio Jung resigned April 6. Eight senators from the party also abandoned the UP, leaving it with only one-third of the seats in the upper house of Congress.

Allende commented bitterly that he accepted the PIR's defection "with satisfaction," since the party was guilty of "opportunism and demagoguery." Allende also accused the opposition DC of provoking the PIR's withdrawal as part of its overall strategy to win the 1973 Congressional elections.

The London Times reported April 8 that Allende was also at odds with the the UP's strictly Marxist parties, which had severely limited his freedom to reach an understanding with the opposition.

General gets Cabinet post—In a surprise move, Allende appointed Gen. Pedro Palacios Cameron, an engineer who had been in charge of the army's recruitment program, mining minister April 7. Jorge Tapia, a lawyer from the Radical party, was named justice minister.

In announcing the appointments, Allende said it had been an aim of his government "to incorporate the armed forces into the country's process of development in its economic, technical, scientific and cultural aspects." Palacios was the first member of the armed forces to serve in the Chilean Cabinet in more than 10 years.

A conference of officials from army, navy and air force organizations representing retired officers had previously voted to support the government, El Nacional of Caracas reported April 6. The conference also voted to back active armed forces officers "faced with attacks that they are suffering at the hands of those interested in discrediting them."

The latter vote was apparently taken in response to Interior Minister Hernan del Canto's charge March 24 that several retired army officers were involved in an alleged right-wing conspiracy against the government.

Opposition march. A crowd estimated at more than 200,000 persons rallied in downtown Santiago April 12 to protest food shortages and call on President Allende to submit his Socialist programs to a plebiscite. The peaceful demonstration, billed by its organizers as a "march for democracy" and against "statist socialism," was said to have attracted all opposition groups.

Addressing the rally, Christian Democratic Senate President Patricio Alwyn said Chileans wanted "a government that is not just at the service of Socialists and Communists, and there is no better way to achieve this than to go to a plebiscite." Alwyn charged that highway policemen had prevented large delegations from neighboring communities from attending the rally by turning back their trucks and buses at checkpoints.

According to El Nacional of Caracas April 1, the rally was organized by the opposition Christian Democratic, National and Democratic Radical parties March 31 in dissatisfaction with the government's justification of its charges of sedition against the right-wing Fatherland and Liberty party.

Opposition legislators had called a special session of the Chamber of Deputies March 30 to ask Interior Minister Hernan del Canto to substantiate the charges and the government's cancellation of opposition marches scheduled for March 21 and 24. The congressmen announced after the session that they were not satisfied with del Canto's answers and that the cancellation of the marches had "threatened the right to assembly guaranteed by the constitution."

The government reportedly barred rally organizers April 8 from routing the march past the downtown headquarters for the third United Nations Conference on Trade and Development (UNCTAD), which was to begin April 13.

In granting permission for the opposition march, Allende said April 8 that he welcomed the opportunity to compare the crowds that the government and the opposition could draw and to see "who is stronger." Allende announced a pro-government rally for April 18.

Leftist rally. Police dispersed a rally of about 300 "extreme leftists" outside the UNCTAD building in Santiago April 21 after demonstrators had burned a U.S. flag. The rally protested the detention of nearly 200 leftist political prisoners.

Emiliano Campos, a student and leader of the Trotskyite Revolutionary Communist Party (PCR), said April 21 that most of the prisoners belonged to the People's Organized Vanguard—responsible for assassinating ex-Interior Minister Edmundo Perez Zujovic—the Revolutionary Armed Forces, the Revolutionary Left Movement (MIR) and the PCR. Many of the prisoners allegedly had been tortured by police.

Church-left alliance urged. More than 400 Latin American priests and laymen ended a week-long conference of "Christians for Socialism" in Santiago May 2 with a call for "a strategic alliance between revolutionary Christians and Marxists for the liberation of the continent."

The assembly, organized by a group of 80 Chilean Roman Catholic priests who publicly supported President Allende's government, renounced Christian Democratic "reformism" and urged Christians to join "the revolutionary process" against "the capitalist society based on exploitation of the weak."

The conference met with the disapproval of both the Vatican and the Chilean Roman Catholic hierarchy, Le Monde reported May 3.

(A group of Chilean priests who had visited Cuba in February at the invitation of Premier Fidel Castro was reprimanded April 26 by church officials who demanded that the "rebel" priests "limit themselves strictly to their religious functions.")

Marxists lose in university votes. Anti-Marxists consistently outpolled Marxists during 1972 in an on-going struggle for control of the University of Chile.

Anti-Marxist university rector Edgardo Boeninger, whose ouster the Marxists had sought, had announced Jan. 4 that he was resigning as rector to be a candidate in an election of university officials.

The government's Popular Unity (UP) coalition Feb. 28 announced its nomination of an extremely strong candidate, Felipe Herrera, former president of the Inter-American Development Bank (1960–71), to contest Boeninger for election as rector.

Herrera, a former member of the Socialist party and a close Allende associate, resigned as coordinator of preparations for the third full session of the United Nations Conference on Trade & Development in order to campaign for the university post.

The UP was defeated in the election, held April 27, as opposition candidates won control of the university. Boeninger was reelected rector with 51.8% of the vote against 43.8% for Herrera, 3.4% for Andres Pascal Allende, a nephew of Allende's and candidate of the Revolutionary Left Movement (MIR), and less than 1% for Communist candidate Luis Vitale.

Anti-Marxist candidates also won a slim majority in the 100-member university council, which had been controlled by UP sympathizers and had figured importantly in the crisis which led to Boeninger's resignation.

Nearly 70,000 students, teachers and employes voted at the university's campuses in Santiago and provincial cities. Balloting was weighted so that faculty votes counted 65% of the total, student votes 25%, and employe ballots 10%.

Chile was so bitterly divided between supporters and opponents of the government that the university vote had taken on the importance of a national plebiscite, the Washington Post commented April 26. However, both Boeninger and Herrera had agreed it was imperative that the university become less politicized.

At a press conference April 28 President Allende said that despite the results, he was convinced "the university will continue to participate actively in the process of national transformation."

Candidates of the opposition Christian Democratic and National parties later won a majority of department chairmanships at the university Sept. 28. Christian Democratic students retained control of the university's Federation of Secondary Students in elections Nov. 16; pro-government students charged them with fraud.

Candidates of the opposition university Front defeated pro-government candidates Nov. 21 in elections for rector and vice rector of the state university at Concepcion. Opposition candidates also won elections at the university's branches in the neighboring towns of Chillan and Los Angeles.

Carlos Von Plessing, a chemistry professor, and Lorenzo Gonzalez, a mathematics teacher, were elected rector and vice rector at Concepcion. Both had reportedly escaped assassination Nov. 14 when fired on by alleged leftist extremists.

The UP and MIR at conception then switched tactics and backed a common list of candidates in the balloting for officers of the student federation, defeating a united opposition list by a comfortable margin, the newsletter Latin America reported Dec. 15.

(Communist party youth leader Alejandro Rojas was re-elected president of the Student Federation of Chile, defeating a Christian Democrat and two right-wing candidates, the New York Times reported July 8.)

Street violence. One person was killed, 62 were injured and 52 arrested May 12 as supporters and opponents of the government fought in the streets of the southern city of Concepcion.

Members of the opposition Christian Democratic and National parties were attempting to hold an illegal march to protest alleged government violations of the democratic process. The gathering was disrupted by pro-government sympathizers, and particularly violent clashes ensued between Revolutionary Left Movement (MIR) militants and members of the right-wing Fatherland and Liberty party. An MIR student was shot to death in the melee.

A declaration signed by all government factions except the Communist party blamed the student's death on police and called for the resignation of the Communist governor of Concepcion province, the Miami Herald reported May 16.

Labor minister resigns. Minister of Labor Jose Oyarce resigned May 9 to take up "important duties" in the central committee of the Chilean Communist party.

Leftist leader killed. Rodrigo Ambrosio, secretary general of the United Popular Action Movement, a party in the ruling Popular Unity coalition, was killed in a car accident May 19.

Government & the Economy

Credit pact signed. Chile and 11 creditor nations including the U.S. reached an agreement in Paris April 20 for the refinancing of an estimated $600 million of Chile's foreign debt. (Chile's total foreign debt was estimated to be $3.7 billion.) The accord, signed by Guy Nebot, chairman of the 16-nation "Paris Club" of creditors, and Chilean Central Bank President Alfonso Inostroza, capped 10 weeks of negotiations.

The agreement obligated Chile to remit by 1975 only 30% of the debt and interest payments falling due from November 1971 through December 1973. After that, Chile would have six years to repay these debts in full. The creditors also agreed to study "with good-will" the refinancing of all Chilean debts due in 1973.

The Chilean government April 20 called the agreement "satisfactory," and Chile's left-wing press described it as "a great victory." The government had asked for a 3-year moratorium on all payments and had insisted that the subject of compensation for nationalized U.S. copper interests not be a factor in the negotiations.

However, at the insistence of the U.S., Chile accepted "the principles of payment of a just compensation for all nationalizations in conformity with Chilean law and international law."

(Ambassador Hernan Santa Cruz, head of the Chilean delegation to the third United Nations Conference on Trade and Development [UNCTAD] in Santiago, commented April 20 on the compensation clause. He said that there was no generally accepted principle of international law on the means and conditions of expropriations, and that "to perpetuate juridical concepts that do not obey the interests of the world today . . . is to swim against the current of history.")

U.S. debts refinanced. The government and a group of 28 private U.S. banks reached agreement on the refinancing of $160 million in Chilean debts, according to the Chilean embassy in Washington June 12. Repayment of three-quarters of the total debt, originally due in 1974, was delayed eight years, and payments due in 1972 and 1973 were reduced.

U.S. bankers quoted in the New York Times June 13 called the refinancing agreement a "fairly reasonable compromise" and the only alternative to complete default by the Chilean government. They added that there was an unwritten understanding that U.S. banks would begin to relax somewhat the restrictions they had imposed on new short-term credits to Chile, to finance normal import and export activity.

Cabinet shuffled. Amid growing economic problems and political opposition, President Salvador Allende June 17 replaced six Cabinet officials, including controversial Economy Minister Pedro Vuskovic. The entire Cabinet had resigned June 12 to facilitate a change in the government's economic policies.

Vuskovic, a member of Allende's Socialist party, was replaced by Carlos Matus Romo, also a Socialist but reportedly more pragmatic and less of a Marxist ideologue than Vuskovic. Vuskovic would remain in the government as director of the Executive Economic Committee—a new presidential unit to coordinate economic programs—and vice president of the State Development Corp.

In a nationwide radio speech June 17, Allende said the new Cabinet had been chosen to carry forward a more clearly defined and better coordinated program against inflation, deficits in Chile's international payments and conflicts over wages and prices, as well as to improve relations between the state and private sectors of the economy.

According to the New York Times June 18, inflation had accelerated in recent months due to huge deficits in the rapidly expanding sector of state enterprises and a 100% increase in currency in circulation. Prices reportedly rose by 25% from January-May, and the rate of inflation on an annual basis climbed to 40%.

Labor was protesting wage contracts that were being eroded by inflation, the Times reported, and a black market had developed in potatoes, onions, beef, textiles and spare automobile parts, as well as in other articles officially under price controls or import regulations.

In addition to Vuskovic, Labor Minister Jose Oyarce, Finance Minister Americo Zorrilla, Education Minister Alejandro Valdivia, Housing Minister Orlando Cantuarias and Mining Minister Pedro Palacios were replaced.

Mireya Baltra, a Communist, became labor minister and the first woman in the Cabinet; Orlando Millas, also a Communist, became finance minister; Anibal Palma, a Radical, education minister; Luis Matte, an independent, housing minister; and Jorge Arrate, a Socialist, acting mining minister.

Paper, editor sued. The government June 27 filed suit against the Santiago newspaper El Mercurio and its editor, Rene Silva Espejo, for publishing an article entitled "Chile has dollars for only 45 days."

The report, based on allegations by Engelberto Frias, a Congressman of the right-wing National party, said Chile had reserves of only $43 million, and was undergoing "the most dramatic crisis in its history." The government charged that by publishing the allegations El Mercurio had violated the state internal security law.

Economic plan set. President Salvador Allende Gossens July 24 announced a new government economic plan to combat inflation and accelerate national development.

Under the program, the government would invest more than $760 million in industrial and farm production over the next two years. Most of the money would come from Communist countries, which Allende said had already pledged $400 million in credits. Among the plan's goals were three new milk bottling plants, a new sugar refinery and more fruit, grain, beef-breeding and poultry farms.

The government also pledged to send to Congress legislation for compulsory salary increases to offset inflation. The official cost of living index had risen by 27.5% during the first half of the year, but actual inflation was reportedly higher.

The plan provided tax increases for the wealthy and the middle classes, compulsory insurance on virtually everything from life to private automobiles, and further price controls to force the nationalization of the 91 large industries still remaining in private hands. Allende said the controls would permit government-administered industries to become self-financing, give small and medium private enterprises a "reasonable" profit, and big industries "strictly enough to operate."

Allende admitted that a sharp drop in foreign currency reserves, which the government had drawn on heavily to buy food, had put the country in "difficult straits." He attacked the U.S. for aggravating the situation by "deliberately restricting" Chile's credits in 1970–72 and imposing "a virtual economic blockade" on the country.

According to the New York Times July 26, Chile's economic difficulties had also been aggravated by a drop in earnings from copper exports, which accounted for more than two-thirds of the country's income.

Currency devalued. The Central Bank devalued the Chilean escudo against the U.S. dollar through "readjustments" in several exchange rates Aug. 2 and 4. The moves were attributed to Chilean inflation and foreign payments deficits due in part to low copper prices on the world market.

The "special payments rate," given to foreign visitors, was raised from 42 to 46 escudos to the dollar. The rate for Chileans buying dollars to go abroad was increased from 42 to 85, but taxes on foreign travel were said to be such that the effective rate was 134. The rate for exporters was raised from 15.8 to 20, and the rate for purchase of essential food imports, from 12.2 to 20.

(International Monetary Fund statistics showed that Chile had completely exhausted its Special Drawing Rights, becoming the only country in the organization to do so, La Prensa of Buenos Aires reported Aug. 5.)

(The government had doubled the price of cigarettes as the first step in a new policy to reduce demand for non-essential foreign goods that required hard currency, the London newsletter Latin America reported Aug. 4.)

Copper mine strikes. a 48-hour strike by 8,000 workers at the Chuquicamata copper mine, Chile's largest, ended May

6 after the government made concessions on bonuses, work regulations and promotions. It was the first general strike at the mine since 1966, when it was owned by the Anaconda Co.

The strike cost $1.5 million in lost production, apart from additional costs involved in the concessions to worker demands, the New York Times reported May 7. A labor contract signed in December 1971 had increased wages by an average of 30%.

The strike had been voted by a workers' assembly May 3 in support of five worker representatives on the 11-member management council that ran the mine, mill and smelter operation. The representatives had protested that because they were outnumbered on the council by government appointees, they were given too little to say in the running of the mine.

The following week three dozen senior technicians resigned to protest what they claimed was "chaotic administration" at Chuquicamata.

More than 3,000 workers staged a work stoppage May 18 at El Teniente, the world's largest underground copper mine, to protest allegedly poor transportation between the mine and nearby housing projects.

Other strikes. Among other labor disruptions by mid-1972:

■ About 1,000 workers at the Santiago and Valparaiso plants of the Andean Bottling Co., which bottled and distributed soft drinks, struck May 19 to pressure the government to nationalize the plants. Strikers claimed the company, whose truck drivers had recently struck for higher wages, was on the verge of bankruptcy.

■ A majority of the 1,800 workers at Mademsa, Chile's largest manufacturer of home appliances, refrigerators, industrial valves and metal cylinders, voted to stop work until the government appointed a state manager to run the company, the New York Times reported

■ Nearly 15,000 striking workers at the Lota and Coronel coal installations, south of Santiago, returned to work July 4 after negotiating a 44% wage hike with Labor Minister Mireya Baltra. The strikers had sought a 120% increase.

■ A two-day nationwide strike by bus drivers, started July 4, ended July 5 after the drivers accepted the appointment of a Public Works Ministry committee to study their economic grievances. However, train transportation throughout the country remained paralyzed as administrative personnel of the state rail agency continued a strike for higher wages begun July 4.

Communists control CUT. A Santiago electoral board declared July 15 that Communists had retained control of the Central Workers Confederation (CUT) and that veteran Communist politician Luis Figueroa had been re-elected CUT president in the union's June elections, in which more than 500,000 workers voted.

Christian Democratic sources immediately challenged the results, accusing the Marxist-controlled board of fraud. Returns cited by the New York Times July 8 had shown Christian Democrat Ernesto Vogel winning, but the board's final results put Vogel in third place, behind the Socialist party candidate.

Government & business. Among developments involving the Chilean government and various companies during 1972:

■ The government took temporary control of Pfizer Laboratories of Chile, a Chilean company that was owned by the New York-based Pfizer Co., after accusing it of illegally exporting pharmaceuticals, the Miami Herald reported May 19. Pfizer had allegedly been shipping terramycin and other drugs to northern Chile "to stimulate their clandestine departure from the country."

Pfizer Laboratories return to company control was reported by the Wall Street Journal June 16.

According to government officials, Pfizer had sought to avoid paying high duties by declaring to Central Bank authorities that certain chemicals it was importing were less expensive than was actually the case.

■ Chile's only private newsprint producer said June 17 that it was near bankruptcy because government economic control administrators had refused to grant price increases during the past year, in which wages and costs of material had risen 50%.

The firm, the Paper and Carton Manufacturing Co., exported $30 million worth of paper, pulp and lumber each year. It was reportedly on the list of 91 "strategic enterprises" the government sought to nationalize.

The financially pressed firm was ordered Dec. 21 to pay a $400,000 debt to the state electric concern ENDESA under threat of having its assets frozen.

■ The government bought the Coca-Cola Co.'s 51% interest in Coca-Cola Inc. of Chile for the equivalent of $1.5 million, the Wall Street Journal reported June 23. The remaining 49% of the firm was held by private Chilean interests.

■ The Banco Suramericano, one of the most important banks in the country, had come under the control of the government, according to a central bank official June 30. The Chilean Development Corp. had purchased 71.5% of the bank's stock.

■ The government Aug. 3 took control of the privately-owned Gas Co. under the pretext of "normalizing" gas deliveries to the public and ending a strike by company employes.

Leaders of Chile's four opposition parties sharply criticized the move Aug. 4, reportedly vowing action to keep the government from taking over the few large enterprises still in private hands.

Del Canto under fire. Interior Minister Hernan del Canto was suspended by the opposition-controlled Chamber of Deputies July 5 on a series of charges including failure to enforce laws protecting private property and personal rights. A chamber proposal to censure and dismiss Del Canto was sent to the Senate, also controlled by the opposition.

Del Canto was charged with refusal to order the arrest and prosecution of leftist agitators who seized private farms and factories to force an acceleration of President Salvador Allende's Socialist program, and with allowing the entry of 18 mysterious packages from Cuba without proper customs checks.

The opposition had charged that the packages, which were taken from a Cuban plane to a secret destination by plainclothes policemen, might contain illegal arms. However, the government maintained they contained only gifts for Allende from Cuban Premier Fidel Castro.

Allende announced July 6 that Foreign Minister Clodomiro Almeyda would assume Del Canto's duties until the Senate voted on the impeachment measure. Allende said the charges against Del Canto were "unjust and the product of political passions."

Del Canto charged July 6 that the vote against him was "a political accusation against the government of the people."

Editor arrested, freed—Mario Carneyro, editor of the opposition newspaper La Segunda, was held by authorities for 15 hours June 21 after La Segunda published a Congressional report finding Del Canto guilty of the charges on which he was ultimately suspended.

The government had said it would try Carneyro for breach of state security laws, but the Court of Appeals had ordered the editor released.

Del Canto ousted—Del Canto was censured and dismissed by 27–14 senate vote July 27. This was the second time in seven months that the opposition-controlled Congress had removed an interior minister, who was first in the line of presidential succession and in charge of the police.

Charges against Del Canto, initiated by the right-wing National party and supported by the liberal Christian Democrats, included abetting violence by extreme leftists and harassing the opposition press.

Del Canto denied the charges before the Senate July 27, saying the proceedings against him were "political" and not constitutional.

Opposition charges increase—Del Canto's impeachment came amid growing opposition charges that the government tolerated illegal activities by armed extreme leftist groups.

In a special Senate session July 26, Christian Democratic Sen. Rafael Moreno exhibited a suitcase containing a pistol, ammunition and several urban guerrilla manuals, which he called "proof" of government tolerance of subversion. Right-wing Sen. Victor Garcia added a tape recording of an alleged conversation between the Socialist civil police chief and a man accused of killing a worker.

The Senate debate followed the arrest July 20 of 18 members of the extremist July 16th National Liberation Movement, including two Nicaraguans, a Brazilian and a Mexican, for violation of the state internal security law. President Salvador Allende ordered a full investigation into leftist terrorist activities July 21.

Del Canto exonerated re smuggling— The Santiago customs administrator was reported Sept. 1 to have ruled that del Canto was not guilty of smuggling goods from Cuba.

Suarez becomes interior minister—President Allende Aug. 2 named Jaime Suarez Bastidas, a Socialist, to replace del Canto as interior minister. Del Canto, also a Socialist, assumed Suarez' post as secretary general of the Cabinet.

Government wins by-election. Communist candidate Amanda Altamirano was elected to the Chamber of Deputies from Coquimbo province July 16, giving the ruling Popular Unity coalition (UP) its first victory in four Congressional by-elections.

Altamirano defeated Orlando Poblete of the Radical Left party by more than 8,000 votes. Opposition leaders claimed the margin showed a drop in UP popularity, but the government hailed the vote as forecasting a UP victory in the 1973 Congressional elections.

Electoral coalitions set—The Christian Democratic party had agreed to join an oposition coalition, the United Democratic Confederation, to oppose the UP in the 1973 elections, the London newsletter Latin America reported July 14. The coalition would be subdivided into two groups, with the Christian Democrats and the Radical Left forming the Democratic Opposition Federation, and the right-wing National and Radical Democracy parties constituting the National Federation.

'Popular assembly' scored. President Salvador Allende Aug. 2 denounced a "popular assembly" formed in Concepcion, Chile's third largest city, by members of four government parties and the Revolutionary Left Movement (MIR). The organization, created July 26 at a meeting of Socialists, Radicals, the United Popular Action Movement, the Christian Left Organization and the MIR, had assailed Chile's Congress as "reactionary" but had not ascribed to itself any legislative or other functions.

Allende condemned the assembly for allegedly undermining his determination to operate constitutionally, asserting it was "unrealistic politics to separate the Chilean revolution from the country's democratic system."

Agrarian policy failings conceded. Sen. Luis Corvalan, leader of the Chilean Communist party, admitted Aug. 13 that the government's land reform program had not "found the road to increased production and rationalization." Chile would reportedly need food imports costing more than $300 million in 1972.

Speaking at a meeting of the Communist party's central committee, Corvalan castigated government officials "sitting in offices in towns far removed from the countryside" for decisions against the interests of peasants. Among these he cited frequent efforts by state purchasing concerns to buy produce from peasants at prices lower than those offered by private outlets.

Corvalan also criticized state-run cooperative farms, where he said alcoholism, absenteeism and the sale of produce on the black market were common.

Confirming Chilean setbacks, the U.S. Agriculture Department's Economic Research Service said Nov. 24 that Chile's crop output might drop sharply in 1972, but that the decline could not clearly be linked to the agrarian reforms of the Allende administration.

Allende had said Nov. 23 that Chile would have to import a million tons of wheat in 1973, adding that the wheat shortage was not a Chilean but a world problem.

High food imports seen—Agriculture Minister Rolando Calderon announced Dec. 1 that Chile would spend $450 million on food imports in 1973, using an estimated 60% of the country's projected income from copper sales. The figure was disputed by Benjamin Matte, president of the National Agriculture Association, who said it should be closer to $700 million.

Calderon estimated meat imports would reach 110,720 tons, costing about $97 million, and wheat imports would be nearly a million tons, costing more than $99 million, Calderon said that a trucker strike had damaged spring plantings. Opponents of the government charged the food crisis was attributable to official agrarian reform policies, under which most of Chile's productive lands had been nationalized. According to Manuel Valdez, president of the Confederation of Farmers' Unions, these lands were now uncultivated because of poor government management.

Poor exploitation of productive lands had contributed to the black market in food, El Nacional of Caracas reported Dec. 2. Middle class youths reportedly bought food in rural areas and sold it door-to-door in Santiago at large markups, increasing resentment against the government.

A high flour content bread developed to reduce Chile's wheat imports had become a controversial issue in Santiago, the Journal of Commerce reported Dec. 10. Housewives complained that the bread, produced since November, was of poor quality and caused internal disorders in infants. The government claimed the bread was safe and nutritious, and complaints against it were a "calculated campaign" to discredit the bread.

U.S. continues arms aid—U.S. officials said Dec. 8 that the U.S. was continuing arms aid to Chile despite its refusal to help finance Chilean food imports and economic projects. The aid came under a $10 million credit agreement signed in May with the Allende government.

The U.S. planned to send Chile at least one C-130 transport plane and possibly tanks, armored personnel carriers and trucks, the officials said. The aid package was double that of 1971, when a C-130 was supplied to the Chilean air force along with other items for the armed forces.

The aid seemed to be at odds with the Nixon administration's expressed policy of denying direct assistance to countries that failed to pay prompt and adequate compensation for nationalized U.S. property, but U.S. officials insisted Dec. 8 that military aid was a separate matter. They strongly denied suggestions that the aid was designed to court the Chilean military in hopes that it might overthrow the Allende government.

Price & wage increases set. Agriculture Minister Jacques Chonchol announced a sharp increase in food prices Aug. 18. Apart from chick peas, which rose by only 3.87%, all other foods rose by 36%–117%.

The government simultaneously announced wages and salaries would go up by 100% from the beginning of October, and everyone would receive an unprecedented 700-escudo bonus for the Sept. 18 independence celebrations. However, there was no guarantee the adjustment in wages and prices would prove adequate, since inflation had already reached 34.4% for the year and was expected to top 50% by the end of August as a result of the price increases.

Court upholds 'excess profits' charge. A special copper tribunal ruled Aug. 11 that the government could bill Anaconda Co. and Kennecott Copper Corp. for repayment of $774 million in "excess profits" from mining operations since 1955.

The tribunal, composed of the Supreme Court's chief justice, an appeals court judge, the president of the Constitutional Tribunal and two government appointees, ruled 4–1 against appeals by the companies, which argued that Chilean law at the time of the operations did not set ceilings on profits. The decision set a legal precedent for denying the companies further compensation for the takeover of their Chilean copper properties.

A spokesman for the Chilean state Copper Corp. charged Aug. 12 that Anaconda had held back more than $323,000 it owed Chile for the 1971 purchase of 24,000 tons of copper ore from the Chuquicamata mine. The spokesman said Anaconda had deposited the money in escrow with a court in New York.

Difficult financial situation seen—Orlando Letelier, Chile's ambassador in Washington, said Aug. 15 that the country faced grave financial problems because the U.S. had cut off credit and opposed loans to Chile in international agencies. Letelier had returned to Santiago to brief President Allende on the current talks between Chilean and U.S. officials on refinancing Chile's external debt and compensation to nationalized U.S. copper companies.

The government was taking special precautions against any embargoes on its property in the U.S. following, a ruling by Chile's special copper tribunal upholding Allende's decision to deduct "excess profits" from compensation to the expropriated companies, according to the London newsletter Latin America Aug. 18.

Chilean funds had been transferred from New York to European banks, and the purchase of any machinery or equipment from the U.S. would not be considered complete until the goods reached Chile, the newsletter said.

U.S. blocked World Bank aid? Alfonso Inostroza, president of the Central Bank of Chile, charged Sept. 28 that Chile's loans from the International Bank for Reconstruction and Development had been suspended, under pressure from the U.S., because of Chile's nationalization of U.S. copper interests.

Inostroza, who was also a governor of the World Bank and the International Monetary Fund, made the charges in an address to the two organizations' joint annual meeting in Washington. (The charges were repeated by Chile Oct. 3 in the U.N. General Assembly.)

His statement, which was sharply critical of World Bank President Robert S. McNamara, said that the bank's actual policy of granting loans was widely different from its stated policy of aiding underdeveloped countries toward an equitable distribution of wealth.

Inostroza said that Chile's Marxist regime had taken steps to redistribute income and was deserving of aid from the World Bank group of lending institutions.

Bank officials had admitted Sept. 28 that no new loans had been made to the country during the presidency of Salvador Allende Gossens, but they denied Inostroza's charges, saying it was bank policy to make loans to countries which had nationalized foreign owned property as long as legal efforts at compensation were also undertaken.

Loans to Bolivia and Guyana had been made in 1972 under those circumstances, despite U.S. opposition, the bank said. The U.S. did not deny its opposition to new loans made to Chile.

Chile's loans were suspended, bank spokesmen contended, because the country's huge external debt rendered it no longer creditworthy. And Chile also did not qualify for "soft" loans, made only to very poor nations by the International Development Association, because its per capita income was too high, according to the bank.

Bank spokesmen said payments made under previously existing loans had not been cut off, and two new loans were presently under consideration.

Kennecott sets write-off, threatens reprisals. Kennecott Copper Corp. announced Sept. 7 that because of Chile's failure to pay compensation for the nationalized El Teniente mine, the company was withdrawing from further legal proceedings in Chile and would "pursue in other nations its remedies for the confiscated assets."

The decision, which meant a write-off in 1972 of the $50.3 million book value of the company's equity investment in Chile, was announced shortly after Chile's special copper tribunal declined to review its Aug. 11 "excess profits" decision.

Kennecott President Frank R. Milliken said Kennecott and its subsidiary, Braden Copper Co., were "informing all persons who may be concerned with copper from the El Teniente mine in Chile of their continued rights to El Teniente copper and of their intention to take such action as may be considered necessary to protect their rights in the copper or its proceeds."

Milliken's statement was denounced by representatives of most Chilean political groups, including the government, the opposition Christian Democratic party and the right-wing National party. President Salvador Allende charged Sept. 10 that Milliken had threatened legal action to embargo Chilean exports, and he appealed to "international conscience" to prevent Kennecott from closing foreign markets to El Teniente copper.

In a stronger denunciation reported Sept. 13, Jorge Arrate, vice president of the Chilean state copper corporation, called Milliken's statement "open aggression intended to create uncertainty among Chile's usual customers, to cause immediate economic damage to the country and to obstruct the normal flow of its foreign trade."

Copper payment freeze lifted. A Paris civil court Nov. 29 released a $1.3 million payment made by French firms for a shipment of Chilean copper but frozen at the request of Kennecott Copper Corp. However, the court ordered Chile to deposit an equal amount in escrow pending settlement of the two-month dispute between the U.S. company and the Chilean state copper firm, CODELCO.

The payment had been frozen by the court Oct. 4 after Kennecott made claims to the 1,250 tons of copper, charging it had not been compensated for the nationalization of its properties in Chile in 1971. The ruling was condemned Oct. 5 by all Chilean political groups. The shipment itself, on its way to France, was rerouted Oct. 13 to avoid confiscation by Kennecott but was finally unloaded in Le Havre Oct. 23 and turned over to its French purchasers.

The ruling releasing the payment was hailed Nov. 29 by both Kennecott and the Chilean government. Chilean diplomats in France said the ruling strengthened President Salvador Allende's stand against "external aggression" by U.S. businesses. Kennecott, on the other hand, praised the court for supporting its contention that CODELCO was not immune from civil actions despite its governmental status.

Allende had said Oct. 9 that he was assuming personal control of Chilean copper sales to thwart future "aggression by imperialist monopolies."

Allende disclosed later that Canadian and Dutch banks had suspended all lines of credit to Chile pending settlement of Kennecott's claim to the Chilean copper destined for France.

Later, in Santiago, the world's four most important copper exporting nations resolved Dec. 2 to suspend dealings with Kennecott "while it persists in acts of aggression against Chile." The decision was contained in an eight-point declaration issued at the end of a ministerial meeting of the Intergovernmental Council of Copper-Exporting Countries, whose members—Chile, Peru, Zambia and Zaire—together accounted for about 60% of world copper exports. The document also promised future consultations to help Chile "alleviate the damage caused by the [Kennecott] aggression."

Anaconda loses on insurance. The U.S.' Overseas Private Investment Corp. (OPIC), the government agency that insured U.S. private investment abroad, announced Sept. 19 that it had denied insurance claims of $154 million from Anaconda Co. for the nationalization of the company's copper investments in Chile.

OPIC did, however, approve an Anaconda claim of $11.89 million—the highest ever awarded by the agency—for the loss of its investment in the Exotica mine in Chile. The much larger disapproved claims involved the Chuquicamata and El Salvador mines.

OPIC's rejection of the larger claims was based on its contention that the mines in question were expropriated in July 1969, when Anaconda sold its majority interest to the Christian Democratic government. At that time, Anaconda was insured by OPIC, but only on a "stand-by" basis. Under the stand-by arrangement, the company was not "fully insured" because it had not paid $4 million in added premiums.

Anaconda, on the other hand, claimed the expropriation took place in July 1971, when the new Marxist government took full control of the properties without paying any compensation. At that time, Anaconda claimed, it was fully insured by OPIC.

Despite its proportions, the financial impact of the OPIC decision on Anaconda was considered relatively slight by industry analysts, the Wall Street Journal reported Sept. 20. At the end of 1971, the company absorbed a gigantic writedown of $303 million resulting from the Chilean expropriation, including the OPIC claim in the figure, the Journal noted.

Kennecott gets OPIC settlement— Kennecott Copper Corp. and OPIC announced Dec. 14 that they had agreed on the terms of a $66.9 million insurance settlement on Kennecott's debt investment in the El Teniente mine.

OPIC guaranteed both principal and interest of a $66.9 million, 5¾% debt issue to be offered to institutional investors by Braden Copper Co., a Kennecott affiliate. The offering would be participation certificates in the outstanding $76.7 million debt to Braden guaranteed by the Chilean government.

The settlement, contingent on the completion of the sale of the certificates, covered a debt that was initially $80 million. Installments paid by Chile earlier in 1972 had reduced the principal to $74.7 million. Taking into account accrued unpaid interest, the obligation currently amounted to $76.7 million.

Takeover program pressed. Despite growing protests against its economic policies, the government continued its takeover of industries, seizing a few local businesses and Chilean facilities of the U.S. firm Dow Chemical Co.

Government inspectors Oct. 20 requisitioned a Concepcion province plant in which Dow had 70% interest and a wholly owned Dow subsidiary that distributed the plant's products and ran a small plastics factory in Santiago. Dow said the Concepcion plant, which produced polyethylene and polyvinyl chloride, was worth "less than $10 million," and the distribution company less than $1 million. The government claimed its action was based on failure by Dow to make deliveries of the plastics produced by the firms. Dow maintained the facilities had "ample supplies" on hand but could not make deliveries because of gasoline shortages.

A Chilean-owned special steels firm was requisitioned Oct. 20, following the government takeover of two supermarkets the day before.

Two enterprises owned by British, Dutch and Chilean interests were also seized but were returned to their owners in apparent fear of further strikes and pressure from abroad, it was reported Oct. 21.

Cerro compensation set. The U.S.-based Cerro Corp. announced Dec. 1 a decision for the Chilean government to pay it $37,544,000 for copper properties nationalized in 1971. The amount, to be owed by Chile as of Dec. 31, 1972, included $13,254,000 for Cerro's 70% equity in the Andean Mining Co., plus $24,300,000 in notes and interest. The equity payment, set by Chile's special copper tribunal Dec. 1, was slightly higher than the amount proposed earlier by the Chilean government.

Cerro had been exempted from any charges for excessive profits since its Rio Blanco mine was a new property that had not begun operations when President Salvador Allende took office in 1970. The mine project had been carried out with government cooperation since its inception under a previous administration, and Chile's relations with Cerro had remained friendly despite its bitter dispute with Anaconda Co. and Kennecott Copper Corp.

Cerro had continued to aid Chile in operating the Rio Blanco mine after its nationalization. The mine was said to be the only copper property in Chile that had maintained full production.

Exchange at critical low. Finance Minister Orlando Millas had told the Senate budget committee that Chile's foreign exchange problem was critical, due mainly to an international campaign against the nationalization of the country's mineral resources, the London newsletter Latin America reported Dec. 1.

Chile's net reserves were reportedly down to about $80 million, and it was calculated that at least $200 million were needed to import essential food supplies and spare parts.

Millas said that in August 1970 Chile could call on lines of credit totalling $219 million but that this had fallen to a mere $32 million by August 1972 due to pressure from international banking organizations. In the seven years before copper nationalization in 1971, he said, Chile had obtained more than $1 billion from the World Bank, the Inter-American Development Bank, the U.S. Export-Import Bank and the Agency for International Development. However, Chile had not been awarded a single credit from any of these organizations for more than a year, and credits worth $205 million were held up, Millas asserted.

The problem was aggravated by the fall in world copper prices, which according to Millas had cost Chile $187 million in 1971–72.

Unrest Grows

Civil clashes, police heads ousted. President Allende fired the chief and subchief of the civil police Aug. 6 in response to protests from most political sectors over a bloody police raid on a Santiago shantytown Aug. 5. The police chief, Eduardo Paredes, belonged to Allende's Socialist party, and his deputy, Carlos Toro, was a Communist.

The raid was conducted by more than 100 policemen searching for members of the extremist July 16th National Lib-Assault on the Moncada Barracks, which had reportedly been organized by the Revolutionary Left Movement (MIR), attempted to prevent a house to house search, and a battle ensued in which one person was killed, 60 injured and 160 arrested.

The incident reportedly caused a political crisis, stirred initially by angry editorials in opposition newspapers Aug. 6 and aggravated by a hostile communique from the MIR, which claimed the government's "reformist sectors," implicitly the Communist party, were responsible for the violence. Allende called newsmen to the presidential palace Aug. 10 to assure them there would be no military coup or civil war in Chile.

MIR members showed up in force at the funeral of the man killed in the police raid, and then attacked the government again at a press conference Aug. 11. MIR leader Miguel Enriquez charged that the Communists and other "reformists" in the Allende administration were guilty of "Stalinist tactics" and of "repression, torture and killing."

The conflict between the MIR and the government continued Aug. 13 when six party members were arrested along with 36 others being evicted from an occupied farm in Osorno, south of Santiago. Police reported confiscating 33 Molotov cocktails, a shotgun, ammunition and a time bomb during the action.

Emergency in Santiago. Allende declared a state of emergency in Santiago province Aug. 21 after violent protests were directed against Chile's acute food shortage. The disturbances grew out of a one-day strike by most of the capital's 150,000 shopkeepers, who complained that inflation, the scarcity of goods, price controls and other official restrictions were squeezing retailers out of business.

Santiago housewives staged a pot-banging demonstration Aug. 21 while police riot squads clashed with anti-Marxist demonstrators. Other anti-government youths put up flaming barricades along Providencia Avenue, an elegant thoroughfare.

About 160 young demonstrators were arrested after police used tear gas and clubs to break up groups shouting slogans against the Allende administration.

Demonstrators threw rocks at federal inspectors who attempted to reopen about 20 of the shops closed by the strike, which had been declared illegal by the government. The protesters were dispersed by police armed with tear gas and a water cannon.

Clashes spread to residential areas by nightfall, with demonstrations outside the homes of four government officials. The automobile of Labor Minister Mireya Baltra was smashed by angry neighbors when she returned home, but her attackers dispersed after police fired shots into the air. The state of emergency, which banned public meetings and suspended constitutional guarantees, was declared shortly before midnight.

Santiago was reported calm Aug. 22 as most shops reopened and government troops and police returned to their barracks.

Further south, in Llanquihue, one person was killed and seven wounded when peasants and landowners clashed Aug. 24. Four farmers were being sought in connection with the shooting, which reportedly began outside an expropriated farm when its former owner attempted to retrieve some implements.

Earlier, a state of emergency had been declared in the southernmost province of Magallanes Aug. 20 to quell protests over government policies and the death of a Punta Arenas supermarket owner while his store was being "requisitioned" by officials.

Further street disturbances. Street fighting broke out in Santiago and Concepcion Aug. 29–Sept. 1 as protests continued against government policies. Concepcion was placed under army control Aug. 31, but the state of emergency in Santiago, lifted Aug. 28, was not reimposed.

A state of emergency was declared, however, in the southern province of Bio-Bio, where merchants closed their stores Aug. 29 to protest the closing by the government of a right-wing commercial radio station. Closure of the station, in the provincial capital of Los Angeles, had been ordered for alleged incitement of an incident in which a peasant was killed. The emergency measures were lifted Aug. 30.

In Concepcion, thousands of pro-Marxist youths battled government opponents Aug. 30 after each group held illegal demonstrations. Police using water hoses and tear gas broke up the fighting, but in the action one policeman was killed and two policemen and seven civilians injured. The army took command of the city early the next day, and Interior Minister Jaime Suarez flew in from Santiago to investigate the disturbances.

In Santiago, high school students from two rival organizations—the Marxist-controlled Chilean Students Federation and the anti-government Federation of Secondary Students—battled each other and police Aug. 29–Sept. 1. The opposition students claimed Education Minister Anibal Palma was not working to solve student problems, and protested the appointment of a woman as principal of a Santiago girls' high school because her political party supported the government.

Roving gangs of students fought in the streets of Santiago the night of Sept. 1, often eluding riot policemen with tear gas and armored trucks. Anti-Marxist students set wood and paper bonfires, blocking intersections, and housewives angered by food shortages shouted encouragement from apartment houses. Police reportedly re-established order after arresting 154 persons.

Allende charges conspiracy. President Allende charged Sept. 2 that there was a right-wing "September plan" to overthrow his government. He asserted that any attempt at a coup would be met by a nationwide general strike and occupation of plants and buildings by workers. Without giving details, Allende said the "plan" was the work of "reactionaries" and foreign financiers who sought to return Chile's copper mines to their former U.S. owners and Chilean industries and large estates to "the plutocrats."

The charge followed government denunciation Aug. 26 of a "wave of sedition" by opposition groups and announcement of a series of repressive measures to control civil disturbances. Among the measures were the closing of the Los Angeles radio station by the police, application of the internal security law against right-wing groups, permission for police to use "all their preventive and repressive measures against [disruptive] groups," and "increased control over the activities of resident foreigners."

The opposition Christian Democratic party had charged Aug. 25 that Allende himself was to blame for the recent disturbances, which stemmed from dissatisfaction with the government's "erroneous and socially negative" economic policies. The party also criticized Allende for turning over to the army the responsibility for re-establishing order when it was the government's incompetence which had caused the disruptions.

Army coup rejected—Rumors that the current wave of civil disturbances might lead to a military coup were rejected Sept. 29 by Gen. Carlos Prats Gonzalez, army commander in chief, who said it was "illegal to use military power . . . against the democratic way of life." In one of his many recent pledges of military support for the government, Prats said the army was not going to "soak [its] arms and uniforms with the blood of thousands of fellow countrymen."

Prats' statement followed the forced retirement Sept. 21, for "institutional" reasons, of Gen. Alfredo Canales, who was widely reported to have plotted to overthrow President Allende. Allende had repeated charges Sept. 14 that "fascists" had plotted against his administration, but named only retired Maj. Arturo Marshall, who was in exile in Bolivia, among the alleged subversives.

Other unrest—Opposition parties staged demonstrations in Santiago Oct. 10 to protest cost of living increases, which, according to the National Statistics Institute, reached 99.8% for the first nine months of 1972. (Economy Minister Carlos Matus had announced an across-the-board price freeze beginning in October, the Wall Street Journal reported Sept. 27.)

The cost of living rose in Chile by 15.2% in October, making it 130.2% for the first ten months of 1972.

Students clashed with riot police and opposition parties staged demonstrations in Santiago Oct. 3 to protest a government order closing Radio Agricultura, an opposition radio station, for 48 hours. The government claimed the station's recent report of a clash between soldiers and civilians in the southern town of Nacimiento was "false and alarmist."

More than 40 youths were injured Sept. 23 when a group of pro-government youths dislodged anti-government demonstrators from a Santiago girls' school, which they had occupied to protest the alleged appointment of a principal on political grounds.

The government had suspended classes for 10 days Sept. 11 after repeated clashes between pro- and anti-Marxist high school students.

Strikes shake regime, cause Cabinet revision. A nationwide truckers strike, started Oct. 10, snowballed into a popular protest against the Popular Unity government and did not end until Nov. 5, three days after President Salvador Allende had been forced to revise his Cabinet.

The trouble began Oct. 10 when the Confederation of Truck Owners called a nationwide strike to demand higher rates and protest the establishment of a state trucking agency in the southern province of Aysen. The government immediately called the strike "seditious" and arrested 159 persons, including the four national leaders of the confederation.

As the strike spread Oct. 11, a state of emergency (a form of martial law) was declared in the central agrarian provinces of Curico and Talca, where striking truckers were allegedly blocking major roads.

Eleven more central provinces, including Santiago, were placed under military control Oct. 12 as filling stations began to run out of gasoline and bakeries closed for lack of flour deliveries. The government requisitioned all trucks belonging to striking enterprises and assumed control of distribution of fuel in Santiago. Interior Undersecretary Daniel Vergara announced in a radio speech that all "promoters, organizers, instigators and executors of [this] criminal strike" would be fined and prosecuted.

Most of the nation's shopkeepers and small businessmen joined the strike Oct. 13. Organizations of taxi drivers, construction workers and independent farmers also called on their members to join the protest. The government took control of all radio stations "until further notice," stifling most opposition opinion about measures being taken against the strike, and 1,000 striking truck drivers were reported arrested. In a nationwide radio speech, President Allende denounced "fascists and neo-fascists" who allegedly sought to paralyze the country.

In an effort to end the strike Oct. 14, Allende offered truck owners and drivers a number of concessions including release of all imprisoned strikers, but strike leaders reportedly refused to end the walkout until plans for the Aysen province trucking agency were dropped. Four more provinces were placed under a state of emergency, but many private radio stations were returned to their owners. Many Santiago shops were reported opened, and a government directive authorized official takeover of any that remained closed. However, the shortage of food and fuel remained serious.

The anti-Marxist opposition parties expressed support for the strikes Oct. 15 after the government threatened to requisition all stores that refused to open for business. Sen. Renan Fuentealba, president of the Christian Democratic party, accused the government of "trampling upon the constitutional guarantees it promised to respect." He asserted that the arrest of strikers and declaration of emergency zones was "a flagrant violation of the rights of Chilean workers."

Violence erupted Oct. 16 as the government resorted to force against the striking shopkeepers. Riot police using tear gas and a water cannon broke up anti-Marxist demonstrations and smashed locks on stores in downtown Santiago, forcing them open. Pro- and anti-government youths clashed in rock-throwing street battles in the center of the city. The government again took control of all radio stations as 7,000 engineers announced their support for the strikers.

Physicians, merchant marine captains, private school students and many bank employes joined the walkouts Oct. 17, and the Santiago lawyers association urged the regional bar association to call a strike of all attorneys. Riot police attempted to force open more stores in the capital, but were reportedly beaten back by rock-throwing demonstrators. The main rail line between Santiago and the port of Valparaiso was bombed for the

second time in 30 hours, and at least two trucks carrying supplies to the capital were fired upon.

Christian Democratic leaders rejected an invitation from President Allende Oct. 17 to confer on the strike crisis.

Allende's first major success against the strike movement was his negotiation late Oct. 17 of a settlement with bus owners who were threatening to join the shutdown. The agreement included a pledge by Allende to keep transportation in the private sector.

Officials of the confederations representing the striking truck owners and shopkeepers said Oct. 18 that their action, basically a political move to force Allende to change some economic policies, would continue with a new list of demands. In a further move against the shopkeepers' strike, the government Oct. 17 had requisitioned the last large wholesale distribution company in private hands. Two more provinces were reported under military control Oct. 18. Army vehicles patrolled Santiago, and riot police broke up more street brawls.

The situation grew worse Oct. 20 when bus service was cut off, following a vote by union members to stage a 24-hour strike despite numerous concessions to bus owners in negotiations with the government Oct. 17. The 180 pilots of the government airline LAN also joined the strike.

Factories that had functioned normally despite the earlier strikes were forced to cut back production Oct. 20 when laborers who depended on public transportation were unable to get to work. Two more provinces were placed under a state of emergency, bringing to 21 the number of provinces under military rule. All five opposition political parties endorsed the protest strikes, blaming the Allende administration for what they called "total chaos" in the economy.

Army commanders Oct. 21 barred sales of gasoline to private consumers for two days as a result of delays in deliveries. Several hundred persons were arrested for violating the midnight–6 a.m. curfew (imposed Oct. 17) and one person was shot to death when he refused to stop for questioning by soldiers.

Following the end of the bus strike Oct. 21, President Allende announced the government had crushed attempts to paralyze the country, and said the stoppages still in effect were doomed to failure. He denied, as he had asserted earlier, that the country was on the verge of civil war. Meanwhile, the controller general, a congressionally appointed watchdog who could pass judgment on presidential acts, declared the government's takeover of all radio stations illegal (and the government relinquished control over the stations Oct. 27).

Representatives of 17 commercial and professional associations, including shopkeepers, taxi drivers, doctors, lawyers and construction workers, announced Oct. 22 that their strikes would continue until the government acceded to eight demands: Respect for the groups' rights and liberties; full restitution of the right to information and free expression; achievement of change only within the law; participation by professionals in the formulation of government reforms; security in places of work and an end to all violence; liberty for Chileans to enter and leave the country as they pleased; an end to government political and economic control; and consideration of separate petitions by each group.

Striking bank employes announced Oct. 22 they would return to work but warned they would resume their stoppage if any reprisals were taken against them. Striking pilots also ended their action following a military takeover of LAN. A railway line south of Santiago was reported bombed, but rail transportation was not interrupted.

A "day of silence" protest called by opposition leaders Oct. 24 was only partially successful as activities in Santiago proceeded normally. A government newspaper reported that 10,000 volunteer laborers from student and union groups were unloading trucks and trains to help overcome the food and fuel shortages caused by the strikes. The government also closed down three opposition radio stations which had begun broadcasting "independent" news.

Allende broke off negotiations with strike leaders Oct. 28, charging they had made "unacceptable" political demands which would mean "the limitation of presidential powers." The demands reportedly included modifications in the government's agrarian policies and suspension of measures taken to centralize foreign trade under the Central Bank.

Allende dissolved the truckers union Oct. 28. He said its strike had affected "the social-economic normality of the population, disrupting vital activities such as the distribution of fuel and supply of food to the community." Truck owners had reported an "agreement in principle" with Allende Oct. 25, but this had apparently broken down in further negotiations.

Hundreds of persons were arrested Oct. 26–Nov. 3 as street disturbances continued in Santiago and other cities.

Strikes end after Cabinet change— The strikes ended Nov. 5 after Allende revised his Cabinet and the new interior minister, Gen. Carlos Prats Gonzalez, negotiated a settlement with strike leaders.

Prats, former commander in chief of the army and one of three senior armed forces officers in the new Cabinet, reached the agreement with strike leaders after threatening them with "severe action." The government acceded to a number of the strikers' "strictly labor" demands but rejected others that it termed "political," including a reported demand for a plebiscite on Allende's economic policies. The government also agreed to continue negotiations with labor leaders on a series of specific grievances.

Terms of the settlement, read by Prats in a nationwide radio address, included:

■ Immediate abandonment by the government of legal actions and sanctions against striking unions.

■ No government reprisals against strikers or strike leaders.

■ No reprisals by striking employers against employes who worked or tried to work during the stoppages, and full pay for those laid off by the strikes.

■ Removal from the list of enterprises to be nationalized of Cenadi, a wholesale distributing firm owned by small businessmen and industrialists.

■ A new pledge by the government not to nationalize trucking.

■ Return of private businesses and property taken over or requisitioned by the government during the strikes.

■ Enactment of legislation to protect small businessmen, industrialists and artisans.

Prats also announced an end to the midnight–6 a.m. curfew in Santiago and other cities, and the return to civilian officials of 21 provinces placed under a state of emergency.

Strike leaders termed the settlement "satisfactory," and the leader of the truckers union called it "a triumph for Chilean union democracy, and perhaps an affirmation of the country's political democracy." Most strike leaders asserted the presence of military men in the Cabinet would ensure enactment of the government's pledges.

A strike by pilots and mechanics for LAN, the state airline, ended Nov. 10 after management agreed to wage increases. The strike, begun during the recent nationwide stoppages, had continued despite the end of the other strikes Nov. 5.

Finance Minister Orlando Millas said Nov. 15 that the recent nationwide strikes had cost the state more than $240 million.

Cabinet changes — President Allende named a new Cabinet Nov. 2 following the resignation of all ministers Oct. 31 to give him a freer hand in resolving the strike crisis. Three portfolios went to military officers and the others to civilians, several of whom retained their old posts. The Interior Ministry, second in power to the presidency, went to Gen. Prats, who had repeatedly pledged military support of the government during the strikes.

The new Cabinet:

Foreign affairs—Clodomiro Almeyda; interior—Gen. Carlos Prats Gonzalez; economy, development and reconstruction—Fernando Flores Labra; finance—Orlando Millas; education—Jorge Tapia; justice—Sergio Isunza Barrios; public works and transportation—Rear Adm. Ismael Huerta Diaz; agriculture—Rolando Calderon; land and coloniza-

tion—Humberto Martones; labor—Luis Figueroa; public health (temporary)—Juan Carlos Concha Gutierrez; mining—Gen. Claudio Sepulveda Donoso; housing and urban affairs (temporary)—Luis Matte Valdez; national defense—Jose Toha; Cabinet secretary general (temporary)—Hernan del Canto.

The new Cabinet retained a left-wing orientation, with a majority of ministers from the Communist, Socialist and Radical parties. The appointment of military officers was seen as a way of placating anti-Marxists, at least until the March 1973 Congressional elections.

Resignation of the old Cabinet followed a move by the five opposition parties Oct. 31 to impeach four officials — Interior Minister Jaime Suarez, Economy Minister Carlos Matus Romo, Agriculture Minister Jacques Chonchol and Education Minister Anibal Palma. The five groups, aligned in the Confederation of Democratic Parties, introduced resolutions in the Chamber of Deputies censuring the ministers for "repeated violations of the constitution and the law." Two of the officials, Suarez and Palma, had announced previously that they would resign to run in the 1973 elections.

Armando Arancibia, of Allende's Socialist party, was named economy undersecretary Nov. 18, replacing Fernando Flores Labra, the new economy minister.

The Revolutionary Left Movement had sharply criticized the inclusion of military officials in the new Cabinet, asserting it was "dangerous for the people to accept alliances made in their name with high military officials without some guarantees and conditions," the Miami Herald reported Nov. 11.

Christian Left leaves Cabinet. The Christian Left party, a member of the ruling Popular Unity coalition (UP), announced Nov. 13 that it would not accept a post in the new Allende Cabinet. However, it reiterated its support for President Allende and most UP policies. The party had been unrepresented in the Cabinet since the resignation Oct. 31 of Agriculture Minister Jacques Chonchol.

Finance, economy ministers switched.
President Salvador Allende had Finance
Minister Orlando Millas switch posts with
Economy Minister Fernando Flores Dec.
29 after the Chamber of Deputies censured and suspended Millas for allegedly
violating the law and the constitution. The
switch prevented the chamber's censure
motion from going to the Senate and
possibly resulting in Millas' impeachment.

The chamber censure motion, introduced by the right-wing National and
Radical Democracy parties and supported
by the moderate Christian Democrats,
was passed by a vote of 75–42. It accused
Millas of illegally firing 26 Central Bank
employes who had participated in the recent nationwide strikes; refusing to extend credits to businessmen opposed to
the government; and illegally reducing the
amount of dollars available to individuals
for foreign travel. Millas denied the
charges.

Emergency in south. The Interior
Ministry declared a state of emergency
in the southern province of Bio-Bio Nov.
25, following clashes between supporters
and opponents of the government at the
regional hospital in Los Angeles. The
province was placed under military control.

The disturbance reportedly began
when a group of employes occupied the
hospital to demand advance wages allegedly approved by the Health Ministry but canceled after they participated in the recent anti-government
strikes. Hospital workers supporting the
government tried to dislodge them, and
at least 50 persons were injured in the
ensuing clashes. Order was restored by
police using tear gas, who arrested about
100 persons.

Gun control enacted. Congress had
enacted an omnibus gun control law,
giving the armed forces absolute control
over all privately owned arms and for-
bidding private militias and all other
nonofficial armed groups, the Miami
Herald reported Nov. 6.

The measure, initiated by opposition
parties to combat violent leftist armed
groups—principally elements of the
Revolutionary Left Movement—banned

the private possession of machine guns
and other high-powered automatic
weapons, grenades, tear gas and bombs
of any kind. Persons possessing such
arms had 30 days to turn them in and
escape prosecution. In the future,
armed forces permission would be required to own or possess a firearm of any
kind.

Frei begins Senate campaign. Ex-
President Eduardo Frei Montalva opened
his campaign for the Senate Dec. 5 with a
sharp attack on the Popular Unity
government (UP).

Speaking to a convention of his Christian Democratic party, Frei accused the
UP of creating a "catastrophic" situation
through policies that had "little to do with
the history . . . and the socioeconomic and
political reality of Chile." He said the
government had sought to divide Chileans
irreconcilably, spreading the "cancer" of
hate and violence. He also predicted an
acceleration of inflation in 1973, bringing
"hunger into many homes."

Frei said the March 1973 elections
would be a plebiscite on UP programs,
which would have to change if the opposition won decisively. His own campaign, for a Senate seat from Santiago,
was seen as a prelude to a presidential bid
in 1976.

Christian Democratic leaders Dec. 16
criticized Interior Minister Prats for not
denouncing a Socialist party attack on
Frei. The attack, on a nationwide television program, allegedly included
"charges of treason, robbery, and hand-
ing over the national wealth to foreigners."

Economic measures set. Defense
Minister Jose Toha, acting as interior
minister while President Allende was
away on a foreign tour, announced
Dec. 12 a series of government measures
to combat the scarcity of essential goods
and the growth of the black market.

The measures were approved at a
Cabinet meeting presided over by Interior
Minister Carlos Prats, acting as vice
president. They included proposed legislation providing severe punishment for
black marketeers and monopolists and
establishment of a special commission to

improve systems of distribution and commerce. Measures would also be taken to overcome production problems in certain industries.

Toha also announced that many industries and firms requisitioned by the government or occupied illegally would be returned to their owners.

Allende Abroad

Tour includes U.N., U.S.S.R. & Cuba. President Allende, on a 15-day trip Nov. 30–Dec. 14, visited Mexico, the United Nations, the Soviet Union and Cuba, with stopovers in Peru, Algeria and Venezuela. The first leg of the tour culminated in an address to the U.N. General Assembly Dec. 4, in which Allende accused U.S. corporations, banking interests and governmental agencies of "serious aggression" against his government.

Allende stopped briefly in Lima Nov. 30, conferring with Peruvian President Juan Velasco Alvarado before proceeding to Mexico. He said the purpose of the meeting was to thank the Peruvian government and people for their support in Chile's battle against "the aggression of a powerful company with multinational interests." Allende assured his hosts that Chile would remain united with Peru and Ecuador in claiming 200-mile offshore territorial limits.

Allende received a tumultuous reception at the Mexico City airport Nov. 30. Mexican President Luis Echeverria Alvarez described Allende as "a leader of a revolutionary battle for freedom." Allende addressed Mexico's Congress the next day, accusing the U.S.-based International Telephone & Telegraph Corp. (ITT) of bringing Chile to the brink of civil war.

Before Allende's departure Dec. 3, a joint Mexican-Chilean communique was issued urging Latin American nations to set aside their ideological differences, promote economic integration and stand together in international forums to defend their interests. Allende and Echeverria reaffirmed the right of all nations to "dispose freely of their natural resources and follow, without foreign interference, the models of development most suited to their national realities."

Allende arrived in New York later Dec. 3, met briefly with George Bush, U.S. ambassador to the U.N., and addressed the General Assembly the next day.

In his 90-minute speech, Allende accused U.S. interests of trying to prevent his government from taking power, and then promoting an economic blockade that had severely limited Chile's ability to secure equipment, spare parts, food and medicine. This "financial strangulation" was "yet another manifestation of imperialism, one that is more subtle, more cunning and terrifyingly effective in preventing us from exercising our rights as a sovereign state," Allende charged.

Because of pressure from U.S. interests, Allende continued, agencies such as the Export-Import Bank, the World Bank, the Inter-American Development Bank, private banking interests in the U.S. and the Agency for International Development had cut off lines of credit to Chile. Such actions, he said, were "legally and morally unacceptable," representing "the exertion of pressure on an economically weak country, the infliction of punishment on a whole nation for its decision to recover its own basic resources, and a form of intervention in the internal affairs of a sovereign state."

Allende centered his criticism on two U.S.-based corporations, ITT and Kennecott Copper Corp., which he said had "dug their claws into my country" and proposed "to manage our political life." ITT, he charged, had "launched a sinister plan to prevent me from acceding to the presidency . . . Before the conscience of the world I accuse ITT of attempting to bring about civil war in my country."

Allende denounced Kennecott for bringing legal action against Chile's state copper company in foreign courts and justified the excess profits ruling by which Chile's special copper tribunal had upheld the government's refusal to compensate Kennecott for its nationalized Chilean properties. He said that the ruling was based on a reasonable margin of profit of 12%, which Kennecott had exceeded in 1955–70 by making an average annual profit of 52.8% on its investment.

Allende included ITT and Kennecott among huge "transnational" corporations which he said were waging war against sovereign states and were "not accountable to or regulated by any parliament or institution representing the collective interest."

U.S. Ambassador George Bush replied after Allende's speech that investment of U.S. capital abroad was not intended to exploit foreign countries, but rather was of mutual benefit to the investor and the people of the country in which the investment was made.

An ITT spokesman also contested Allende's charges, saying "ITT has been interested only in the safety and well-being of its employes in Chile and in receiving just compensation for those assets which the Chilean government might acquire." Kennecott president Frank Milliken said "no amount of rhetoric can alter the fact that Kennecott has been a responsible corporate citizen of Chile for more than 50 years and has made substantial contributions to both the economic and social well-being of the Chilean people."

Allende flew to Algiers Dec. 5, meeting with President Houari Boumediene during a 19-hour stopover on the way to Moscow. He said "future relations between Algeria and Chile will be those of revolutionary friendship because we have the same enemies." Allende also expressed support for the Palestinian guerrilla movement, which he said was "fighting for national independence and against imperialism."

Allende arrived in Moscow Dec. 6, where he was greeted by Soviet Communist Party General Secretary Leonid Brezhnev, President Nikolai Podgorny, Premier Aleksei Kosygin and about 100,000 cheering citizens. He conferred with Soviet leaders in Moscow Dec. 6–8 and then traveled to Kiev, departing for Cuba Dec. 10.

In a communique issued shortly after Allende's departure, the Soviet Union pledged continued political and economic aid to Chile. It promised further economic assistance in the construction of certain unspecified industrial concerns, and for power plants, agriculture and fisheries.

The Soviet Union also joined Chile in condemning "actions taken by foreign monopolies to deprive Chile of her right to use her natural resources at her own discretion, specifically her right to sell her copper freely."

(U.S. military sources claimed that during his visit to the Soviet Union, Allende was offered $50 million in low-interest credits to buy Soviet military equipment, the Washington Post reported Dec. 12. The Soviets reportedly had been urging Chile to replace its obsolete British-made warplanes with MiG-21 jet fighters, but Chilean air force officers reportedly preferred to obtain new equipment from the U.S.)

Allende arrived in Havana Dec. 10 to an enthusiastic welcome from Premier Fidel Castro, President Osvaldo Dorticos and a large crowd. A joint Cuban-Chilean communique issued at the end of Allende's visit Dec. 14 called for Latin American unity against "foreign economic exploitation and oppression," which it said were aimed at crushing Latin America's "struggle for emancipation." It attacked large international consortiums which had "exploited for years the national wealth of our peoples, obtaining exorbitant profits," and denounced "imperialist maneuvers" designed to punish economically those countries that did not share U.S. social and ideological policies.

Allende stopped briefly in Caracas Dec. 14, where he conferred with Venezuelan President Rafael Caldera. The two signed a joint declaration defending their countries' policies on natural resources and pledging action on Venezuela's bid for membership in the Andean Group.

Allende received a rousing welcome on his return to Santiago Dec. 14, but was immediately faced with charges by the opposition Christian Democrats that he was "leading [Chile] to a dependence on and a subordination to the Soviet Union." The Christian Democrats called for an investigation of the accords made by the president in the Soviet Union, calling them "an attempt against the sovereignty and the dignity of Chile and ... the most dangerous threat for our economic future and, because of this, for the possibilities of raising the living standards of the Chilean people." Allende rejected the charges.

The U.S.S.R. gave Chile credits of $30 million for food and cotton purchases and more than $180 million for capital goods, including industrial equipment, Foreign Minister Clodomiro Almeyda announced Dec. 20. He said the U.S.S.R. had also agreed to renegotiate payment of Chile's $103 million Soviet debt.

U.S. talks. Following Allende's trip, U.S. and Chilean representatives held three days of negotiations in Washington Dec. 20–22 and agreed to resume talks in Washington early in 1973.

The talks were agreed to after a diplomatic exchange initiated by the U.S. Sept. 15, U.S. officials had said Dec. 15. The purpose of the talks was to seek solutions to the increasing U.S.-Chilean problems. The principal questions discussed were Chilean nationalization of U.S. property, Chile's $1.7 billion debt to the U.S. and Washington's blockage of international credits to Chile. The talks were the first full-fledged review of relations by the two countries since Allende's inauguration.

Earlier Developments in Foreign Relations

Allende opens UNCTAD parley. Chilean President Salvador Allende opened the third United Nations Conference on Trade and Development (UNCTAD) in Santiago April 13 with a strong denunciation of industrial nations for creating a world where "the toil and resources of the poorer nations pay for the prosperity of the affluent peoples."

Speaking before 1,500 delegates from 141 countries, Allende singled out the U.S., international corporations and the General Agreement on Tariffs and Trade (GATT) as perpetrators of "unfair international division of labor, based on a dehumanized concept of mankind."

Allende said 75% of the world's economic system "is in the hands of the developed countries of the West, and of this proportion, more than 60% is controlled by the big U.S. private corporations, with whose policy we are familiar."

Noting the "plundering indulged in by these consortiums, and their powerful corruptive influence on public institutions in rich and poor countries alike," Allende referred indirectly to U.S. columnist Jack Anderson's recent report on anti-government activities in Chile by the International Telephone and Telegraph Corp. (ITT).

A huge corporation, Allende said, had begun "worldwide campaigns against the prestige of a government, to make it the victim of an international boycott and to sabotage its relations with the rest of the world." Allende said the action "constitutes an alarm signal for the international community, which is under an imperative obligation to react with utmost vigor."

Allende noted, however, that Socialist and capitalist countries had recently shown an ability to cooperate, and proposed similar cooperation between "the former colonizing and imperialist countries on the one hand and the dependent peoples on the other."

Specifically, Allende recommended an UNCTAD study on the origin of the Third World's alleged $70 billion foreign debt and how to eliminate it, and a "fund for homogeneous development" to be financed from the savings from disarmament.

U.N. Secretary General Kurt Waldheim spoke briefly after Allende in an apparent effort to soften the criticisms of the industrial states, whose cooperation would be needed for the conference to achieve its goal of aiding more balanced development.

Mexican President Luis Echeverria Alvarez addressed UNCTAD April 20.

Echeverria urged the conference to adopt a "charter of economic duties and rights of states," which would include the demands of Chile's Socialist government for the renunciation of economic pressure on other states and the express prohibition of interference by multinational corporations in the internal affairs of the countries in which they operated.

Echeverria hailed Chile's nationalization of U.S. copper interests, recalling Mexico's expropriation in 1938 of foreign oil companies.

Echeverria and Allende April 21 issued a joint communique calling for closer relations between Mexico and the Andean Group, reaffirming the right of nations to control their natural resources and condemning economic or political pressures by any nation to prevent another from transforming its own internal structures.

Bolivian exiles barred. The Chilean government refused Feb. 18 to allow 208 Bolivian political prisoners to enter the country as exiles. Brazil and Peru had also refused to take the exiles.

A Chilean Foreign Ministry spokesman said the Bolivian request seemed to contradict that country's charges that Chile was training guerrilla fighters to overthrow the Banzer government.

The Bolivian government held that hundreds of exiled Bolivians were being trained as guerrilla fighters in Chile, the Miami Herald reported Feb. 17. Interior Minister Mario Adett Zamora charged that "Bolivian exiles in Chile are receiving military and subversive instruction with the consent of the [Chilean] government and with the support of Cuba and . . . the countries behind the Iron Curtain." Officials were said to believe the guerrillas would return to Bolivia to commit acts of urban terror and to foment labor uprisings in the nation's economically vital tin-mining regions.

As evidence of subversive preparations, the government cited the presence in Chile of known revolutionaries and enemies of the regime of Hugo Banzer Suarez (including deposed President Gen. Juan Jose Torres), and the formation in Santiago of the Bolivian Anti-imperialist Revolutionary Front.

Plotter in Bolivia—Chile sharply criticized Bolivia June 8 for allowing an exiled Chilean army officer to make political statements, violating accepted international conditions for political asylum.

The officer, retired Maj. Arturo Marshall Marchesse, had admitted to a La Paz newspaper that he had led a right-wing plot against President Allende, who, he said, was "doing so much harm" to Chile. Marshall had fled to Bolivia after the government announced discovery of the plot.

Foreign Undersecretary Anibal Palma charged June 8 that Marshall's statement "violated the right of asylum," and noted the "paradox that the Bolivian government would permit such declarations after complaining repeatedly of alleged activities of Bolivian exiles in Chile."

In an apparent reply June 21, Luis Mayser, secretary general of the pro-government Bolivian Socialist Falange, charged that Bolivian guerrillas were reorganizing in Chile "with the support" of the Allende government. Mayser said Chile was "the country most interested in provoking socio-economic disorder in Bolivia."

Argentina voids border pact. Argentina was reported March 12 to have decided to withdraw from a 1902 treaty with Chile under which the two countries had agreed to settle by arbitration a long-standing dispute over the Beagle Channel and three small islands at the southern tip of South America. The treaty had been automatically renewed every 10 years.

Argentina's action invoked an article in the treaty that allowed either nation to withdraw on six months' notice at the end of each 10-year period. Argentina said ways of resolving international disputes had evolved so much since 1902 that it was necessary to bring the treaty up to date.

Chile had recently invoked an article in the treaty to ask Queen Elizabeth II to arbitrate in a fresh effort to resolve the dispute. Chile and Argentina had agreed on the composition of a tribunal, and British officials were working on details of its operating methods when the Argentine withdrawal was announced.

President Alejandro Lanusse assured Chilean President Salvador Allende in a telephone call March 10 that Argentina would still accept British arbitration in the dispute. Allende said later that Lanusse sought "an instrument more suitable for modern techniques," and that Chile was in full agreement.

Chilean Foreign Minister Clodomiro Almeyda and Argentine Foreign Minister Luis de Pablo Pardo signed a 10-year arbitration agreement April 5 to replace the 1902 treaty. Under the new treaty, the two countries would take unresolvable differences to the International Court of Justice in The Hague.

Soviet dealings. Soviet and Chilean officials signed a $11.5 million contract March 30 for the shipment of Soviet tractors to Chile.

The Soviet Union had offered Chile a 12-year loan of $220 million at 2½% interest for the purchase of machinery and industrial equipment, the newsletter Latin America said July 14. The U.S.S.R. also agreed to buy 130,000 tons of Chilean copper over the next three years, the Miami Herald reported July 20.

Relations with China, Korea & Vietnam.

Chilean Foreign Minister Clodomiro would lend Chile $70 million for establishment of small- and medium-sized industries.

The Miami Herald reported Feb. 2 that Chile would receive the money in pounds sterling over the next four years, and would repay it in 10 annual installments—either in cash or in produce—beginning in 1981.

The North Korean regime in Pyongyang announced April 4 that it had signed an agreement to supply Chile with machinery, metals, and chemical and textile products. Chile was to send copper, minerals and chemicals.

Chile established diplomatic relations with North Korea and North Vietnam June 1, becoming the first South American nation to recognize either country.

South Korea's ambassador in Santiago, Choon Kee Kang, had been recalled to Seoul for "consulations" the previous week. Diplomatic sources did not expect him to return to Chile, the Miami Herald reported June 2.

A Chilean mission headed by Planning Minister Gonzalo Martner visited China May 28–June 8, securing an interest-free $65 million loan and signing trade contracts and agreements on technical, economic and commercial cooperation.

According to the agreements, Chile would sell China nitrate and copper, while China would sell Chile rice, soybeans and pharmaceutical and food products. Chile would send copper and nitrate technicians to China, and China would supply Chile with light-industry factories—particularly for textiles and machine tools—and equipment for the manufacture of agricultural and mining tools.

The mission arrived in North Korea June 9 and signed a trade protocol and an agreement for economic and technical cooperation with North Korean officials June 15. The agreement reportedly included long-term economic and technical loans to Chile for industrial and agricultural purposes.

Latin credit set. The government announced June 14 that it had obtained $100 million credit from Brazil, Mexico, Colombia and Peru for the purchase of capital and consumer goods in those countries. The largest of the contributions was from Brazil.

Central Bank Vice President Hugo Fazio, who negotiated the credit, said the loans and others being sought in other Latin American nations were beginning to break an alleged credit embargo imposed on Chile by U.S. commercial banks.

Argentine skyjackers reach Chile. Ten alleged Argentine terrorists landed in Chile in a hijacked plane Aug. 15.

As an upshot of the hijacking, 16 other suspected guerrillas, including at least three women, were shot to death Aug. 22 while allegedly trying to escape from an Argentine naval air base prison near Trelew.

According to police officials, all of the victims had been arrested Aug. 15 at the Trelew airport, where they had helped the 10 hijackers commandeer an Austral Airlines jet with 96 aboard.

The hijacking was carried out in conjunction with a mutiny at an army maximum security prison at Rawson, 15 miles from Trelew, during which a group of inmates escaped. Some escapees were reportedly among the hijackers, who commandeered the jet to Santiago, Chile, where they surrendered to police and requested political asylum.

The presence of the alleged terrorists in Chile presented a delicate problem for Chilean President Salvador Allende. Allende said Aug. 16 that if Argentina asked for the extradition of the hijackers, it would be up to the Chilean courts to decide whether they were political prisoners or common criminals. However,

Sen. Carlos Altamirano of Allende's Socialist party visited the hijackers Aug. 19 to express the party's "solidarity" with them.

The Chilean government sent the 10 hijackers to Cuba Aug. 25.

In a nationwide radio-TV message Aug. 25, Allende said that his regime's decision to grant the guerrillas political asylum and then sent them to Cuba was motivated by "profound humanity and morality" and followed "international conventions and principles and the dispositions of our internal laws." Allende added that Chile remained "deeply" committed to maintaining friendly relations with Argentina, which had been "strengthened with satisfactory results" by his administration.

The Argentine government, which had demanded extradition of the guerrillas, angrily recalled its ambassador from Santiago Aug. 26 and delivered what it called a "very severe" protest to Chile Aug. 27.

Castro denies criticizing Allende. Cuban Premier Fidel Castro Sept. 10 dismissed as "base, gross, truculent lies" allegations by Washington columnist Jack Anderson that Castro had privately criticized President Allende during his visit to Chile in 1971.

Anderson's report, allegedly based on a Central Intelligence Agency (CIA) document, appeared in U.S. newspapers Sept. 8. It claimed that before his departure from Chile, Castro had told local Communist leaders that Allende had not imposed Marxism on Chile forcefully enough, and was "physically spent." Castro had reportedly added that other Chilean leaders lived "too well," and were "not under sufficient tension."

According to the alleged CIA document, "Castro said the [government] does not have a solid front to face the opposition, which he claimed is growing rapidly. Castro added that the situation in Chile is rapidly approaching a critical stage . . ." Among factors which could precipitate a crisis and confrontation with the opposition, Castro allegedly cited a breakdown of public order, which could come about "at any time because the opposition, especially the middle class, has lost its fear of the government."

Foreign credits. Among foreign credits negotiated by Chile in 1972:

The government announced Nov. 10 that Finland would lend Chile $10 million for forestry development.

Chile and Spain signed an agreement Dec. 6 providing for Spanish credits to Chile worth $40.8 million. The credits would help finance engineering projects and purchase of equipment and parts.

The International Monetary Fund Dec. 20 granted Chile credits worth $42.8 million to compensate for the drop in revenues from copper exports.

In related developments:

The Central Bank had signed two credit agreements with the National Bank of Hungary totaling $20 million, it was reported Dec. 22. The credits were for purchase of capital goods.

Other Developments

Gen. Viaux jailed in Schneider death. An army judge June 16 sentenced retired Brig. Gen. Roberto Viaux to 20 years in prison for complicity in the 1970 assassination of Army Commander in Chief Rene Schneider.

Thirty-three others were sentenced to prison terms ranging from three years to life or to expulsion from the country in connection with the assassination. Two important former officers—Brig. Gen. Camilo Valenzuela, who had commanded the army's Santiago garrison in 1970, and Vice Adm. Hugo Tirado Barros, who had headed the navy—were banished from Chile for three years. All said they would appeal.

The Military Tribunal Dec. 7 unexpectedly reduced the prison sentences of all those convicted in the case. Viaux' was reduced from 20 to two years, but he was ordered to serve a one-year sentence for leading a 1969 military rebellion and, after that, to leave Chile for a minimum of five years.

Foreign doctors to be hired. The National Health Service announced Aug. 7 that it would hire 300 foreign physicians to alleviate Chile's shortage of medical personnel. The doctors would be assigned mostly to rural areas, where the need was greatest. Service director Sergio Infante said that despite an increase in medical students, the country needed 7,000 more doctors.

(The director of Chile's Engineering College said Aug. 9 that at least 500 professionals had left the country during the past 18 months. However, he added that the number of students applying to the college was continually increasing.)

Chilean drugs increase in U.S. Chile had become the major source of cocaine smuggled into the U.S. and was gaining importance as a supplier of heroin, the New York Times reported Aug. 7.

According to U.S. Bureau of Narcotics and Dangerous Drugs agents and unidentified Chilean officials, Chilean cocaine shipments intercepted in Central America, Mexico and the Caribbean averaged 80–100 pounds—indicating well-organized smuggling operations—and contained increasing amounts of heroin.

Most of the cocaine was reportedly produced in Peru, Bolivia and Ecuador and sent to Chile for refinement in clandestine laboratories and shipment to the U.S. and other countries.

Heroin entered Chile for refinement and shipment from Argentina, Paraguay and Uruguay, which in turn obtained it from southern Europe and the Middle East, the Times reported.

The traffic had reportedly been facilitated by difficulties of the Chilean currency. It was said that ordinary goods were being smuggled out of the country at an unprecedented rate, giving cocaine merchants a useful cover. Moreover, the value of the U.S. dollar in Chile was such that the cocaine price in Santiago and frontier towns was far lower than in other countries.

Chilean police Oct. 28 announced discovery of two cocaine laboratories, one possibly the largest in Latin America, with narcotics destined for the U.S., Spain, Italy and Mexico.

Campaign against alcoholism. Government officials, public health organizations and rehabilitation agencies were contributing to President Allende's five-month campaign against alcoholism,

Chile's major public health problem, according to El Nacional of Caracas Aug. 20. Among new programs to combat the disease were electric shock treatments for alcoholics.

According to Carlos Montalva, coordinator of the National Commission against Alcoholism, 20% of Chile's population drank excessively, and 5% were alcoholics. About 20% of children over nine years of age drank alcoholic beverages, Montalva added.

According to an official report, Chileans annually consumed alcoholic beverages worth $400 million, or about a year's budget allocation for the National Health Service. Chile's hepatic cirrhosis rate was the highest in Latin America. Alcoholism was also the major cause of the country's acute labor absenteeism problem and a significant factor in labor accidents and suicides, the report said.

Crash survivors found in Andes. Sixteen men who had been given up for dead when their plane vanished over the Andes Mountains on the Chilean border Oct. 13 were rescued Dec. 22–23 after two of the group climbed 10 days to reach civilization. The survivors had lived in below-freezing weather 69 days and subsisted on melted snow, food from the plane and, police later revealed, by eating the remains of their dead companions.

Of the 45 people aboard, the survivors said 21 died immediately in the crash and eight were killed later in an avalanche.

Some of the 16 survivors were members of Uruguay's Old Christian Brothers rugby team of Montevideo, which chartered the plane.

Foreign news to be checked. The government informed foreign news agencies Nov. 9 that in the future they would be required to provide the presidential palace with copies of all news dispatches sent abroad. The presidential press secretary denied any censorship was implied.

Under the order, allowed by a 1937 security law, messengers would pick up the dispatches twice a day. The first pickups were made Nov. 10.

In another press development Nov. 9, police forcibly ejected about 100 leftist workers from a newspaper building in Concepcion. The workers, who belonged to a labor faction dominated by the Revolutionary Left Movement, had occupied the building Oct. 17, stopping publication of two newspapers.

1973: Allende's Fall

Turmoil Precedes Coup

Salvador Allende Gossens, Chile's Marxist president, was overthrown by a military coup d'etat Sept. 11. Allende died in the coup.

The coup was preceded by months of economic disruption, strikes and political violence.

Food limitations ordered. Finance Minister Fernando Flores announced Jan. 10 food distribution rules to combat speculation, inflation and the growing black market. The measure was one of several drastic moves that would put Chile on what the government called a "war economy."

Flores said a quota on about 30 essential foods—including oils, sugar, rice, meat and coffee—would be established for each family, and enforced by the Price and Supply Boards (JAPs), which were dominated by members of the ruling Popular Unity parties. The JAPs were authorized to determine the local needs for essential foods, supervise supplies and denounce merchants and speculators who subverted the plan.

Flores also announced elimination of trusteeships in state enterprises, establishment of the National Distribution Secretariat, elimination of direct sales to the public in factories, elimination of payment in products to industrial laborers, and state control of distribution and sales of agricultural and livestock products.

The measures were immediately denounced by Sen. Osvaldo Olguin, acting president of the opposition Christian Democratic party, as "so absurd as to give the impression the government wants a war with the public." Olguin said the system would only aggravate the food shortage, causing "desperation among the Chilean people." The other opposition parties protested Jan. 11, calling the government's economic policies "dictatorial."

The government, which had asserted Chile's economic difficulties were caused by the "imperialist blockade" and "internal aggression" by the opposition, rejected the opposition charges Jan. 11. The three military officers in the Cabinet declared the same day that they agreed with President Salvador Allende Gossens on the need to apply "urgent measures and the full weight of the law" to eliminate hoarding, speculation and the black market.

A government report recommending rationing, published in the left-wing weekly Chile Hoy, was cited in the London newsletter Latin America Jan. 5. It said the total food supply had increased by 27% in 1971–72—twice as much as it had in the previous five years—but that for a variety of reasons supplies in shops and markets had declined. The reasons included a lack of development in the transport system and warehousing arrangements; an uncontrolled increase in demand, caused by the extra spending power of the lower classes, the undiminished spending power of the upper and middle classes, an increase in employment and the results of many government social schemes; and the growth of the black market, which allegedly had halved the number of goods available through the official distribution network.

The government Jan. 12 took control of all wheat sales in what it called a "profound political and social move" to strengthen food rationing. Producers would be required to sell wheat to the state, which would then distribute the grain to mills and bakeries.

More than 8,000 workers at the Chuquicamata copper mine struck Jan. 16–17 to protest "serious food shortages" in the area and the food limitations. A government spokesman called the walkout "unjustified and unpatriotic," claiming it would cost Chile $2 million a day and was aimed at embarrassing the government before the March parliamentary elections.

'Rationing' label disputed—The government denied Jan. 11 that its new food distribution measures constituted "rationing," as the opposition charged and most newspapers reported. Debate over the implications of the measures continued for several days, with the government maintaining the measures would only assure "equitable" distribution of essential articles to Chilean families.

(According to the London newsletter Latin America Jan. 19, the measures constituted a form of wholesale rationing, although they left retailing to local shopkeepers. They did not include the ration books and strong bureaucratic control normally involved in rationing, and offered as many loopholes for abuse as the former system of distribution, which had led to artificial shortages and the large black market. Furthermore, the opposition in Congress had refused to grant the government power to make black market activities "economic crimes," the newsletter noted.)

The government also denied an opposition charge that with the measures, President Allende had taken Chile "to the edge of a dictatorship." Allende asserted Jan. 15 that the charge, made a few days earlier by the opposition newspaper El Mercurio, was "a lie," and that Chile would never have "a dictatorship of any kind, least of all, of course, a fascist one."

Allende admitted in a speech Jan. 20 that he had made many mistakes since taking power in 1970, including failing to disclose the extent of the huge foreign debt he inherited and to begin renegotiations immediately; failing to formulate a long-term policy for livestock; and failing to dissolve Congress and call a plebiscite soon after he was elected, to try to obtain the Congressional majority he lacked.

Allende also criticized working class supporters of his Popular Unity coalition (UP), as well as government officials, for "featherbedding inefficiency" and a lack of "revolutionary spirit." He was said to be disturbed by special privileges enjoyed by industrial workers—such as the large amounts of free cloth given annually to textile workers—and angry that copper workers, the elite of Chile's working class, should have struck earlier in the week for economic reasons.

(Millas, suspended as finance minister by the Chamber of Deputies late in 1972, was censured and dismissed from that office by the Senate Jan. 10. But he remained in the Cabinet as economy minister, and Fernando Flores, with whom he switched posts following his suspension, remained finance minister. Millas was the third Cabinet official impeached in 12 months.)

Armed forces control distribution. President Salvador Allende Jan. 22 placed the armed forces in charge of distribution of essential articles, naming air force Gen. Alberto Bachelet to head the new National Distribution Secretariat and three other military men to assist him. Creation of the secretariat was announced Jan. 10 as part of the government's food quota plan.

Economy Minister Orlando Millas said Jan. 23 that the appointments were "temporary" and that the officers would leave the secretariat "once the problems of supply and the black market are solved."

The appointments reportedly deflated increasingly bitter opposition criticism of the quota system. Critics of the scheme were said to feel confident the appointments would guarantee impartiality under the new food distribution measures. The right-wing National party asserted Jan. 23 that the appointments would prove to be "positive" if they "prevented all Marxist functionaries from interfering in the supplying of the population."

Copper shipment attached. A district court in Hamburg, West Germany Jan. 8 ordered a shipment of 3,000 tons of Chilean copper ore handed to a court-appointed officer pending settlement of a lawsuit brought against Chile by Kennecott Copper Corp. in connection with the nationalization of the U.S. firm's Chilean mining interests in 1971.

The shipment, reportedly valued at $3.5 million, had been provisionally unloaded by its purchaser, the North German Refinery. Kennecott claimed it owned the copper and the Chilean mine that produced it.

Attachment of the copper was criticized Jan. 9 by the Chilean government, which accused Kennecott of renewing its "moves to block the normal commercialization of Chilean copper." Kennecott had sought attachment of Chilean copper shipments in other European countries in 1972.

Chile's ambassador to Bonn, Federico Klein, noted Jan. 12 that West Germany was his country's most important copper customer, with annual imports of 520,000 tons of ore out of a total production of 700,000 tons. "It is clear that both countries are interested in an undisturbed transaction of the copper business," he said.

Klein announced Jan. 15 that Chile and the world's three other major copper exporting countries—Peru, Zambia and Zaire—had agreed not to replace copper on the world market where Chilean copper was seized as a result of legal action begun by Kennecott. He denied, however, reports that Chile would stop all copper exports or ban sales to West Germany if it lost its case in the Hamburg court. He

said such moves were reserved only for extreme circumstances, and were not currently being considered.

Attachment lifted—The Hamburg court Jan. 22 released the disputed copper ore, and the ore was then handed over to the North German Refinery, which had purchased it from the Chilean state copper company, CODELCO.

The court ruled that Kennecott did not own the disputed copper, since the mine that produced it had been nationalized by Chile. It agreed with Kennecott that nationalization without compensation constituted "an important discrimination," but said it could not rule on the legality of the seizure of Kennecott's copper properties because they were all located in Chile. Kennecott, the court added, had failed to prove the existence of any "fundamental violation of law and order in Germany."

The court ordered Kennecott to pay the costs of the case, which Chilean President Allende estimated Jan. 25 at $50,000.

A Kennecott spokesman in New York disclosed Jan. 22 that the firm had filed another suit in Germany Jan. 16, seeking to hold the North German Refinery liable for the value of the disputed copper if it were processed and sold to consumers.

Chile denied a French report that it had made a $5 million "good-will payment" to Kennecott, the Miami Herald reported Jan. 20.

CODELCO disclosed that only two of the five copper mines nationalized by Chile had registered production increases in 1972, the Herald reported Jan. 27. Output had risen at the El Teniente mine, formerly owned by Kennecott, and the Andina mine, formerly owned by Cerro Corp., but had fallen at the Chuquicamata, Exotica and El Salvador mines, formerly owned by Anaconda Co.

Anaconda attachments let stand—The U.S. Supreme Court May 29 declined to review a preliminary court order attaching the New York City property of two Chilean state companies—the copper firm, CODELCO, and the development corporation, CORFO.

The attachment, ordered by a U.S. district court in 1972, had been obtained by Anaconda Co., which claimed Chile had stopped payment on promissory notes issued in 1969 for purchase of Anaconda's major Chilean properties, including the Chuquicamata mine. CORFO and CODELCO had sought the high court review on grounds they were part of the Chilean Republic and entitled to sovereign immunity from such court orders.

Kennecott Copper Corp., which once owned El Teniente, saw little hope for an amicable settlement of its long conflict with Chile. Kennecott President Frank Milliken told the company's stockholders May 1 that he saw "nothing going on that would lead me to believe there could be a rapprochement with the Allende government, and I do not know what kind of government might succeed him."

Soviet contract signed—CODELCO had signed an agreement to purchase machinery, equipment and spare parts from the Soviet Union, it was reported May 25.

Other economic developments—The cost of living had risen by 163.4% in 1972, according to government statistics reported by the Miami Herald Jan. 13.

Workers for bus companies providing service from Santiago to other provinces struck Jan. 6–9 to protest the refusal of Alberto Fernandez to resign as intervenor of the Via Sur Co. Fernandez had been replaced by the government following charges that he had led the firm to bankruptcy and illegally fired some 100 workers belonging to opposition parties, but he had declined to abandon his post. His replacement said Jan. 9 that the fired workers would be reinstated.

The government was developing a computer-controlled system to manage the entire economy, the newsletter Latin America reported Jan. 12.

Foreign relations. Chile announced Jan. 9 it was establishing diplomatic relations with the Cambodian government in exile of Prince Norodom Sihanouk. The prince would send a representative to open an embassy in Santiago.

China had granted Chile credits worth $62 million to purchase food, medicines, machinery and equipment from China, the newsletter Latin America reported Jan. 5.

Finland, Bulgaria and Rumania reportedly had offered credits totaling $40 million for expansion of the copper refinery and by-products at Ventanas, while East Germany had offered a loan of $15 million.

Chile and China had signed a maritime accord under which the state-owned Interoceanic Line of Chile and the Oriental Ocean Line of China would carry passengers and cargo between the two nations, it was reported Jan. 28.

Chile and Argentina signed an agreement Jan. 17 under which Argentina gave Chile credits worth $100 million to purchase food, automobile spare parts and capital goods. It was the largest loan ever made to Chile by Argentina.

Delegations from Chile and its 11 "Paris Club" creditors met in Paris Jan. 25–26 for further talks on repayment of Chile's foreign debt.

Visiting Chilean Education Minister Jorge Tapia announced in Lima that Peru and Chile had agreed to a large-scale exchange of teachers, the Miami Herald reported Jan. 18. Tapia said the exchange would help Chileans learn "the reforms implanted by Peru's revolutionary law."

A letter bomb addressed to the honorary Israeli consul in Santiago exploded Jan. 24 while being dismantled, blinding a police bomb expert and blowing off both his hands. Police said the device was mailed from Athens.

A group of terrorists in Guatemala City reportedly opened fire on the Chilean embassy there Jan. 25, damaging the ambassador's car but causing no injuries. The embassy had suffered two similar attacks in October 1972, when it was located in another part of the city.

Del Canto suspended. A Santiago court Jan. 27 fined and temporarily suspended Government Secretary General Hernan del Canto in a ruling on a suit filed by the Chilean Broadcasters Association. The suit cited Del Canto's closure in October 1972 of several stations which resisted the government's illegal takeover of radio broadcasting during the nationwide protest strikes.

Public works minister replaced. Rear Adm. Ismael Huerta, installed as public works minister shortly before the strikes ended, resigned Jan. 31. He was replaced by another naval officer, Rear Adm. Daniel Arellano.

Neruda to leave Paris post. President Allende announced Feb. 5 that Pablo Neruda, the poet and Nobel Prize winner, would resign as ambassador to France for health reasons. Neruda was 68.

Pre-election violence. Authorities were concerned about the increasing amount of campaign violence among supporters of the two political federations, La Prensa of Buenos Aires reported Jan. 21. Dozens of persons had been injured in street fights, some sustaining bullet wounds, and several political offices had been damaged by Molotov cocktail explosions. Interior Minister Carlos Prats made an appeal for electoral peace Jan. 18.

Prats announced Jan. 21 that the government was investigating a recent incident in Concepcion in which Arturo Frei Bolivar, running for re-election to the Chamber of Deputies, was allegedly stoned and fired at. Frei, a nephew of ex-President Eduardo Frei Montalva, charged his assailants were supporters of the government.

State ownership measure splits up. The ruling Popular Unity (UP) coalition suffered a split Jan. 26 when Allende's Socialist party publicly rejected a government bill which provided, among other measures, for the return to private owners of several dozen enterprises that had come under state control through interventions or requisitions.

The party said it had not been consulted on the bill before it was sent to Congress, and asserted it was opposed to the return of any state-controlled firm to the private sector. The party ordered one of its members, Economy Undersecretary Armando Arancibia, to resign from the government in protest. Arancibia's resignation was reported in Allende's hands Jan. 28, but the president took no immediate action on it.

The disputed bill was said to be the work of Economy Minister Orlando Millas, a member of the Communist party,

with which the Socialists were at odds on a number of issues. The parties had criticized each other sharply in their respective newspapers, and there was fear within the UP that their feud would harm the coalition in the upcoming elections, in which it faced a relatively united opposition federation, according to La Prensa of Buenos Aires Jan. 29.

The Revolutionary Left Movement (MIR) issued a communique Jan. 26 supporting the Socialists and calling the Communists "revisionists" and "reformists." The MIR supported the re-election of Santiago Sen. Carlos Altamirano, the Socialist secretary general, who, because of electoral circumstances, would effectively be running against Communist Sen. Volodia Teitelboim, also of Santiago.

Congressional Elections

CODE wins vote; UP shows strength. The opposition Democratic Confederation (CODE) retained its Congressional majority in the March 4 elections, but President Salvador Allende's Popular Unity coalition (UP) showed surprising strength, gaining seats in both the Senate and the Chamber of Deputies.

Official results reported March 7 gave CODE 54.7% of the vote and the UP 43.4%. However, the UP gained six seats in the Chamber of Deputies, cutting CODE's majority there to 87–63, and two in the Senate, cutting CODE's margin to 30–20. All 150 Chamber seats and half of the 50 Senate seats were at stake in the elections.

CODE consisted of the National, Christian Democratic, Radical Left, Radical Democratic and National Democratic parties. The UP was composed of the Socialist, Communist, Radical, Independent Action and Christian Left parties and the United Popular Action Movement. The Popular Socialist Union, though not a member of the UP, usually was counted with it.

Votes were cast by 3.66 million of the 4.51 million eligible voters, an estimated 20% of whom were newly enfranchised

18–21-year-olds and illiterates. The voting was peaceful throughout the country.

Among Chile's four major parties—the Christian Democrats, Nationals, Communists and Socialists—Allende's Socialists made the greatest gains, picking up 14 Chamber and three Senate seats. The Communists gained three Chamber and three Senate seats, and the Nationals one Chamber and three Senate seats. The Christian Democrats, the country's largest party, made the poorest showing, gaining three Chamber seats but losing a Senate seat.

Both sides claimed victory late March 4 as the unusually long vote count began. Ex-President Eduardo Frei, elected to a Santiago Senate seat on the Christian Democratic ticket, called the vote a "clear" mandate for a change in government policies. Allende, on the other hand, claimed it was unprecedented in recent Chilean history for a government to surpass its winning presidential vote in subsequent parliamentary elections. Allende was elected with 36% of the vote in 1970.

(Frei received the highest vote among Santiago Senatorial candidates. He was followed by Communist Sen. Volodia Teitelboim and Socialist Sen. Carlos Altamirano, who were re-elected to their seats.)

The government won an important psychological victory in denying CODE the overwhelming public mandate it expected, according to the New York Times March 6. Opposition leaders had predicted a two-thirds majority for CODE, which would have enabled it to veto government legislation and even impeach Allende.

Throughout the often bitter campaign, CODE had characterized the elections as a "morally binding" plebiscite on government policies. The government, on the other hand, had minimized the importance of the vote, often calling it a routine democratic exercise, and predicting only that the UP would improve on its 1970 vote margin.

A high military source had told the Times Feb. 22 that the armed forces high command would not consider a simple majority victory by the opposition as "an expression by the country against the government" or its Marxist programs.

The source asserted the ranking military officials felt the opposition did not "represent a durable or consolidated force."

Numerous sources had noted that CODE's major parties, the center-left Christian Democrats and the right-wing Nationals, were united mainly in opposition to the UP, and would oppose each other under normal circumstances. During Frei's presidential term, the Nationals had strongly opposed the government. However, observers also noted that one wing of the Christian Democrats was moving to the right.

Allende had issued a campaign platform Feb. 5 which pledged creation of "a new state" to guarantee workers and all Chilean people "the exercise of economic power and political power." The document proposed, among other measures, establishment of a unicameral "people's assembly" to replace the existing bicameral legislature, a new constitution, and simultaneous election of the president and Congress.

In releasing the platform, Allende had warned that if the Chilean right continued what he called its policy of obstruction and provocation, the "Chilean revolution would be forced to abandon the democratic road and embrace physical violence as an instrument." The warning followed attacks on a Christian Democratic senator and a National senatorial candidate for which the UP considered itself unjustly blamed. Attacks against two other opposition candidates caused Interior Minister Carlos Prats to meet Feb. 19 with leaders of all parties, who subsequently took measures to reduce campaign violence.

Six persons were reported killed during the campaign, considered normal for important Chilean elections.

Military officials leave Cabinet. President Salvador Allende March 27 accepted the resignations of the three military officers in his Cabinet, naming civilians to replace them.

The move was part of a general Cabinet shuffle following the resignation of all ministers March 23, to allow Allende to form a new government in the wake of the

March 4 Congressional elections. Nine ministers were reappointed to their posts, one was shifted to another post, and five new ministers were appointed. The new Cabinet represented all component parties in Allende's Popular Unity coalition (UP), but was said to be more moderate than its predecessor.

Allende said the three officers—army Gen. Carlos Prats, navy Rear Adm. Daniel Arellano and air force Gen. Claudio Sepulveda—would "return to their normal activities" because they had accomplished their appointed tasks: to resolve the crisis brought on by the October 1972 nationwide strikes and to guarantee the March 4 elections. Allende said, however, that the armed forces would continue to play an important role in government efforts to alleviate the existing economic crisis—in food distribution, transportation, port activities and certain industries.

Prats, Sepulveda and Rear Adm. Ismael Huerta had joined the Cabinet in November 1972 to help end the "bosses' strike" against the government and the resulting crisis. Prats was named interior minister, Sepulveda mines minister and Huerta public works minister. Huerta resigned in January in an apparent disagreement with the administration and was replaced by Arellano.

It was not immediately clear why the three officers left the Cabinet. Some reports said Allende had wanted to retain them in office, but they had made demands he was unwilling to accept. Others noted, however, that the president was under strong pressure in the UP, particularly from his Socialist party, to return to an all-civilian Cabinet.

Prats' crucial Interior Ministry post, second in power to the presidency, was assumed by Gerardo Espinoza Carrillo, 42. Espinoza was one of four Socialists in the new Cabinet, all counted in the moderate wing of the party, with which Allende generally sided. Allende reappointed two moderate Socialists, Foreign Minister Clodomiro Almeyda and Defense Minister Jose Toha, and replaced two members of the party's radical wing, Agriculture Minister Rolando Calderon and Government Secretary General Hernan del Canto.

The rest of the new Cabinet consisted of three Communists, three Radicals, two

independents and one member each of the Independent Popular Action (API), Christian Left and MAPU (formerly United Popular Action Movement) parties. Observers reportedly were surprised that the smaller parties, which contributed little to the UP's March 4 vote, received eight Cabinet posts.

The new ministers and their parties:

Interior—Gerardo Espinoza Carrillo (Socialist); public works—Humberto Martones (Radical); agriculture—Pedro Hidalgo Ramirez (Socialist); land and colonization—Roberto Cuellar Bernal (API); mines—Sergio Bitar Chacra (Christian Left); government secretary general—Anibal Palma (Radical); foreign affairs—Clodomiro Almeyda (Socialist); economy—Fernando Flores Labra (MAPU); finance—Orlando Millas (Communist); education—Jorge Tapia (Radical); justice—Sergio Insunza (Communist); labor—Luis Figueroa (Communist); health—Arturo Jiron (independent); housing—Luis Matte (independent); defense—Jose Toha (Socialist).

In a speech shortly before swearing in his new Cabinet, Allende said Chile faced "difficult hours" in which it would have to overcome "serious economic difficulties," including a high inflation rate, speculation, hoarding and the black market. He called on "democratic sectors in the opposition" to "understand that flexibility is necessary to accept the changes that this country needs and demands." He also urged the UP parties to make clear within their ranks that "beyond us—the actors in this process—millions of human beings look with respect and admiration on our country's process of transformation."

Referring to conflicts within the UP, Allende said the new Cabinet would have to "concern itself with strengthening the unity and cohesion of the popular movement, recognizing and overcoming the errors we have committed."

New foreign minister. President Salvador Allende announced May 3 that Orlando Letelier would replace Foreign Minister Clodomiro Almeyda, who would resign to devote himself fully to Socialist party affairs. Letelier, currently Chile's ambassador to the U.S., was also a Socialist.

Crisis in MAPU. The tiny MAPU party expelled 15 members of its radical wing March 7, accusing them of "divisive activities" and of having contact with "ultra-leftist sectors that do not belong to the Popular Unity." Those expelled included the party's undersecretary for government, Eduardo Aquevedo.

The expulsions followed the disclosure shortly before the March 4 elections of an "internal" MAPU document criticizing a number of government actions, including the appointment of military officers to the Cabinet. The document, published by the conservative newspaper El Mercurio and exploited by opposition Congressional candidates, reportedly irritated President Allende. Allende was said to have told MAPU leaders that unless they provided a satisfactory explanation for the document, he would demand the resignation of every MAPU member in high government office. The expulsions reportedly were the party's response to that threat.

The 15 expelled MAPU members were said to be close to the extremist Revolutionary Left Movement (MIR), to have doubts about the participation of the armed forces in the government, and to oppose strongly the Communist strategy of consolidation within the UP and reconciliation with the major opposition party, the Christian Democrats.

U.S. talks held, 'impasse' reported. The U.S. and Chile held a second round of negotiations on financial and political problems March 22–23. A terse communique issued after the talks said "both parties expressed their respective points of view in an atmosphere of mutual respect, but no specific decisions or accords were reached." The left-wing magazine Chile Hoy reported March 31 that there was "a cruder truth: total impasse."

According to Chile Hoy, the U.S. negotiators "adopted from the very beginning a hostile, stubborn attitude which became threatening in the end." The London newsletter Latin America reported April 6 that the U.S. was more intransigent than it had been at the first round of talks in December 1972, demanding this time that Chile pay $700 million in compensation for nationalized U.S. assets before renegotiating its $1.7 billion U.S. debt.

A different report on the talks, published by the Washington Post April 1, said Chile had broken off negotiations in response to testimony before a U.S. Senate subcommittee on intervention in Chilean politics by the International

Telephone and Telegraph Corp. (ITT). The testimony, which coincided with the U.S.-Chilean talks, reportedly convinced President Salvador Allende the U.S. had conspired with ITT to prevent his election in 1970.

Allende denied the Post report April 7, but denounced the U.S. April 10 for "collusion" with ITT's plans against his government. However, Chilean officials cautioned the attack should not be interpreted as a sign of "paralysis" of the U.S.-Chilean negotiations, and pointed out that Foreign Minister Clodomiro Almeyda, in Washington for an Organization of American States meeting, had met April 9 with John M. Hennessy, U.S. assistant secretary of the Treasury for international affairs, and John H. Crimmins, head of the U.S. negotiating team.

U.S. Probes ITT Actions

ITT's anti-Allende plans. A special U.S. Senate Foreign Relations Committee subcommittee on multinational corporations began a two-year investigation into the effects of those firms on the U.S. economy and conduct of foreign policy. Opening testimony was given by officials of International Telephone & Telegraph Corp. (ITT).

John A. McCone, former director of the Central Intelligency Agency (CIA) and a consultant to the agency since his retirement in 1965, told the subcommittee March 21 that he had met with Henry A. Kissinger, President Nixon's national security adviser, and Richard Helms, then director of the CIA and a "close friend," in mid-1970 to offer the U.S. government $1 million in financial aid from ITT. The money would be used to block the runoff election of Salvador Allende Gossens as president of Chile.

Allende, a Socialist, was elected Sept. 4, 1970 by a small plurality. He headed a left-wing coalition dominated by the Chilean Communist party. Allende took office in October 1970 after a joint session of Congress elected him president.

A year after his election, Allende expropriated the ITT-controlled telephone company in Chile. ITT filed a $92 million claim with the U.S. government's Overseas Private Investment Corp. (OPIC), which insured U.S. firms against foreign takeovers; any "provocation or instigation" by a client company, however, unless requested by the U.S. government, could invalidate such an insurance claim.

McCone made the $1 million offer in his capacity as a director of ITT. The money had been authorized by ITT President and Chairman Harold S. Geneen. McCone denied that the money was intended for "surreptitious" purposes or would be used to create "economic chaos."

"What he [Geneen] had in mind was not chaos but what could be done constructively. The money was to be channeled to people who support the principles and programs the U.S. stands for against the programs of the Allende-Marxists," McCone testified.

The money would be used in Chile, McCone said, for programs such as housing projects and technical agricultural assistance.

"International communism has said time and again that its objective is the destruction of the free world, economically, politically, militarily. . . . That was what Mr. Geneen was thinking of," according to McCone.

Members of the subcommittee expressed incredulity at McCone's testimony. Sen. Clifford P. Case (R, N.J.) noted that the U.S. had already given Chile more than $1 billion in economic aid over the past 10 years and that Allende had been elected anyway.

"How can a man of Mr. Geneen's intelligence possibly think that $1 million for these kinds of purposes in six weeks could make any difference?" Case asked.

The ITT plan proposed to Kissinger and Helms was termed the "Alessandri Formula." It called for financial support to be given to a coalition of the conservative National party, headed by Jorge Alessandri Rodriguez, and the Christian Democratic party, led by Radomiro Tomic. It was planned that they would oppose Allende in the expected runoff election and that Allesandri would be elected. He would then resign and call for new elections, permitting former President Eduardo Frei Montalva to challenge Allende in the subsequent two-man race.

"A number of people were trying to explore alternatives about what might be done. The Chilean military was discussing the Alessandri Plan. Mr. [William V.] Broe [director of clandestine operations in Latin America for the CIA] had a shopping list and the staff of the CIA had a shopping list," McCone told the subcommittee.

The plan was abandoned when Alessandri withdrew from the runoff race because of his lack of support in the Chilean Congress, where the final decision would be made.

McCone testified that Helms had told him "the matter was considered by an interdepartmental committee of senior representatives of the Defense and State Departments as well as the CIA, and the decision was reached that nothing should be done."

Although the ITT plan was rejected, McCone said that at his request, Helms put Geneen in contact with Broe. This corresponded with testimony given the previous day.

William R. Merriam, vice president of ITT and former director of its Washington office, had testified March 20 that ITT President Geneen had arranged to establish a working relationship between the corporation and the CIA in order to prevent the election of Allende as president of Chile, and, failing that, to bring about the "economic collapse" of Chile.

Merriam said his association with the CIA's Broe began at a Washington meeting held July 16, 1970 which was arranged and attended by Geneen. Geneen instructed him to "stay in touch" with Broe, Merriam testified, and subsequent phone conversations and meetings with the CIA agent occurred "many times."

Merriam told the subcommittee that Broe was impressed with the quality of information gathered by ITT operatives in Latin America. When shown a Sept. 17, 1970 cable from ITT officials Bob Berrellez and Hal Hendrix, Broe "approved" the recommendation, Merriam declared.

The cable urged ITT "and other U.S. firms in Chile" to head off Allende's election by contributing advertising funds to a conservative Chilean newspaper in financial difficulties. The report also recommended that ITT "bring what pressure we can" on the U.S. Information Agency to circulate the Chilean newspaper's editorial in Latin America and Europe. (In testimony given March 21, Hendrix claimed the plan was never carried out because its intent was too obvious.)

According to an ITT memo dated late September 1970, when the Chilean election results were still in doubt, ITT Senior Vice President Edward Gerrity told Geneen that Broe had suggested the company "apply economic pressures" to influence the voting.

Broe "indicated that certain steps were being taken, but that he was looking for additional help aimed at inducing economic collapse," Gerrity told Geneen, "Realistically I don't see how we can induce others involved to follow the plan suggested," Gerrity concluded.

As part of this plan, Merriam said the CIA made "repeated calls to firms such as General Motors, Ford Motor Co. and banks in California and New York." All refused to cease or reduce operations in Chile, according to ITT documents submitted to the subcommittee.

Other CIA recommendations called for cessation of U.S. aid to Chile, under the guise of a policy review, and government intervention with the World Bank group and the International Monetary Fund to halt their loans to Chile.

Merriam testified that ITT, at the instigation of the Anaconda Copper Co., organized an "Ad Hoc Committee on Chile" which met in his office in February 1971. "The thrust of the meeting was toward the application of pressure on the [U.S.] government wherever possible to make it clear that a Chilean takeover wouldn't be tolerated without serious repercussions following," according to Ronald Raddatz, a representative of the BankAmerica Corp., who was present. Others represented were Anaconda, Kennecott Copper Corp., W. R. Grace & Co., Pfizer Inc. and Ralston Purina Co.

No conclusions were reached, according to Merriam and he discounted the significance of the meeting itself. "We were just kicking around some ideas. We have these ad hoc committees all the time in Washington."

After the expropriation of the ITT Company in September 1971, Merriam wrote White House assistant Peter Peterson that there were "numerous justifiable leverages" the government could exert to protect American property in Chile.

The 18 suggestions included fostering "discontent" in the Chilean military, cutting off bank loans, restricting Chilean travel and slowing trade between the U.S. and Chile. "Everything should be done quietly but effectively to see that Allende doesn't get through the crucial next six months," the memo concluded.

Merriam justified the corporation's actions saying, "If Allende was faced with economic collapse, he might be more congenial toward paying us off."

In other testimony and documents submitted to the subcommittee, Merriam indicated that he made at least 25 visits to the State Department and had conferred for a "year" with officials in Kissinger's office.

According to another ITT memorandum submitted to the committee March 21, President Nixon had given the U.S. ambassador to Chile, Edward M. Korry, a "green light" in September 1970 to do everything possible short of military intervention to prevent the victory of Allende.

Helms had testified privately before the subcommittee March 5 prior to leaving to assume the post of ambassador to Iran. Broe was also questioned by the committee in secret session, the Washington Post reported March 22.

McCone and Geneen were interrogated March 16 in a private subcommittee meeting.

Geneen admits ITT offer. Harold S. Geneen, chairman of ITT, admitted to the subcommittee April 2 that he had twice offered money to the U.S. government to prevent Allende's 1970 election.

Geneen's admission regarding the first offer of funds was cautious. Having "no recollection to the contrary," Geneen told the subcommittee he would accept the testimony of William V. Broe, director of covert CIA operations in Latin America, that the money was offered at a July 1970 meeting and was intended to finance a CIA effort to stop Allende.

Geneen justified the gesture as an "emotional reaction" resulting from his conversations with Broe in which the CIA representative said the U.S. planned no efforts to circumvent the Chilean election of Allende, who was running on a Socialist-Communist platform.

According to Geneen, this policy of nonintervention represented the reversal of a 14-year U.S. "policy to maintain a democratic government in Chile." Geneen said he had been particularly disturbed by the talks with Broe because ITT had invested in Chile as part of the U.S. government's economic assistance policy to develop the country. In contrast to its past encouragement, the Nixon Administration appeared unwilling to aid ITT when the company anticipated the expropriation of its Chilean properties.

The matter "died right there," Geneen claimed, although he admitted making a second offer to the government in September 1970 when Allende had won his first election test and required ratification by the Chilean Congress in an October vote.

Geneen was unable to clarify contradictory testimony given earlier regarding the use of the slush fund. He claimed that the "amount mentioned of up to seven figures was intended to show a serious intent and to gain serious attention from the government" to finance "some socially constructive joint private industry and government projects" to induce Allende to make adequate compensation for ITT properties in Chile.

The hearings recessed following Geneen's appearance, but earlier testimony elicited further information regarding the extent of ITT's involvement in Chile's internal affairs.

ITT memo cites efforts—An ITT memorandum submitted to the subcommittee March 22 revealed that ITT had attempted to obtain compensation for the firm's telephone company in Chile, expropriated in September 1971 by President Allende, at the expense of other U.S.-owned companies also slated for nationalization.

The memo detailed a mutual assistance pact in which ITT would be compensated for loss of property and Allende would benefit politically by demonstrating his willingness to conclude a "fair deal" with the U.S. firm.

According to the memo, ITT hoped to persuade Allende that favorable world opinion would then allow him to confiscate the copper companies owned by Kennecott Corp. and Anaconda Copper Co. under the pretext that the seizures involved crucial natural resources and were distinct from the deal concluded with ITT.

The Chile plan failed when the Allende government broke off negotiations after columnist Jack Anderson made public ITT documents revealing ITT's intervention in the 1970 presidential elections in Chile aimed at the defeat of Allende.

According to the ITT memo, the company claimed success for its arrangement in 1968 when it had "handled the situation in Peru" on the "same basis." A petroleum subsidiary of the Exxon Corp. had been confiscated without compensation while ITT had received payment for the takeover of its telephone company.

ITT Senior Vice President Edward J. Gerrity gave testimony March 22 which contradicted the public statements of ITT director John A. McCone. McCone had said he had offered U.S. officials $1 million to finance an anti-Allende coalition.

Gerrity said he was "baffled" by McCone's disclosures. "The first I heard about it [the covert purpose of the fund] was here yesterday." Gerrity said ITT had intended that the money be used to finance "constructive" humanitarian programs in Chile.

Gerrity claimed that Jack D. Neal, ITT's director of international relations, had conveyed the offer of social assistance to the National Security Council and the State Department during September 1970.

In testimony March 20, Neal had said he "didn't elaborate" on the purpose of the money in his talks with government officials.

Arturo Matte Larrain, a prominent conservative Chilean politician, corroborated McCone's testimony March 23. Matte said he had rejected an offer by Robert Berrellez, an ITT official, to help anti-Allende forces block the final presidential vote in October 1970.

Matte, campaign manager for Jorge Alessandri, who was opposing Allende in the runoff race, said Berrellez "offered assistance but money was not mentioned. We turned him down."

Broe testified before a closed session of the subcommittee March 27. Portions of the transcript were made public March 28 after the CIA had reviewed it.

Broe described Geneen's offer made at a July 16, 1970 meeting in Washington to provide a "substantial fund" for the support of Alessandri's candidacy. The money was rejected, Broe testified, because the CIA refused to "serve as a funding channel."

"I also told him that the United States government was not supporting any candidate in the Chilean election," Broe said. He added that Geneen never suggested at that time that the money be used for social assistance programs.

According to Broe, Geneen told him that ITT and other American companies had raised money to influence the 1964 Chilean election of Eduardo Frei but that CIA Director John A. McCone had refused the offer.

After the Sept. 4, 1970 election in Chile when Allende won a small plurality of the vote, the CIA altered its policy of neutrality and met with ITT officials to devise anti-Allende plans, Broe testified.

During the same period in 1970, ITT held a board of directors meeting Sept. 8–9 when Geneen asked McCone to repeat the offer of financial assistance to the government with the new aim of funding an anti-Allende coalition before the second presidential vote. This plan, detailed by McCone at the hearings March 21, was termed the "Alessandri Formula."

Broe admitted devising a series of secondary proposals in September 1970 for Gerrity which would create economic chaos in Chile, also with the aim of preventing Allende's presidential victory.

Broe claimed he had acted with the full knowledge of CIA Director Richard Helms and that Geneen had initiated the company's first contact with the CIA in 1970.

Broe met with Geneen Sept. 29, 1970 to discuss plans for accelerating Chile's economic deterioration in order to "influence a number of Christian Democratic [party] congressmen who were planning to vote for Allende." Among the proposals Broe presented were delays in bank credits and delivery of spare part shipments, and withdrawal of technical assistance.

Broe also confirmed the testimony of another top ITT official, William M. Merriam, who had said Broe gave his approval Sept. 29, 1970 to a plan supporting an anti-Allende newspaper and "propagandists."

Other portions of the Broe testimony were released March 29 relating to the September 1970 conversations with Gerrity. Broe insisted that the CIA plan for the disruption of the Chilean economy had been approved by superiors in the intelligence gathering agency.

Charles A. Meyer, former assistant secretary of state for inter-American affairs and currently with Sears, Roebuck & Co., told the subcommittee March 29 that he saw no inconsistency between Broe's disclosures and his own testimony that the Nixon Administration had steadfastly maintained a policy of nonintervention in Chile.

Former Commerce Secretary Peter Peterson, then presidential adviser on international economic affairs, confirmed March 29 that he had met with Geneen Dec. 14, 1971 to discuss ITT's 18-point "action plan" to cripple the Chilean economy. Gen. Alexander Haig, presidential security adviser Henry Kissinger's principal adviser, was also present at the meeting. Peterson said the ITT proposal was never seriously considered by the Administration.

Edward Korry, U.S. ambassador to Chile from 1967 to 1971, testified March 27. He revealed that the CIA had commissioned polls to determine the outcome of the 1970 election and voiced his disagreement with the survey results. According to the CIA, Allende would win 40% of the vote. (He actually received 36%.) Korry said he had doubted the validity of the polls because they were based on a 1960 census.

Korry declined to answer other questions related to intervention in Chilean politics by the U.S. government or U.S. businesses. However, he did state that an ITT document claiming that President Nixon had given him a "green light" to oppose Allende was "erroneous."

As ambassador, Korry said he had tried to minimize intervention by his staff and by all Americans in Chile in the presidential election. Contacts with the Chilean military were specifically avoided, Korry said.

OPIC rejects ITT claim. The Overseas Private Investment Corp. (OPIC) April 9 denied International Telephone & Telegraph Corp.'s (ITT) insurance claim for $92.5 million sought as indemnity for its Chilean subsidiary seized in 1971 by the government of President Salvador Allende.

OPIC, a quasi-governmental agency which insured investments of U.S. companies from political risks abroad, based its rejection on ITT's "noncompliance with contractual obligations." It charged the firm with failing to "disclose material information to OPIC. In addition, ITT increased OPIC's risk of loss by failing to preserve administrative remedies as required by the contracts, and by failing to protect OPIC's interests as a potential successor to ITT's rights."

John W. Guilfoyle, ITT vice president and group executive for Latin America, announced that ITT would seek "immediate" arbitration of the decision. He said the company had paid nearly $6 million in premiums to OPIC.

Because further action was pending on the case, OPIC spokesmen refused to detail their reasons for denying the ITT claim; however, contractual grounds for default would include ITT's failure to pursue negotiations with Chile on compensation and evidence of "provocation or institgation by the investor [ITT]" causing expropriation of the property, unless undertaken at the "specific request" of the U.S. government. Dismissal of the OPIC claim did not invalidate ITT's right under international law to compensation from Chile, OPIC officials noted.

According to OPIC, 18 insurance claims had been filed in the past 2½ years by U.S. investors in Chile. Five claims were settled with payments of more than $80 million; the Chilean government and U.S. business interests, with the aid of OPIC guarantees, had agreed on settlements in two cases involving $26 million; OPIC was processing nine claims and had rejected a $154 million case brought by Anaconda Co.

Allende bars compensation for ITT. President Allende asserted April 10 that Chile would pay no compensation to ITT because of the revelations which emerged from the Senate subcommittee hearings.

"No one can dream that we are going to pay even half a cent to this multinational company which was on the verge of plunging Chile into civil war," Allende declared. He added that he "now could say North American officials and agencies of the U.S. tried to thwart the will of the Chilean people."

In making his address before a meeting of the World Labor Union Assembly, attended by 1,500 representatives from 70 countries, Allende extended his remarks on "imperialist" corporations to include Anaconda, Kennecott Copper Corp. and Cerro Corp., whose properties also had been seized.

Chilean Foreign Minister Clodomiro Almeyda declared April 9 in Washington that other ITT assets in Chile—two Sheraton hotels and a telephone equipment manufacturing company—"are in a very precarious position" because public opinion, outraged by disclosures made during the hearings, could force the government to make further expropriations.

'64 anti-Allende U.S. aid reported. The U.S. contributed considerable money and manpower to help elect Eduardo Frei president of Chile in 1964, the Washington Post reported April 6. Frei's Christian Democratic party disputed the report April 11.

The report, by Post staff writer Laurence Stern, said "knowledgeable officials" in Washington asserted the U.S. had dispatched up to $20 million and 100 agents of the Central Intelligence Agency (CIA) and State Department to help Frei defeat the current president, Salvador Allende.

"U.S. government intervention in Chile in 1964 was blatant and almost obscene," an intelligence officer told the Post. "We were shipping people off right and left, mainly State Department but also CIA with all sorts of covers," the officer asserted.

The Post said Cord Meyer Jr., whom it called a "Cold War liberal," directed the

CIA's covert programs to neutralize Communist influence in important opinion-molding sectors such as trade unions, farmer and peasant organizations, student activist groups and communications media before the elections.

One conduit for CIA money, the International Development Foundation, was employed in the 1964 campaign to subsidize Chilean peasant organizations, according to a former official responsible for monitoring assistance to Chile from the State Department's Agency for International Development (AID), the Post reported.

Covert financing reportedly was also arranged for a newspaper friendly to the interests of the Christian Democrats. "The layout was magnificent. The photographs were superb. It was a Madison Avenue product far above the standards of Chilean publications," another State Department veteran of the campaign recalled.

Among State Department personnel, another source told the Post, "individual officers . . . would look for opportunities. And where it was a question of passing money, forming a newspaper or community development program, the operational people would do the work. AID found itself suddenly overstaffed, looking around for peasant groups or projects for slum dwellers. Once you established a policy of building support among peasant groups, government workers and trade unions, the strategies fell into place."

A former U.S. ambassador to Chile privately estimated the covert program on Frei's behalf had cost about $20 million, the Post reported. In contrast, the figure that emerged in U.S. Senate hearings as the amount ITT was willing to spend to defeat Allende in 1970 was $1 million. AID funds alone were substantially increased for 1964, the Post reported.

The number of "special agents" dispatched to Chile at various stages of the campaign was estimated by one official at about 100.

The Post story was given extensive coverage in Chile by the official Communist newspaper El Siglo, which charged the story proved Frei guilty of treason, it was reported April 14.

Christian Democratic denial—The Christian Democratic party president, Renan Fuentealba, denied at a press conference April 11 that the U.S. had contributed $20 million to Frei's 1964 campaign. He also called for an investigation of the Post's charges and asked the Post to examine the financing of campaigns by Chile's Marxist parties.

Fuentealba asserted that Christian Democratic races in Chile were "fundamentally" funded by the monthly dues of some 70,000 paying party members. Party sources acknowledged some income from abroad, such as Chileans living outside the country and from companies doing business in Chile.

(It was also generally accepted that foreign counterparts of the party, as well as the Radical and Communist parties, contributed money, the Post reported April 14. German correspondents had tried to prove that the West German Christian Democratic party was a prime funder of its Chilean counterpart but had failed to do so, the Post reported.)

The party's vice president, Felipe Amunategui, noted that the $20 million figure included money given to Chile "under U.S. aid . . . approved by the Chilean Parliament with Allende voting in favor," the Post reported. This raised the question of when development assistance crossed the line into political bribery, the Post said.

Other sources disputed the original Post article's two specific cases of covert financing of Frei's campaign. Politicians from both left- and right-wing parties had been unable to find the "Madison Avenue" style newspaper which allegedly had supported Frei in the campaign and later disappeared. Extensive research in the Congressional archives, which filed every newspaper published, produced none fitting the description, the Post reported April 14.

The International Development Foundation, which allegedly had channeled CIA money to peasant organizations, had begun to operate in Chile only a month before the 1964 elections and had had impact on the country only after Frei's inauguration, the Post reported April 14.

Prats in U.S. Gen. Carlos Prats Gonzalez, army commander and former interior minister, visited Washington, D.C. May 3–6 as the guest of Gen. Creighton W. Abrams, U.S. Army chief of staff. Prats conferred with other U.S. military officials including Adm. Thomas H. Moorer, chairman of the joint chiefs of staff, and discussed Chile's need for U.S. military equipment, mostly logistical.

Prats said May 6 that Chile had not ruled out buying arms from the Soviet Union, emphasizing the nation did not want to "depend on any one line of supply." He was scheduled to visit Great Britain, the U.S.S.R. and other countries before returning to Chile.

'Plots' & Strikes

'Extremist' plan charged. Santiago riot police were placed on alert late April 10 against what the government called a plan by the extreme right and left to block roads and occupy factories.

Earlier in the day, members of the extremist Revolutionary Left Movement (MIR) had led residents of Constitucion, on the coast south of Santiago, in blocking the roads and railway into the town to demand government solutions to local housing and food problems. No serious incidents were reported.

Government Secretary General Anibal Palma charged extremists planned the Santiago occupations to disrupt food distribution, create a climate of agitation and embarrass the government, which they would then criticize for lack of authority. The plan had been originated by the extreme right, which had duped the MIR into cooperating, Palma asserted.

Palma said the government was once again "calling for the maintenance of order. Occupations and violent acts are not the way to solve problems."

President Salvador Allende had warned April 3 that MIR activists were planning assaults on private and state food distributors, and that strong measures would be taken against such actions. MIR militants surrounded the warehouse of the private distributor CENADI the next day

but were dispersed after a battle with police. Thirty persons were reported arrested and 10 injured.

Santiago merchants April 5 praised the government's action against the MIR. The MIR denounced it as "police repression", and asserted occupations of factories and food distributors were not provocations but attempts by the people "to defend themselves against inflation and the shortage of essential articles." The MIR urged formation of "commando groups in each factory, farm, village and school" to combat government repression.

Works Ministry occupied—MIR militants occupied the Public Works Ministry April 23 and held it most of the day to demand a voice in the ministry's affairs and increased benefits for laborers working part-time on emergency repairs. They abandoned the building only after a personal appeal from Allende. No arrests were reported.

Christian Democratic challenge—The Christian Democratic party May 15 issued a statement pledging to use "all its power" to stop what it called the government's "totalitarian escalation."

The statement, approved at the party's national meeting ending May 13, accused the government of "seeking the totality of power, which means Communist tyranny disguised as the dictatorship of the proletariat."

The party approved a new executive board and president May 13. The president was Sen. Patricio Aylwin, who replaced Sen. Renan Fuentealba, not a candidate for re-election. Aylwin said the new board represented "categorical opposition to the government." Fuentealba warned the government that if it persisted in its policies it would be unable to "resist the current of popular discontent."

Education reforms postponed. The government announced April 13 that it would not decree its projected education reforms in 1973. It acted following expressions of doubt about the measures by the armed forces commanders and protests by high school students, the political opposition and the Roman Catholic Church.

Education Minister Jorge Tapia said the reforms would be sent to Congress, as demanded by the opposition and the student federations it dominated. However, he denied opposition charges that the measures were designed to impose a "Marxist consciousness" on students and constituted a "death-blow to freedom of education."

According to a government education official, Ivan Nunez, the reforms would establish the National Unified School (ENU), whose general purpose would be to replace the current "scientific-humanist" curriculum with a "polytechnic and general" one. Nunez said March 21 that ENU would effect "the changing of education from a socialist perspective."

The primary and intermediate education levels would be eliminated in favor of a straight 12-year program, Nunez said. The new program would be divided into three study areas: "common" courses similar to those currently offered; work courses to introduce students to industries, the agrarian reform and public services; and independent study consisting of courses selected by the students from the "common" program.

Msgr. Emilio Tagle, archbishop of Valparaiso Province, said March 21 that the Church opposed the ENU plan, fearing it could "give control of education to a partisan ideology." Other church officials protested the education reforms, as did opposition political parties. Students from the opposition-dominated Secondary School Students Federation in Santiago protested the measures April 13 in a demonstration broken up by police.

Tapia acknowledged at a press conference April 13 that high military officials had also expressed reservations about the projected reforms. He said he had talked for more than two hours with the armed forces commanders and about 150 officers, who had questioned him closely about the reforms.

Press scored on military. The government April 18 accused the opposition press of trying to "break the discipline of the armed forces" and discredit their commander, Gen. Carlos Prats Gonzalez.

The opposition newspaper La Segunda had alleged Prats had taken a political stance in favor of the government, telling a meeting of 800 officers that he supported the process of change instituted by President Allende. Other opposition papers had alleged that several senior officers, including Rear Adm. Ismael Huerta, had been prematurely retired because of their opposition to the government's projected educational reforms.

Defense Minister Jose Toha April 18 condemned the "repeated dissemination of false or alarmist" news about the armed forces, and asserted "the government has the obligation, which it will discharge effectively, of defending the prestige, discipline and unity of military institutions."

2 provincial intendants suspended. The Chamber of Deputies' approval of a motion by the Christian Democratic party to impeach Jaime Faivovich, the intendant of Santiago Province, was reported April 12.

Faivovich, a member of President Allende's Socialist party, was suspended pending Senate action on the impeachment measure. He was accused of excessive leniency toward extreme leftist elements and responsibility for an incident in which two young Christian Democrats were killed.

The Chamber vote was 65–0, with no government deputies in attendance. A government official charged Faivovich was prevented by the opposition from appearing in the Chamber to refute the charges.

The Chamber then suspended the intendant of Valparaiso Province, Carlos Gonzalez Marquez, June 5 on charges of ordering arbitrary arrests of members of the extreme right-wing Fatherland and Liberty party. The motion, introduced by the Christian Democrats, was approved 76–0 after all pro-government deputies walked out, according to the Cuban press agency Prensa Latina.

Impeachment procedures had also been introduced in the Chamber against the intendants of Talca and Nuble, Francisco Reyes and Luis Quesada respectively, it was reported June 15.

Rightist 'plot.' Some 40 to 50 members of the right-wing Fatherland and Liberty party were arrested May 11 in several cities in connection with an alleged plot against the government. Most were released after questioning. Interior Undersecretary Daniel Vergara said May 13 that the arrests were ordered for violation of the internal security and press laws. He said arms and ammunition held by detainees had been confiscated in Concepcion, Osorno and Chillan.

The alleged plot was reported in the left-wing press after two Fatherland and Liberty leaders, Walter Robert Thieme and Miguel Juan Sessa, were detained in Mendoza, Argentina, where they had flown in a private plane. The two requested political asylum and were granted it May 9. Chile asked Argentina to hold them pending a request for extradition.

Thieme had been reported dead Feb. 23 after his plane seemingly disappeared into the Pacific Ocean.

La Prensa of Buenos Aires reported May 9 that Thieme and Sessa had admitted to Argentine officials that they had plotted against Allende. They reportedly produced documents and plans for action against the government to begin May 15.

Thieme said at a Buenos Aires press conference May 12 that if "the price of liberation [in Chile] is civil war, we will have to pay it." He did not specify the role of the armed forces in such a conflict, but said he was convinced the military "know very well the responsibility that falls to them and will fall to them in the future when the people and all Chile react" against the government.

Outgoing Foreign Minister Clodomiro Almeyda said May 13 that Thieme's declarations exemplified "the subversive aims of the fascist sectors in Fatherland and Liberty, in sectors of the National party and even the leadership of the Christian Democrats."

(The president of Fatherland and Liberty's Valparaiso organization, Claudio Fadda Cori, had been arrested June 4 on charges of possessing various arms, Prensa Latina reported. Interior Minister Gerardo Espinoza had warned May 17 that police would arrest any party members carrying weapons. He accused Fatherland and Liberty of planning "armed violence" against the government.)

Defense Minister Jose Toha had denied before a Senate committee May 10 that his ministry had any evidence of "the possibility of armed aggression coming from a neighboring country" and asserted the press reports of a plot against the government were "alarmist."

Toha also denied a charge by Sen. Pedro Ibanez of the National party that Chile had agreed to turn over to the Soviet Union the southern port of Colcura, which was being constructed with Soviet technical assistance under a bilateral agreement signed in 1967.

Private buses halted. Private collective transport was paralyzed throughout Chile beginning May 22 as owners demanded higher fares and a solution to the shortage of spare parts. The government requisitioned all buses and microbuses not in operation, and placed an army general in charge of them. A settlement involving a 166% fare increase reportedly was reached with the owners May 24, but it was rejected by the drivers.

The Communist party, the second most important in the ruling Popular Unity coalition, called on Chilean workers May 31 to postpone their economic demands to help contain inflation. The cost of living reportedly rose by 34.4% in January–April.

Emergency declared in copper strike. The government May 10 declared a state of emergency in O'Higgins Province, where a strike at the El Teniente copper mine had entered its fourth week. The measure placed the province under military control.

The emergency declared earlier in Santiago Province was lifted May 17 by President Salvador Allende, who said the disorders there had ceased.

Interior Undersecretary Daniel Vergara May 10 said the O'Higgins emergency was imposed because the copper strike, though "partial," was having "such an impact on the national economy that its maintenance and prolongation mean . . . a public calamity." Workers at Chuquicamata, the nation's other crucial mine, struck to support El Teniente May 11–12.

El Teniente's strikers claimed they had been cheated of a 41% pay raise, agreed to in 1972 but later deducted from a 100% raise granted by the government to all wage-earners to offset inflation. The government, which blamed "fascist" forces for the strike, reportedly offered a compromise bonus amounting to six weeks' pay, but this was rejected by the strikers. About half the miners at Chuquicamata began striking June 1 to support El Teniente.

According to the French newspaper Le Monde May 15, the most committed strikers at El Teniente were not the 8,000 workers, some of whom had returned to their jobs, but some 5,000 mine officials and administrators demanding a 41% wage supplement retroactive to October 1972. The copper strike threatened to spread to other sectors, having already stimulated transport strikes in Valparaiso and Concepcion, Le Monde reported.

About 120 striking miners and a policeman were injured May 9 in clashes in the town of Rancagua in O'Higgins Province, the Times of London reported May 12.

The opposition Christian Democratic party May 25 filed impeachment charges in Congress against two Cabinet officials—Labor Minister Luis Figueroa and Mines Minister Sergio Bitar—for allegedly precipitating the copper strike.

Copper exports halted—The government was forced to suspend foreign copper shipments June 5 as a strike at the El Teniente mine entered its 48th day and a solidarity strike at the Chuquicamata mine entered its fifth day.

The shipments, suspended at least until the end of June, were destined mainly for Great Britain and West Germany.

O'Higgins Province, in which El Teniente was located, continued under military rule following several eruptions of violence in the provincial capital, Rancagua, in which one person was killed and numerous others injured.

The worst violence occurred late June 1 and early June 2, after the funeral of a miner shot to death by a military patrol May 30. Strikers erected flaming barricades across at least 20 intersections, fired guns and hurled dynamite, reportedly blowing up the offices of several progovernment parties. Police and troops fought back with tear gas and water cannons. Two policemen were reported injured, and 86 persons were arrested.

The miner had been shot when he refused an order to halt and "imperiled"

the lives of several soldiers on patrol, according to authorities. The government closed the right-wing radio station Radio Agricultura late May 30 for broadcasting "false and alarmist" reports of the killing. The closure order covered six days, but it was lifted by an appeals court officer June 3.

Students and striking miners had erected flaming barricades in Rancagua May 25, clashing with police and attacking a number of businesses which refused to strike in solidarity with El Teniente.

Clodomiro Almeyda, acting as vice president while President Salvador Allende attended Argentina's presidential inauguration, warned May 25 that striking miners would be fired if the conflict continued much longer. (Sixty-five strikers were reported dismissed June 5 in the first punitive action in the stoppage.)

Palma arrested—Government Secretary General Anibal Palma was ordered arrested by an appeals court judge June 5 on charges of "prevarication" and "disrespect" in connection with the closing of a right-wing radio station. Palma was later released on bail.

The station, Radio Agricultura, had been ordered closed by Palma for allegedly broadcasting false and alarmist reports on disturbances in Rancagua related to the copper strike. Radio Agricultura appealed the decision before an appeals court, and a court-appointed magistrate, Hernan Cereceda, lifted the closure order. Palma appealed that action before the supreme court. The court rebuked the minister for "disrespect," and assigned Cereceda to make a new investigation. Cereceda then accused Palma of "prevarication" in addition to "disrespect," and ordered him arrested.

The political commission of the governing Popular Unity coalition (UP) said June 6 it would begin impeachment procedures against the entire Supreme Court, which it denounced as having "lost all legitimacy and moral authority by becoming another bastion of reaction." The court, the UP charged, was guilty of a "new abuse of power, which once again tweaks the nose of the law."

Labor & mines ministers impeached—The Chamber of Deputies June 6 suspended

Labor Minister Luis Figueroa and Mines Minister Sergio Bitar for allegedly failing to comply with a law which would have raised the salaries of El Teniente's miners, and thus precipitating the current copper strike.

The motion, introduced by the Christian Democrats and backed by the right-wing National party, was approved 74–0 after all pro-government deputies walked out of the chamber.

Before the vote, a melee broke out among at least 60 government and opposition legislators. The fight was started by Communist Deputy Alejandro Rojas and Christian Democratic Deputy Carlos Dupre, who attacked each other during a heated argument.

About 20,000 workers had demonstrated in support of Bitar and Figueroa in Santiago June 5. The rally was organized by CUT.

Figueroa and Bitar were censured and dismissed by the Senate June 20. They were the fourth and fifth Cabinet officials impeached under President Salvador Allende.

The Senate motions were approved 26–0, with pro-government legislators boycotting both the debate and the vote. Allende made no immediate move to replace the two ministers.

Copper strike crisis deepens. Thousands of professionals, teachers and students in the five major provinces went on strike June 20 to support the 63-day stoppage at the El Teniente copper mine and to protest the government's economic policies.

Physicians, nurses, dentists and druggists struck in the provinces of Santiago, Valparaiso, Concepcion, Arica and Magallanes. Hospitals handled only emergency cases, and the national medical college warned it would suspend even those services if the government took reprisals against physicians.

In the capital, the Communist-led Central Labor Federation (CUT) called a general strike for June 21 to support the government. Jorge Godoy, the federation's leader, said workers would paralyze "everything, even lights and telephones, so the reactionaries can gauge the strength of the working class."

President Salvador Allende flew to El Teniente June 20 for a first-hand report on the strike, the longest and costliest of his administration.

Allende had met with six strike leaders June 15 after severe street fighting in Santiago between government supporters and backers of the copper strike. The meeting was denounced by the political commissions of the Communist and Socialist parties, which asserted the government should offer no new concessions to strikers with "fascist and seditious" motives. Allende said June 16 that he had not altered his previous position but simply stressed to the strike leaders "the grave consequences of [this] conflict for the country."

Supporters of the government and the copper strike battled June 15; one person was reported killed and 63 injured. The presidential palace was surrounded throughout the day by chanting workers and students, and by most of Santiago's heavy trash trucks and road scrapers. Nearby, national police and pro-Allende activists fought off anti-government workers and students who sought to welcome a miners' march which had set out from El Teniente the day before.

The government said the miners had no permission to march. When they attempted to enter the city, they were cut down by tear gas and water cannon. Most of the miners gave up the march, but about 2,000 reportedly were smuggled into Santiago in private vehicles.

Police battled striking miners near the presidential palace June 16, breaking up miners' barricades located near the headquarters of the opposition Christian Democratic party, which supported the strike. Ex-President Eduardo Frei, the Christian Democratic leader and newly elected Senate president, charged 50 persons were injured and accused the police of "brutal repression."

Allende June 17 linked the strike to an alleged plot by his opponents to bring down the government. He said the plot would fail because neither Congress nor the armed forces would support it.

(Allende again sought to bring the military into his Cabinet, as he did in November 1972 to help end the nationwide protest strikes, the Washington Post reported June 17. However, the officers reportedly were asking that he abandon his programs for rapid socialization of the country, which Allende found difficult to accept.)

New clashes occurred in Santiago June 19 as riot policemen used tear gas on rock-throwing demonstrators who demanded settlement of the copper strike. The violence followed an anti-government rally near the presidential palace, organized by the Christian Democrats.

At El Teniente, meanwhile, an estimated 50%–60% of the work force was either on strike or manning the emergency maintenance crews which miners provided even in total shutdowns.

A government offer of productivity bonuses and a lump payment, which officials said would cost the state copper company more than the strikers' original demands, had split copper workers into two factions. The majority of unskilled workers, and virtually all card-carrying members of the parties in the ruling Popular Unity coalition (UP), had voted to accept the offer and had returned to work. Virtually all the skilled workers stood by the original demands and continued to strike.

Rancagua, where most of the miners lived, was controlled by the strikers. They received food from sympathetic farmers to the south, brought in trucks provided by the same owners who played a critical role in the October 1972 strikes. Rancagua's radio station was occupied by wives of the strikers, and the local newspaper supported the stoppage.

Milton Puga, a Christian Democrat and leader of the striking skilled workers' union, justified the strike's continuation by noting the government's dismissal of 75 strikers, it was reported June 16. "In the worst struggles of the Yankee epoch, we never saw a strike in which men were fired for striking," he asserted.

Asked if strikers were receiving help from groups that sought the collapse of the government, Puga said strikebreaking efforts were so intense that strikers took help from any source but that it did not imply any political commitment. The military commander of the area, Col. Orlando Ibanez, said he was aware of no subversion by outside agitators in Rancagua.

A high government copper official, Waldo Fortin, admitted June 14 that some striking workers had been fired. However, he said each person had been dismissed for assaulting nonstrikers or damaging government property.

Workers at Chuquicamata, Chile's other crucial copper mine, voted by a narrow margin June 6 not to continue their strike in solidarity with El Teniente, according to the Cuban press agency Prensa Latina.

Strikes, violence continue—Most transportation and commerce were halted in the provinces of Santiago, Valparaiso, Concepcion and Arica June 21, as government opponents struck to support the El Teniente walkout and leftist workers struck in support of the government.

Those striking against the government included doctors, engineers, other professionals and some students, many of whom had struck the day before. Workers supporting the government generally were affiliated with the Communist-led Central Labor Federation (CUT), which called a 24-hour strike to "erase the attempt by fascism to cause a civil war in the country."

Troops were called out to help quell shootings and riots in the capital and other cities. Bombs exploded in Santiago outside a Socialist party office, a government office and a government television installation. A fourth bomb wrecked two cars outside the home of a Cuban embassy official, but no injuries were reported.

In Curico, south of Santiago, shootings and riots left at least six persons wounded, police reported. In Osorno, further south, five persons were injured as Communists and Christian Democrats clashed with rocks and knives.

Allende told workers gathered outside the Government House that he would start court action against Fatherland and Liberty and against the National party. He accused the Nationals of sedition in issuing a statement charging that the government had repeatedly violated the Constitution, thus making itself "illegitimate."

The leading opposition newspaper, El Mercurio, was closed for six days June 21 by court order, for allegedly "inciting subversion" by printing the National statement. The newspaper failed to appear June 22, for the first time in its 73-year history. However, the closure order was overturned by an appeals court later in the day, and El Mercurio reappeared June 23.

Police clashed with government opponents and supporters in Santiago June 26, following the arrival from Rancagua of some 500 wives of striking miners. Police reported no injuries, but at least four ambulances removed injured demonstrators, according to news reports. Allende met with 10 of the miners' wives for about an hour.

More than 1,000 striking miners who arrived in Santiago June 15 despite a police blockade, had remained in the capital and were living in university buildings controlled by anti-government students, the New York Times reported June 27.

El Teniente strike ends. Striking workers at the El Teniente copper mine agreed July 2 to return to their jobs, ending a 74-day walkout that cost the country an estimated $70 million.

The strikers, representing more than half the mine's work force, accepted a government offer of a series of bonuses retroactive to April 1, and a pay increase. One issue, however, remained unresolved: the strike leaders wanted immediate reinstatement of strikers fired during the walkout, while the government wanted a commission created to deal with strikers who had committed illegal acts. The government had charged all those fired had committed such acts.

The state copper concern, CODELCO, said June 3, as strikers began returning to work, that no copper would be available for sale in July.

Economy minister suspended. The Chamber of Deputies voted to suspend Economy Minister Orlando Millas June 20 on charges of responsibility for alleged discrimination in the distribution of scarce food items. An earlier and very similar motion against Millas, introduced by the right-wing National party, had been defeated May 18 when Christian Democratic deputies abstained from the vote on grounds the motion was "unsuitably" worded. Millas was accused by Christian Democrats of violating the law in favor of

the government's Price and Supply Boards (JAPs), created to facilitate and control the distribution of scarce food items. Opposition legislators believed the JAPs were illegal and behaved in discriminatory fashion.

Impeachment measures against yet another Cabinet official, Interior Minister Gerardo Espinoza, were introduced in the Chamber by Christian Democrats June 20. Espinoza was accused of responsibility for a police raid the day before on television Channel 6 of the University of Chile. Police allegedly violated university autonomy and destroyed equipment belonging to the channel, which had begun transmission June 17 after left-wing workers occupied the university's Channel 9.

Allende, Supreme Court clash. The 13 Supreme Court justices June 26 accused President Allende of having, "without warning or motive," participated in a "systematic campaign" to destroy the power and prestige of Chile's highest tribunal.

The court made the charge in response to a letter from Allende alleging that "on each occasion that the harsh social and political struggle of our country has become exasperating ... [the court] has been absent, or more exactly, has been present to make observations of doubtful benefit which rarely favor social peace and the re-establishment of democratic dialogue."

The exchange coincided with the publication of articles in the left-wing press criticizing recent Supreme Court decisions, particularly in political cases.

Cost of living up 238%. Official statistics reported June 7 showed the cost of living in Chile had risen by a record 238% in the 12 months ending in May.

Industrial production fell by 5.6% in January-March, compared with the same period in 1972, according to a private sector study reported June 15. Sales were reported down by 4.9%.

The French firm Peugeot signed an agreement with the state development corporation to produce 15,000 medium-sized vehicles in Chile in 1973, rising to 30,-000 in 1980, it was reported June 1. The vehicles would contain 65.6% Chilean parts in 1973 and 92.6% in 1975.

Finland contributed a $10.6 million credit to develop Chile's forestry industry, according to a report June 6. Chile agreed to use 80% of the loan to purchase Finnish equipment.

Bulgaria granted Chile a $17 million loan for construction of a sulphuric acid plant, it was reported June 29.

Canada granted an $8 million loan for the purchase of twin Otter 300 planes and for re-equipment of the state telecommunications company, it was reported July 27.

Spain granted Chile a loan equivalent to some $45 million for the purchase of motor manufacturing machinery and equipment, and for imports of wheat, oil and other foodstuffs, it was reported July 20.

The U.S. Commerce Dept. reported Aug. 3 that U.S. exports to Chile had declined by 50% since the election of President Allende in 1970.

Coup attempt crushed. Troops loyal to President Salvador Allende crushed an attempted military coup June 29, the first bid to overthrow an elected Chilean government in 42 years.

About 100 rebel troops attacked the presidential palace and the Defense Ministry in downtown Santiago shortly before 9 a.m. They were held off by the palace guard until loyal troops under the army commander, Gen. Carlos Prats, surrounded them and forced their surrender. Twenty-two persons, mostly civilian passers-by, were reported killed and 34 wounded in the battle, which left the immediate area in a shambles.

The rebels, in four tanks and other armored vehicles, first took control of Constitution Plaza, in front of the presidential palace. They herded some civilians out of the area and then shelled the palace and raked the surrounding streets with automatic weapons fire. Several squads of rebels with tanks broke off to attack the Defense Ministry nearby, breaking down its doors and freeing an army captain held there for alleged implication in a planned coup denounced by authorities the day before.

While the rebels battled the palace guard, Allende, at his private residence, declared a nationwide state of emergency and ordered the revolt crushed. Prats personally led loyal troops in the counterattack. The government was in control of the palace by 11:30 a.m.

Allende later made a nationwide broadcast, announcing that most of the rebels had surrendered and that "the situation in the whole country is one of calm and absolute tranquillity." He said the navy and air force commanders in chief had given him their backing immediately after the outbreak. He added that the aborted revolt would have no impact on his government's policies.

Spokesmen for the main opposition party, the Christian Democrats, called for support of the constitutional order during and after the revolt. Allende also received messages of support from Cuban Premier Fidel Castro, Mexican President Luis Echeverria Alvarez, and Argentine ex-President Juan Peron.

Government supporters demonstrated in the streets of Santiago after the revolt was crushed. Leftists reportedly tried to storm the offices of La Tribuna, an anti-government newspaper, and the headquarters of the right-wing National party, but were turned back by policemen firing tear gas. El Mercurio, the leading opposition paper, was temporarily occupied by police, and other newspaper offices were temporarily evacuated. The pro-government radio station Radio Portales was reportedly bombed.

Allende spoke to a crowd of thousands of supporters from the balcony of the presidential palace in the evening. He denounced the "fascists, traitors and cowards" who he said planned the aborted revolt, and asserted "the people and the armed forces can never be defeated." He said the rebels included civilian members of the extreme right-wing Fatherland and Liberty party, who were now seeking asylum at foreign embassies.

(Five Fatherland and Liberty leaders, including party chief Pablo Rodriguez, were reported July 2 to have taken refuge in the Ecuadorean embassy, where they sought political asylum.)

Allende later sent Congress legislation declaring a 90-day state of siege. Despite a government warning that the nation was "on the brink of civil war," the bill was rejected July 2 by an 81–52 vote in the Chamber of Deputies. Leaders of the four opposition parties maintained Allende had ample powers to preserve order under the state of emergency.

Under the emergency, the armed forces assumed control of the public order, and the government could prohibit public gatherings, censor the news and order curfews. The more extreme state of siege, normally reserved for wartime, would have given the president broader authority in suspending civil rights.

The military authorities banned all "commentary" about the revolt June 30. Newspapers published accounts and photographs of the uprising, but some papers appeared with blank spaces, indicating censored passages. Seven radio stations and La Tribuna were reported closed July 1. La Tribuna reportedly had described the uprising as a vulgar show by the government to obtain greater power and institute a dictatorship. An 11 p.m.–6 a.m. curfew was also imposed.

Meanwhile, the rebels and their reputed leader, Col. Roberto Souper, were under arrest in an army camp.

'Barracks revolt' thwarted—The army had announced June 28 the crushing of a "barracks revolt" against the commanding officers and the government.

Gen. Mario Sepulveda, army commander of Santiago Province, said the effort to "break the institutional processes" had been "totally aborted" with the arrest of several low-ranking officers early June 27, shortly before a bizarre incident which the government described as an attempt on the life of the army commander in chief, Gen. Prats.

According to Government Secretary General Anibal Palma, Prats was being driven to the Defense Ministry when his car was boxed in by several others at an intersection. The general feared he was about to be assassinated, and consequently left his automobile, fired two warning shots with a pistol—one striking the door of a woman's car—and fled in a taxi. This account was roughly corroborated by an early United Press International report.

According to other press accounts and opposition charges, however, Prats be-

came enraged when the woman motorist recognized him and stuck out her tongue. The general allegedly pursued her in his vehicle and fired at her. When she stopped, he allegedly aimed the gun at her head and demanded an apology. An angry crowd gathered, and Prats departed in a taxi.

The incident caused a near-riot as angry motorists and bystanders surrounded Prats' car, painted anti-government slogans on it and deflated its tires. Three busloads of riot police firing tear gas arrived to end the disturbance.

Prats reportedly submitted his resignation to Allende shortly after the incident. Allende, however, rejected it, and declared a state of emergency in Santiago Province, calling it "a necessary measure to confront the excesses of fascism." Gen. Sepulveda was named commander of the emergency zone.

Emergency lifted; Cabinet shuffled—Allende dissolved the nationwide state of emergency July 4 and named a new all-civilian Cabinet the next day.

The emergency, declared during the unsuccessful military coup attempt June 29, was ended because the country had returned to "absolute normality," according to Interior Undersecretary Daniel Vergara.

The Cabinet had resigned July 3 and Allende had announced that day he would not appoint military officers to the new Cabinet. He explained he did not want the armed forces "involved in political disputes"; however, Congressional sources reported Allende had asked officers to join the Cabinet, but they had made unacceptable demands, including appointments to key undersecretary posts in several ministries as well as governorships and other provincial posts.

The new Cabinet preserved the political balance of its predecessor, with four Socialists, four Radicals, three Communists, two independents and one member each of the Christian Left and MAPU parties. There were seven new ministers.

The Cabinet:

Interior—Carlos Briones; foreign affairs—Orlando Letelier; defense—Clodomiro Almeyda; agriculture—Ernesto Torrealba; finance—Fernando Flores Labra; economy—Jose Cademartori; labor—Jorge Godoy; health—Arturo Jiron; justice—Sergio Insunza; mines—Pedro Felipe Ramirez; public works—Humberto Martones; housing—Luis Matte Valdez;

education—Edgargo Enriquez; lands and colonization—Roberto Cuellar; government secretary
general—Anibal Palma.

Among the ministers replaced in the new Cabinet were two who had been censured and dismissed by the Senate and two suspended by the Chamber of Deputies. The last to be suspended was Interior Minister Gerardo Espinoza late July 3, on charges of violating university autonomy in authorizing a police raid on television Channel 6 of the University of Chile.

(Jaime Toha Gonzalez, brother of ex-Defense Minister Jose Toha Gonzalez, was sworn in as agriculture minister July 15, replacing Torrealba, who had resigned July 11.)

Upon swearing in the new ministers, Allende announced a 14-point emergency plan developed by leaders of his Popular Unity coalition after the coup attempt.

Among the plan's provisions: Strengthening of the government's political, economic and administrative authority, and guarantees of public order and "civic coexistence"; economic discipline and austerity to combat inflation; "drastic" curbs to prevent crimes against the national economy; price policies favoring "popular consumption" goods over non-essential and luxury articles; wage readjustment policies favoring sectors with lowest incomes; amplification and "rationalization" of state takeovers of enterprises in the reformed agrarian sector; broader participation by workers in the management of the economy; incorporation of popular organizations in the administration of the state.

Christian Democratic Sen. Aylwin commended Allende July 5 for pledging to govern in "pluralism, democracy and liberty," but expressed disappointment in the absence of the military officers from the new Cabinet.

Allende aide murdered. President Salvador Allende's naval aide-de-camp, Capt. Arturo Araya, was assassinated by unidentified gunmen at his home in Santiago early July 27.

The presidential press office made public a statement describing the assassination as "a typical fascist action of Fatherland and Liberty," the extreme right-wing party linked with the aborted June 29 military coup. Sen. Luis Corvalan, leader of the Communist party, blamed the killing on "sectors that seek the overthrow of the government," including, it was assumed, the opposition parties.

The four opposition groups—the Christian Democrats, National party, Social Democratic (formerly Radical Left) party and Radical Democracy party—issued a statement July 28 condemning the assassination, but also accused the government of responsibility for the nation's current crisis and of using even "the death and pain of others" to vent its "characteristic hatreds and ill will."

Fatherland and Liberty leader Robert Thieme, in hiding in Chile after a brief exile in Argentina, charged July 27 that "Marxist-Leninists" had committed the murder. He volunteered to surrender to the navy to prove his party's innocence.

Thieme had announced July 17 that Fatherland and Liberty would unleash a total armed offensive to overthrow the government. The party had published an advertisement in the Santiago newspaper La Tribuna July 13 claiming responsibility for the June 29 coup attempt. The government had closed La Tribuna for six days as a result.

Five Fatherland and Liberty leaders had flown to Ecuador July 7 after the Ecuadorean embassy in Santiago granted them political asylum and Allende authorized safe conduct out of Chile. Other party members gained asylum July 6 in the Colombian and Paraguayan embassies.

Truck owners strike. Truck owners throughout Chile went on strike July 26, threatening to paralyze the country and precipitate a crisis as grave as the one engendered by their strike in October 1972.

The National Confederation of Truck Owners charged the government had not observed its November 1972 agreement to make available new trucks and spare parts, and had tried to set up a parallel trucking organization. The federation said it was prepared to strike "indefinitely."

The strike immediately affected Santiago and other cities, and by July 31 shortages of food, gasoline and kerosene reached serious proportions. Santiago was reported receiving only 30% of its supplies.

The government requisitioned 950 trucks for the most urgent needs, but many of their operators were victims of stonings and sabotage by presumed right-wing agitators. Rail lines and several bridges were reported dynamited in an apparent attempt to isolate the capital from its seaports and generally disrupt communications. Gas stations throughout the country also were reported attacked.

The National Confederation of Ground Transports, controlling some 86,000 buses, taxis and trucks, threatened to join the strike if an agreement with the government was not reached soon. The Superior National Security Council had issued a "formal and severe warning" July 28 against solidarity strikes by any unions.

Political negotiations. Amid growing tension, the Christian Democratic party acceded to President Allende's often-voiced request for political negotiations to avert a civil war. Allende and the Christian Democratic party president, Sen. Patricio Aylwin, met July 30, but no details of the talks were revealed.

Christian Democratic sources said Aug. 1 that the party had sent a letter to Allende demanding the disarming of paramilitary groups on both the left and the right; restoration of factories and farm properties seized after the aborted military coup; approval of a constitutional reform bill to define the private, mixed and state sectors of the economy; and formation of a Cabinet that would provide "constitutional guarantees," i.e. one including military representatives.

Allende was said to have the backing of the majority of the Popular Unity parties in his talks with Aylwin, but not of his militant Socialist party.

A dozen private businesses and professional associations announced Aug. 1 they had formed a "civic front" to overthrow the Allende administration. The group, including lawyers, teachers, doctors and builders associations, published a full-page advertisement in the opposition newspaper El Mercurio.

Strikes, violence widen. Public transportation in Santiago was virtually suspended Aug. 3 when 60,000 bus, truck, taxi and jitney owners joined the crippling, nine-day strike by private truckers.

The new action was called Aug. 2 by the National Confederation of Ground Transports after President Salvador Allende rejected its demand to fire Transport Undersecretary Jaime Faivovich, whom it held responsible for clashes July 31 in which four truckers were injured. The clashes occurred when truckers resisted authorities ordered by Faivovich to confiscate some 100 striking trucks.

Bus owners did not officially join the stoppage, but only 30% of the capital's private buses were running Aug. 3. State-owned buses continued to operate, but they amounted to only 10% of Santiago's fleet.

Employes of the Santiago water works had struck Aug. 1. Physicians and copper miners threatened to strike Aug. 4; the doctors protested shortages of equipment and medicine and low salaries in state hospitals, while miners demanded the immediate rehiring of co-workers fired during the recent El Teniente strike.

The truckers' strike, which caused critical fuel shortages and sent food prices skyrocketing, was denounced as "seditious" by Allende at a press conference Aug. 3. The president said the stoppage, like the truckers' strike of October 1972, would be defeated by voluntary work by "workers and youth."

Allende declared that "all public services and officials are under a state of emergency, and will work Saturdays and Sundays if necessary to collaborate with the government and the armed forces." He named army Gen. Herman Brady to direct efforts to provide emergency transportation.

Allende asserted he would not bring military officers into his Cabinet, as strike leaders and the opposition Christian Democratic party demanded. He insisted on "the importance of the cooperation" of the armed forces but asserted: "I think it is up to the politicians to solve the country's political problems, and I believe the armed forces agree."

(The Cabinet reportedly resigned Aug. 3 to give Allende a free hand as the strikes widened, but Allende was said to have rejected the resignations.)

Allende charged that certain elements of the opposition, particularly the extreme right-wing Fatherland and Liberty party, were using "all means to try to overthrow the government and regain their old privileges." He asserted there was a "concerted plan" to sabotage his talks with the Christian Democrats.

Christian Democratic officials said after the press conference that the talks were "over" because Allende had not acceded to their "minimum demands."

Allende had agreed Aug. 2 to sign a constitutional reform passed by the opposition-controlled Congress which delineated the state, private and mixed sectors of the economy and prohibited further nationalization of private industry without Congressional approval—provided a general agreement was reached on several other points. These included application of the reform; passing of a constitutional amendment requiring future constitutional reforms to be passed by a two-thirds majority in Congress instead of the present simple majority; and approval of a series of government bills on cooperat: es, profit-sharing for workers, and the state's role in the economy.

Allende charged at the Aug. 3 press conference that 180 acts of terrorism against railroads, highways, bridges, pipelines, schools and hospitals had been committed since the assassination of his naval aide-de-camp July 27.

Most of the violence was connected to attempts by strikers to isolate Santiago and other major cities, according to the New York Times Aug. 3. Saboteurs were dynamiting transport routes in strategic areas, and stoning, firing upon or setting fire to strikebreaking trucks.

An estimated 20 workers were seriously wounded Aug. 7 when an oil pipeline exploded about 100 miles south of Santiago. All railroad traffic between the capital and the South had been stopped the day before when a power plant substation was blown up near Rancagua.

Gen. Brady announced Aug. 5 that truckers who returned to work would get armed protection against terrorists. He was authorized by Allende the same day to requisition buses and taxis if they did not resume service.

Soldiers raid factories. Allende asked for the retirement of two air force officers Aug. 7 amid growing acrimony between his left-wing supporters and the armed forces over military raids on factories.

The retirements followed a raid on factories in and near Punta Arenas in which a worker was shot to death when he failed to comply with army orders to halt. The raid had been authorized by air force Gen. Manuel Torres de la Cruz, the regional military commander, who claimed to have acted under the Arms Control Act. The Central Labor Federation (CUT) and Allende's Socialist party had demanded Torres' resignation and the immediate repeal of the law, which allowed the armed forces to conduct raids in search of weapons without authorization from the government.

Leftist naval plots charged. The navy announced Aug. 7 it had quashed a revolt planned by servicemen aboard a cruiser and destroyer stationed at Valparaiso.

A naval communique said 22 persons were under arrest and faced courts martial for plotting to take the vessels out of the harbor while many crew members were on shore leave. It blamed the plot on "extremist groups alien to our institution . . . who have been calling for disobedience in the armed forces." The extremist Revolutionary Left Movement (MIR) had issued numerous such calls recently.

The commander of the second naval zone based in Talcahuano claimed Aug. 9 to have detected and halted attempts by "civilians of the extreme left" to infiltrate naval units in the local shipyards.

The London Times reported Aug. 15 that the navy had presented two lawsuits against the MIR, calling its members irresponsible adventurers seeking only to cause chaos by attacking Chile's basic institutions.

(The navy was reported Aug. 24 to have requested the lifting of the Congressional immunity of two government supporters—Carlos Altamirano, secretary general of Allende's Socialist party, and Oscar Garreton, leader of the small, radical MAPU party. The legislators were accused of "intellectual" responsibility for an alleged leftist plan to subvert the navy.)

Military rejoins Cabinet. President Salvador Allende, yielding to pressure from opposition leaders and anti-government strikers, gave Cabinet posts to the commanders of the three armed forces and the national police Aug. 9.

The Cabinet reorganization, the third of 1973, was precipitated by the crippling truckers' strike, other stoppages and related terrorism. Allende entrusted the new ministers with restoring political and economic order in Chile.

Gen. Carlos Prats, the army commander and former interior minister, rejoined the Cabinet as defense minister. Navy commander Adm. Raul Montero Cornejo was named finance minister; air force commander Gen. Cesar Ruiz Danyau, transport minister; and National Police Chief Gen. Jose Maria Sepulveda, lands and colonization minister.

Four civilian ministers resigned, seven retained their posts and four were shifted to new posts. Foreign Minister Orlando Letelier became interior minister; Defense Minister Clodomiro Almeyda, foreign minister; Government Secretary General Anibal Palma, housing minister; and Finance Minister Fernando Flores Labra, government secretary general.

The new Cabinet, aside from its military members, retained roughly the same political composition as its predecessor, with three Socialists, three Communists, two Radicals, one independent, and one member each of the Christian Left and MAPU parties.

Allende called the new Cabinet one of "national security" whose task was to "defend Chile from fascism [and] prevent the separation of the people from the government and from the armed forces." The ministers, he added, would "reject any attempted political, subversive infiltration of the armed forces, national police and civil police."

Allende said the Cabinet had to "end the fascist transport strike and outlaw all fascist groups such as [the] Fatherland and Liberty [party]." In an indirect threat to left-wing extremists, the president added that authorities would act against "any individual or groups seeking to subvert order, whatever their political orientation."

Allende also stressed the necessity of controlling Chile's skyrocketing inflation, which, he said, might "lead to a chaos without exit."

Reactions to the new Cabinet by the opposition were divided. Christian Democratic party President Patricio Aylwin, representing the party's conservative sector, said Aug. 9 that the appointments were not enough, and called for the "real participation" of the armed forces at every level. However, Sen. Renan Fuentealba, leader of the party's left wing, said Aug. 10 he believed the Cabinet would "give security to all Chileans and [meant] a rectification by the government so that the process of change will be normalized but not held back."

The right-wing National party, which had called for the overthrow of the government, warned Aug. 9 that the military officers in the Cabinet ran the risk of "serving as screens for the maneuvers of extremist groups."

On the government's side, the Socialist and Communist parties jointly backed the new Cabinet Aug. 12, following earlier protests against military participation in the Cabinet from the radical wing of the Socialists and the smaller MAPU party. The Central Labor Federation (CUT) held a massive rally in support of the government in Santiago Aug. 9.

The armed forces also were divided by the current crisis, according to the London newsletter Latin America Aug. 10. Senior officers were classed by left-wing politicians as "golpistas" (plotters) or "no-golpistas." The armed forces had recently been denounced by leftists for concentrating in their search for illegal weapons on leftist workers' groups, rather than on right-wing and openly seditious organizations such as Fatherland and Liberty.

Strikes & terrorism. The truckers' strike, related stoppages and terrorism continued despite a government ultimatum to the strikers and the appointment of military commissioners in each province to get the trucks back on the roads.

The government warned Aug. 10 that if the strike did not end Aug. 12, striking trucks would be confiscated and their owners prosecuted. The government agreed to meet strikers' demands for the import and distribution of spare parts and new trucks but refused a demand for the resignation of Transportation Undersecretary Jaime Faivovich.

The truckers rejected the ultimatum Aug. 11, vowing to continue the strike "to the last ditch." They continued to concentrate their vehicles at El Monte, some

30 miles west of Santiago, where they brought in first aid tents and medical equipment to prepare for battle with authorities. More than 500 police backed by three tanks had tried to requisition trucks there late Aug. 10, but Faivovich had called off the operation after they clashed with truckers.

The Christian Democrats declared their support for the strike Aug. 12. Eduardo Cerda, the party's general secretary, said in a radio speech that the truckers were expressing "legitimate grievances " and warned that the government would be responsible for any violence resulting from attempts to break the strike.

The government Aug. 12 appointed a military commissioner in each province to requisition trucks and, if necessary, use soldiers to seize them.

Meanwhile, fuel was rationed, food supplies rotted in warehouses, prices skyrocketed, and 40%–50% of industry and business were paralyzed because of the strike. Some relief was provided by voluntary work organized by the government political parties.

Strike-related sabotage continued, with daily attacks on strikebreaking trucks and buses, and dynamiting of roads, tunnels, railways, bridges and power stations. Electric power was cut off for nearly an hour in the major provinces late Aug. 13, when saboteurs dynamited three high-tension electric pylons outside Santiago. The action interrupted a televised speech by Allende, who was denouncing the strike.

Allende and government spokesmen blamed Fatherland and Liberty for the sabotage, citing a declaration by the party Aug. 12 pledging to renew its offensive against the government. However, the right-wing press attempted Aug. 13 to put the blame on left-wing extremists.

Meanwhile, the left-wing press was accusing the U.S. embassy in Chile of backing the strikes and terrorism. An editorial in the newspaper Ultima Hora suggested Aug. 13 that U.S. Ambassador Nathaniel Davis and the Central Intelligence Agency were helping finance the current right-wing press and radio campaign against the government. The editorial was signed by Hernan del Canto, a former Cabinet official and an influential member of Allende's Socialist party.

The left-wing press campaign against the U.S. and its alleged support of the strikes continued, but the government denied responsibility for it. Bombs were discovered and dismantled late Aug. 15 in the gardens of the homes of three U.S. embassy officials. U.S. Ambassador Nathaniel Davis met Aug. 16 with Foreign Minister Clodomiro Almeyda, who assured him attacks on U.S. diplomats would not be tolerated.

The government requisitioned more than 2,000 striking trucks Aug. 16–18 in an attempt to get food and fuel supplies moving again. Many strikers removed parts from their trucks and deflated their tires, but did not otherwise resist authorities seizing the vehicles.

The government released a report Aug. 17 saying the truckers' strike had cost Chile $6 million a day, and had helped destroy half of the winter's green vegetable crop and half the country's milk production. Planting was reported to be impossible in several provinces without delivery of seeds and fuel, and heavy livestock losses were reported in the extreme south.

National Planning Office Director Gonzalo Martner, who released the report, called the truck stoppage a "political strike aimed at overthrowing the government, with the help of imperialism." Allende charged Aug. 16 that the political opposition had planned and directed the strike, and was "endangering the foundations of the state."

Other strike-related terrorism continued, meanwhile, with more than 360 terrorist attacks and six deaths reported since the strikes began July 26. Strikebreaking trucks and buses were attacked daily by presumed right-wing militants, and land transport routes and high-tension electric pylons were dynamited. A pro-government transport union leader, Oscar Balboa, was murdered Aug. 18 by what the government called "reactionary bands."

The government Aug. 17 sent to Congress draft legislation that would give it broader powers to combat terrorism, particularly attacks against water supplies, electricity and gas installations, factories, and distributors of mining, agricultural, or industrial products.

Officials replaced—The government Aug. 18 granted what appeared to be the truckers' major demand, the removal of Faivovich as transport undersecretary and general commissioner of highway associations.

The truckers said Faivovich's dismissal only allowed a resumption of talks with the government and the stoppage would continue. Army Gen. Herman Brady was given Faivovich's post as highways commissioner, or chief "intervenor" in the truckers' strike.

The public works and transport minister, air force Gen. Cesar Ruiz Danyau, also resigned Aug. 18, claiming President Salvador Allende had not given him sufficient power to end the truckers' strike. Allende denied the charge, and political sources reported that Ruiz had resigned because of serious differences with the president on ways of ending the strike.

The new transport minister was Gen. Humberto Magliochetti Barahona, the air force operations chief.

Ruiz also was dismissed as air force commander and replaced in that post by Gen. Gustavo Leigh Guzman. An undetermined number of air force officers opposed this action, forcing a postponement of the transfer of command. However, Leigh assumed his post without incident Aug. 20.

(Political observers quoted in the Washington Post Aug. 21 said the incident was a warning to the other military chiefs in the Cabinet that if they proposed projects disapproved by Allende, they might lose their military as well as ministerial posts.)

More than 3,000 doctors in Santiago began a 48-hour strike in solidarity with the truckers Aug. 20, and were joined the next day by colleagues elsewhere in the country. Many physicians protested the shortage of medicine and instruments in Chile's hospitals. Shopowners had begun a strike in the six southernmost provinces Aug. 16. Santiago's shopowners and most organizations of professionals, including lawyers, businessmen, engineers and pilots, joined the strikes Aug. 21. They reportedly demanded a quick solution to the truckers' strike, guarantees to private enterprise, more power for the military, and reinstatement of Gen. Ruiz.

Right- and left-wing militants clashed in Santiago Aug. 21, hurling rocks and in some cases firing on each other. Police using tear gas broke up the fights, with several injuries reported.

Street battles again broke out between right-wing and left-wing students in the capital Aug. 24, and were broken up by national police.

Strike-related terrorism also continued, with daily attacks on strike-breaking trucks and buses, dynamiting of roads and bridges, and sabotage of power installations. In Santiago, the North Korean embassy, several stores and the homes of government supporters were bombed Aug. 22, and the homes of two Cuban diplomats were bombed Aug. 27.

Fourteen members of the neo-fascist Fatherland and Liberty party were reported arrested Aug. 22, and seven others, including party leader Roberto Thieme, were reported seized Aug. 26. The Santiago police chief said that with Thieme's arrest "we have accounted for nearly all recent terrorist acts."

Thieme had admitted that his men had staged numerous terrorist attacks recently, including the dynamiting of a pylon which interrupted a nationwide address by Allende, it was reported Aug. 27. Their purpose, Thieme said, was to "accelerate the country's chaos and provide a military takeover as soon as possible." "If we have to burn this country to save it from [Allende], then we'll do that," Thieme asserted.

The pro-Allende Central Labor Federation (CUT) Aug. 21 ordered its members to stay on their jobs but to "keep vigilant" as the strikes spread. CUT-affiliated employes of the International Telephone and Telegraph Corp. (ITT) seized control of the U.S. firm's Santiago headquarters to assure continuation of telegraph and Telex communications. They kept open cable communications with the outside world, but ITT management instructed its branch offices to refuse cable traffic.

The Communist newspaper El Siglo published a denunciation Aug. 21 of an alleged "foreign conspiracy" against Chile's independence and sovereignty. It specifically accused ITT of backing the transport strike.

The CUT directed its members Aug. 23 to prevent any attempt to overthrow the president. CUT members had occupied at least 100 major industries since the aborted military coup attempt June 29.

Leaders of the striking truckers gave notice Aug. 27 that they would not return to work until the government worked out a constitutional reform providing guarantees for private enterprise. Shops and transportation were shut down in nine provinces Aug. 24, while most of Chile's 7,000 doctors continued their indefinite strike in support of the truckers and in protest against the shortage of medicine and instruments in the nation's hospitals.

In an effort to break the transport strike the Allende regime late Sept. 6 offered some 6,000 new trucks, buses and taxis to persons willing to drive them. A ministerial council said the vehicles could be purchased for 20% down and 24% monthly payments. The government added that it had "never had under consideration as an objective the nationalization of truck transport," as striking truckers had charged.

In another conciliatory move Sept. 7, Labor Minister Jorge Godoy announced plans for legislation setting a general 250% wage increase, effective in October, to keep pace with Chile's skyrocketing cost of living.

Engineers and construction workers joined in the wave of anti-government strikes Sept. 10. Pilots of the national airline, LAN, had declared an indefinite strike Sept. 7, and shopkeepers had extended their previous strike for 48 hours that day.

Prats quits. President Salvador Allende, beset by crippling anti-government strikes and terrorism, received an additional blow Aug. 23 when his staunchest military defender, Gen. Carlos Prats Gonzalez, resigned as defense minister and army commander in chief.

Gen. Augusto Pinochet Ugarte was named army commander Aug. 24, but no one was immediately named to the defense post.

Prats' letter of resignation, released Aug. 24, said he had been forced to step down by a "sector of army officers." He said his participation in the Cabinet had caused a left-right split in the army, and he had resigned "so as not to serve as a pretext for those who seek to overthrow the constitutional government." The newspaper La Nacion added that Prats had told reporters he was influenced by recent demonstrations outside his home in which wives of army officers, including many generals, had demanded his resignation.

Two other army generals, Guillermo Pickering and Mario Sepulveda, resigned Aug. 24, and all other generals reportedly submitted resignations subsequently. Rear Adm. Raul Montero Cornejo, the finance minister, returned to his post as navy commander in chief Aug. 24, leaving in doubt whether he would continue to serve in the Cabinet.

Prats' resignation followed adoption by the opposition-controlled Chamber of Deputies Aug. 22 of a resolution accusing the government of "constant violations of the fundamental rights and guarantees established in the Constitution " and calling on the Defense Ministry to "direct the government's action" as a way of guaranteeing democratic institutions.

In a strong reply Aug. 24, Allende accused the opposition of seeking to provoke a military coup by inciting the armed forces to disobey civil authorities.

It was widely accepted that a mutual allegiance had been hammered out between an important military sector and the leadership of the opposition Christian Democrats, the Washington Post reported Aug. 26. The Christian Democrats did not explicitly favor a military takeover, but their leader, Patricio Aylwin, was quoted as saying he would choose a military regime over "a Marxist dictatorship," the Post reported.

Aylwin said Aug. 25 that only "sufficient military presence" in the government could restore stability and guarantee observance of the Constitution and the law. Such presence meant at least six military men in the Cabinet "with real powers" and military men at the level of undersecretary and at the head of government agencies, Aylwin said.

The New York Times noted Aug. 27 that the Christian Democrats were playing a dual role in the current crisis, calling for a democratic solution while simultaneously supporting the strikes and demonstrations aimed at total capitulation by the government.

Furthermore, the party's newspaper had used blatant anti-semitism in its campaign against the government, charging the government had been taken over by a "Jewish-Communist cell" which allegedly was waging a racial war against the Arab community in Santiago and occupying key posts in government and industry, the Times reported.

Cabinet shuffled. President Salvador Allende named a new Cabinet Aug. 28 as anti-government strikes, related terrorism and sporadic street clashes continued for the fifth week.

The Cabinet shuffle, the fourth of 1973, followed the resignation Aug. 27 of the finance minister, navy Adm. Raul Montero Cornejo, the last of the armed forces commanders in the Cabinet. The government disclosed Sept. 2 that Montero had also offered to give up his naval post, but Allende had asked him to stay on.

The new Cabinet consisted of one officer of each of the armed forces, the commander of the national police, and 11 civilian members of Allende's Popular Unity coalition. Four new ministers were appointed, one rejoined the Cabinet, one shifted posts, and nine ministers retained their portfolios. The civilian ministers included three Socialists, three Communists, two Radicals, one independent, and one member each of the Christian Left and MAPU parties.

The Cabinet:

Interior—Carlos Briones; defense—Orlando Letelier; foreign affairs—Clodomiro Almeyda; finance—navy Rear Adm. Daniel Arellano; economy—Jose Cademartori; mining—army Gen. Rolando Gonzalez; public works & transportation—air force Gen. Humberto Magliochetti; justice—Sergio Insunza; labor—Jorge Godoy; housing—Pedro Felipe Ramirez; agriculture—Jaime Toha; lands & colonization—national police Gen. Jose Maria Sepulveda; health—Mario Lagos; education—Edgardo Enriquez; government secretary general—Fernando Flores.

Allende said the new Cabinet's mission was to "prevent civil war and guarantee security." He denounced the strikes and right-wing sabotage, and asserted he would not resign. He said he represented "a process of revolutionary transformations which will not be stopped either by terror or by fascist threats."

Shopkeepers throughout the nation began a 48-hour strike Aug. 28, joining most of Chile's doctors and thousands of professionals, including engineers, technicians and architects, whose previous stoppages continued. Some 15,000 members of the opposition-dominated Federation of Farmworkers also struck. The pro-Allende Central Labor Federation, which held a rally to support the government, denounced the stoppages as "fascist."

Transport Minister Magliochetti announced Aug. 29 that official negotiations with striking transport workers were "definitively canceled" and that the government was withdrawing legal recognition of the National Confederation of Truck Owners, which began the current strikes. Magliochetti asserted the government would assign 2,000 requisitioned taxis and 2,700 trucks to drivers prepared to return to work.

Shopkeepers extended their strike a third day Aug. 30 as general strikes in several southern provinces entered their third week. The shopkeepers returned to work Aug. 31, but doctors, nurses and pharmacists continued to strike. Pilots of the national airline, LAN, began a 72-hour stoppage Sept. 3.

The Confederation of Professional Employes, claiming more than 90,000 white-collar members, began an indefinite strike Sept. 4, as scores of thousands of leftists marched in Santiago to celebrate the third anniversary of Allende's election. The National Confederation of Retailers announced a 48-hour strike the same evening to protest the wounding of four persons in a clash between truck drivers and police about 60 miles from the capital.

Strike-related terrorism and sabotage continued, meanwhile, although apparently diminished since the arrest Aug. 26 of Roberto Thieme, leader of the neo-fascist Fatherland and Liberty party.

Bombings of several private homes in Santiago and electricity installations in the southern town of Temuco were reported Aug. 28; an army lieutenant was murdered Aug. 30; and two oil pipelines were reported dynamited Sept. 4. Interior Minister Briones said Aug. 30 there had been more than 500 terrorist attacks and eight related deaths since the strikes began July 26.

Street clashes also continued. Left- and right-wing extremists fought in the mining town of Rancagua Aug. 29 after leftists attacked the local opposition newspaper.

The navy, in an independent move criticized by government supporters, joined police in occupying the Catholic University in Valparaiso Aug. 31 to quell disturbances between armed groups of leftist and anti-government students. In Santiago, police used tear gas Sept. 5 to disperse a massive group of women and students marching on the presidential palace to demand Allende's resignation.

The armed forces and even the opposition reportedly remained divided over the strike crisis. Different military factions supported participation in the Cabinet, strict adherence to the armed forces' constitutional role, or seizure of power. The opposition Christian Democrats were divided into conservative and moderate factions, the latter with a less combative attitude toward the president.

The Christian Democratic disunity was made clear in a public letter, reported Aug. 30, in which ex-presidential candidate Radomiro Tomic expressed his support for Gen. Carlos Prats Gonzalez, former defense minister and army commander, who had been denounced by other Christian Democrats for his support of Allende.

The right-wing National party continued to call for Allende's resignation, while the extremist Fatherland and Liberty party was revealed to have worked extensively to try to overthrow the government. Statements by Roberto Thieme to police, reported by the London newsletter Latin America Aug. 31, indicated Fatherland and Liberty had coordinated sabotage attacks with the activities of striking truckers, and had worked with rightist elements in the armed forces to discredit military "constitutionalists." Thieme reportedly asserted the truckers' strike was planned solely to overthrow the government.

The Christian Democrats proposed Sept. 9 that Allende and all elected officials resign and allow new elections to resolve the strike crisis. The party had asserted Sept. 5 it would begin impeachment proceedings against "six or eight" Cabinet ministers it said had broken the law in attempting to end the strikes.

Sources close to the Christian Democratic leadership, quoted in the Washington Post Sept. 7, explained the impeachment proceedings were to help either to "separate the armed forces from Allende's newly formed Cabinet" or to "force the military to accept Cabinet posts only if they can appoint other officers to the civil service."

Tension between the government and the armed forces had been increased by an incident Sept. 7 in which air force troops searching for illegal arms caches had invaded a Santiago nylon factory, opening machine gun fire and wounding three workers and causing damage to the building and machinery. The air force claimed leftist workers occupying the factory had provoked a gun battle and wounded an officer. However, the head of the state development corporation, Pedro Vuskovic, claimed the troops had fired without provocation.

Navy plot charged—The executive committee of the Popular Unity coalition issued a statement Sept. 5 accusing the navy of planning to overthrow Allende and of torturing sailors detained after an alleged attempt to start a left-wing mutiny a month before.

The statement, not a government document, implied the sailors were arrested for refusing to obey orders to involve their ships in a coup maneuver. It alleged the detainees were subjected to "unprecedented tortures " and demanded "correct and just treatment and respect for the [sailors'] human rights."

Military Coup d'Etat, Allende Dies in Revolt

Allende regime overthrown. The armed forces and national police ousted the Popular Unity government Sept. 11, in the first successful military coup against a Chilean civilian administration since 1927.

Police officials in Santiago said President Salvador Allende Gossens had committed suicide rather than surrender power. A newspaper photographer allowed to see the body and a military communique Sept. 12 confirmed that the president was dead, but there was some confusion over whether he had taken his own life.

A four-man military junta seized control of the government and declared a state of siege, imposing censorship and a round-the-clock curfew. The junta members were the army commander, Gen. Augusto Pinochet Ugarte; the air force chief, Gen. Gustavo Leigh Guzman; the acting navy commander, Adm. Jose Toribio Merino Castro, and the national police chief, Gen. Cesar Mendoza. Pinochet was sworn in as president of Chile Sept. 13.

The four commanders had demanded early Sept. 11 that Allende resign by noon. The president refused, going on nationwide radio to declare: "I will not resign. I will not do it . . . I am ready to resist by any means, even at the cost of my own life, so this will serve as a lesson in the ignominious history of those who have strength but not reason." He then urged workers to occupy their factories and resist the coup.

Rebel forces attacked moments after the noon deadline; air force jets dropped bombs and fired rockets on the presidential palace in downtown Santiago, severely damaging the building, and also bombed Allende's official residence, about a mile away, after guards there reportedly resisted rebel troops.

Soldiers and police seized radio and television stations and broadcast the following communique:

Proclamation of the military government junta:
Bearing in mind
1. The very grave economic, social and moral crisis which is destroying the country,
2. The incapacity of the government to adopt measures to stop the growth and development of chaos,
3. The constant increase of armed para-military groups organized and trained by Popular Unity which will bring the people of Chile to an inevitable civil war, the armed forces and carabineros [national police] declare:
1. That the president of the republic must proceed immediately to hand over his high office to the Chilean armed forces and carabineros.
2. The Chilean armed forces and carabineros are united to initiate the historic and responsible mission to fight for the liberation of the fatherland from the Marxist yoke, and for the restoration of order and constitutional rule.
3. The workers of Chile may be certain that the economic and social benefits they have achieved up to the present will not suffer fundamental changes.
4. The press, radio transmitters and television channels of the Popular Unity must suspend their informative activities from this moment onward; otherwise they will be assaulted by land and air.

5. The people of Santiago must homes to avoid [the killing of] innoc

Fighting was heavy be. surrounding the presidential pala. snipers supporting the president, according to a United Press International correspondent. There appeared to be no other organized resistance to the rebel attack. No official reports of casualties were given, but unofficial accounts Sept. 12, as sniper fire continued and scattered resistance to the coup developed, put the number of casualties at 500–1,000.

After the rebels took control of the palace Sept. 11, a police prefect announced that Allende and a close adviser, Augusto Olivares, had killed themselves. Newsmen from the leading opposition newspaper, El Mercurio, were allowed in, and the paper's chief photographer, Juan Enrique Lira, said he saw Allende lying dead, having apparently shot himself in the mouth.

The military junta did not confirm Allende's death until the next day, and did not confirm the police claim of suicide. An official communique said Allende had agreed shortly before 2 p.m. to resign, but when a patrol arrived later in the palace, after a delay caused by sniper fire, it found the president dead. The communique said Allende was buried at noon Sept. 12 "in the presence of his family."

A series of orders was issued immediately after the coup by the military junta. Congress was recessed "until further order," all bank accounts were frozen, foreigners were ordered to the nearest police station to identify themselves, and 68 prominent Socialist and Communist leaders were ordered to appear at the Defense Ministry or face arrest.

More than 100 Communist and Socialist party members were reported arrested Sept. 11 in Santiago and Valparaiso, the port city where naval units made the first moves against the government early in the day. (Allende had gone on the Socialist radio station shortly after 8 a.m. to charge "a sector of the navy" had rebelled in the port, and ask "the army to defend the government.")

The junta announced Sept. 12 that 19 Socialist and Communist leaders had "presented themselves" to the police, including Interior Minister Carlos Briones and Foreign Minister Clodomiro Almeyda. Military sources said some would be released after questioning and others detained. Sources quoted by the Associated Press said 60 officials of Allende's government had sought asylum in the Mexican embassy and others had asked refuge elsewhere.

Explosions were heard in some industrial neighborhoods of Santiago Sept. 12 and snipers barricaded in office buildings exchanged fire with military patrols. The junta declared that "all persons who persist in a suicidal and irresponsible attitude will definitely be attacked. They will be shot on the spot if taken prisoner."

Six hundred leftists reportedly surrendered after a gunfight at the technical university near downtown Santiago. There also were reports of gun battles between soldiers and armed workers occupying factories to protest the coup.

Erratic communications made it impossible to determine conditions outside Santiago, but the junta said in a broadcast Sept. 12 that the country was "returning to normal." Long-distance telephone and telegraph services in Santiago had been shut down during the rebel attacks Sept. 11, but had been reopened at nightfall.

The junta said Sept. 12 it had expelled 150 Cuban extremists. It broke diplomatic relations with Cuba Sept. 13. Leftists from other countries also were being rounded up for expulsion, according to press reports.

(Cuba charged in a complaint to the United Nations Security Council Sept. 12 that the Chilean armed forces had attacked its embassy in Santiago and a Cuban merchant ship off the Chilean coast during the coup Sept. 11. The complaint also said two Cubans in Chile on World Health Organization scholarships had been arrested.)

A military-controlled television station in Santiago broadcast film clips Sept. 12 showing huge arms caches that, according to officers appearing in the films, were seized from the presidential palace and Allende's private residence. The commentators said most of the arms were made in the Soviet Union. Film clips were also shown of Allende's private residence, emphasizing the well-stocked pantry the president kept despite Chile's severe food shortage.

Allende suicide disputed—President Allende's widow, Hortensia Bussi de Allende, asserted Sept. 19 that her husband had not committed suicide but had been "murdered" by soldiers or police invading the presidential palace during the coup Sept. 11.

Mrs. Allende, who took political asylum in Mexico, had asserted Sept. 15, while in the Mexican ambassador's residence in Santiago, and Sept. 16, upon arrival in Mexico City, that military reports of her husband's suicide were true. However, she said her mind had been changed by "eyewitness" reports that Allende's body bore 13 bullet wounds. She added that Allende had told her he would not commit suicide but would resist a coup by force.

The chief Chilean correspondent for Prensa Latina, the Cuban news agency, reported in El Nacional of Caracas Sept. 15 that Allende had died fighting off palace invaders with a submachine gun. The correspondent, Jorge Timossi, added that Allende's former housing minister, Anibal Palma, had been executed in the palace during the coup.

The charge that Allende was murdered was aired in the United Nations Security Council Sept. 17 by the Cuban representative, Ricardo Alarcon. Alarcon denounced the Chilean junta and the U.S., asserting: "It is not difficult to know where the main responsibility lies. The trail of blood spilled in Chile leads directly to the dark dens of the Central Intelligence Agency and the Pentagon."

Alarcon's remarks, interrupted at one point by shouts from angry Cuban exiles in the gallery who opposed the island's Communist government, were subsequently denounced by Chile's new representative to the U.N. and by the U.S. delegate, John Scali. The Chilean delegate, Raul Bazan, charged that Cuba's embassy staff in Chile had been training leftist guerrillas in sabotage. Scali charged Alarcon had "descended" in his remarks to "a new low, even for those who wallow in such words as normal talk."

Charges that Allende was murdered also came from President Tito of Yugoslavia, who said Sept. 14 that "imperialist reaction" had instigated Chile's "hireling generals" to seize power.

Most Latin American governments declared brief periods of national mourning for Allende, and only Brazil and Uruguay, with governments dominated by right-wing military men, recognized the Chilean junta, both doing so Sept. 13. The governments of Sweden and Finland cut off aid to Chile Sept. 13.

The junta issued an official medical report Oct. 31 confirming its assertion that Allende committed suicide during the coup Sept. 11. The report said the president shot himself twice under the chin with a machine gun shortly after the armed forces and national police attacked the presidential palace.

Princeton Professor of Politics Paul E. Sigmund asserted in Problems of Communism (May–June 1974 issue) that "Allende ... put two bullets into his head. The automatic rifle that he used was a gift from Fidel Castro." He claimed "numerous factual errors" in reports that Allende was murdered.

U.S. denies coup complicity—The U.S. State Department and White House Sept. 11–12 declined to comment on Allende's overthrow, asserting it was an internal Chilean matter, and denied charges from Communist and other countries that the U.S. had a hand in the military coup.

However, a State Department official admitted to senators Sept. 12 that the U.S. had advance knowledge of the coup. Jack Kubisch, an assistant secretary of state, told members of the Western Hemisphere Subcommittee of the Senate Foreign Relations Committee that a Chilean officer had told a U.S. official in Chile of the coup some 10–16 hours before it occurred.

(State Department and White House spokesmen subsequently denied the U.S. had known of the coup beforehand. Paul J. Hare, State Department spokesman, admitted the U.S. embassy "did receive reports that Sept. 11 was to be the date," but said it had previously been advised of coups planned for Sept. 8 and Sept. 10, and thus considered the last prediction a rumor likely to be false. "There was absolutely no way of knowing beforehand that on any of these dates, including the Sept. 11 date, a coup attempt would be made," Hare asserted.)

The U.S. reluctance to comment on the coup was attributed to sensitivity over charges that the Central Intelligence Agency (CIA) and the International Telephone and Telegraph Corp. (ITT) had previously conspired against Allende.

(A number of large U.S. corporations whose properties had been seized by Allende's government said Sept. 11 they might consider resuming operations in Chile if the new government were receptive to investment. The companies included ITT, Ford Motor Co., and E. I. Du Pont de Nemours & Co., according to the New York Times Sept. 12.)

U.S. critics of the Nixon Administration's policies in Latin America blamed the U.S. Sept. 12 for helping create the conditions in which military intervention in Chile became likely, according to the Washington Post Sept. 13. One critic, Joseph Collins of the Institute for Policy Studies, a Washington research organization, charged U.S. "tactics" in Chile under Allende were aimed at causing "economic chaos."

Charges of CIA involvement in the coup were made in the capitals of several Communist countries and by supporters of Allende in South American and Western European nations.

Some 30,000 leftists marched past the Chilean embassy in Paris Sept. 11, denouncing the CIA for allegedly overthrowing Allende. In Rome, thousands of demonstrators held similar rallies.

The clandestine Chilean news agency Arauco alleged two U.S. airmen, Capts. M. B. Lemmons and D. C. Baird, had helped coordinate attacks by the Chilean air force during and after the military coup, the London newsletter Latin America reported Nov. 30.

Defense of the coup came from leading newspapers in Brazil, where a right-wing military regime held power.

Truckers' leader asks strike end—Juan Salas, a leader of the six-week truckers' strike, which helped cause Allende's downfall, Sept. 12 urged striking truckers to return to work Sept. 13 in compliance with military demands.

Salas, speaking on the official radio network, congratulated the truckers for maintaining the strike until then, asserting: "The effort that all of you made has been crowned with the satisfaction of seeing the fatherland free." Another strike leader, Leon Vilarin, congratulated the armed forces for deposing the president.

Organizations representing doctors, dentists, pharmacists, nurses and other professionals said Sept. 12 that their groups were prepared to return to work immediately.

Valparaiso installations attacked— Navy and army installations in the port city of Valparaiso were reported attacked by supporters of the deposed government Sept. 14. According to reports, the attacks were crushed by the military, with many of the assailants arrested and a few summarily executed. The city was placed under a round-the-clock curfew.

Scattered resistance to the junta continued in Santiago and other localities Sept. 13–17, but was downplayed by military authorities. Heavy shooting between pro-Allende snipers and military and police officers was reported the night of Sept. 13–14, and more shooting and several bomb explosions were reported the next night. Resistance to authorities in the interior of the country was reported Sept. 15. Fighting in the capital persisted Sept. 16, but was said to taper off the next day.

Trucks began delivering supplies to Santiago Sept. 15, and the city was reported returning to normal Sept. 17. The night curfew there was shortened, but the 24-hour curfew in Valparaiso was maintained.

The London newsletter Latin America reported Sept. 21 that most reports from Chile indicated there had been hard fighting between authorities and backers of Allende in industrial and working class areas. According to some reports, the attack by government supporters in Valparaiso Sept. 14 had nearly succeeded in recapturing control of the port from naval and other military authorities, and was beaten off only after heavy casualties on both sides.

The government conceded Sept. 24 that some resistance continued from supporters of the Allende government. Adm. Jose Toribio Merino Castro, navy commander and junta member, said Chile was still in a "state of internal war . . . There

are still people killing Chileans, most of them foreigners."

Military sources admitted to the news agency LATIN Sept. 28 that a number of guerrilla groups in the South had not yet been crushed. Most of their members were presumed to be from the Revolutionary Left Movement.

Military opposition to coup reported. Accounts emerging from Chile indicated there had been opposition within the armed forces to the military coup, and hundreds of officers had been killed both before the takeover and in open fighting after it, the London newsletter Latin America reported Nov. 9.

According to Latin America, "well-informed persons now leaving Santiago" said several hundred officers thought likely to oppose the coup had been shot the night before it occurred, and much of the fighting during the first three days after the takeover was among military units. A Santiago school for noncommissioned officers of the national police reportedly had held out against the insurgents for three days, and several regiments supporting the Allende government had fought bloody engagements.

These reports were corroborated by a dispatch by Jorge Timossi, former Santiago correspondent of the Cuban press agency Prensa Latina, Latin America reported. Timossi said many officers were killed or detained the night before the coup, including the then navy commander, Adm. Raul Montero, and air force Gen. Alberto Bachelet, who headed the National Distribution Secretariat under Allende. (Bachelet was to be court-martialed for "sedition" and "inciting to rebellion," according to the Santiago newspaper La Segunda Nov. 13.)

Junta in Office

New Cabinet sworn in. The military junta swore in a new Cabinet Sept. 13, two days after violently overthrowing the Popular Unity government of the late Allende.

The Cabinet consisted of 10 armed forces officers, three national police officers and two civilians. The ministers:

Interior—army Gen. Oscar Bonilla; foreign affairs—navy Rear Adm. Ismael Huerta; economy—army Gen. Rolando Gonzalez; finance—Rear Adm. Lorenzo Botuso; education—Rene Tovar; justice—Gonzalo Prieto; defense—Vice Adm. Patricio Carvajal; public works—air force Brig. Gen. Humberto Gutierrez; agriculture—air force Col. (ret.) Sergio Crespo; lands & colonization—national police Gen. (ret.) Diego Barra; health—air force Col. Alberto Spencer; labor—national police Gen. Mario McKay; mines—national police Gen. Arturo Goanes; housing—air force Brig. Gen. Arturo Vivero; and government secretary general—army Col. Pedro Cuevas.

Gen. Augusto Pinochet Ugarte, junta president, said Sept. 14 his government would implement policies of "national unity, not geared to the outdated patterns of the right or left." He charged the deposed civilian government had "gone beyond the limits of the law in a clear and deliberate manner, accumulating in its hands the greatest amount of political and economic power and putting in great danger all the rights and liberties of the inhabitants of the country."

Pinochet asserted Sept. 16, in response to questions by the New York Times, that the coup against Allende had been decided on "unanimously" by the armed forces and national police "when the military intelligence services verified the existence of large arsenals in the power of Marxist elements." He said it was "insolence" to even ask whether there had been U.S. aid or cooperation in the revolt, because "the armed forces and police of Chile, with a pure tradition of respect for legitimate authority, will never accept foreign intrusion."

Asked when parliamentary government might be restored, Pinochet declared: "When the country returns to normality and the unity of all Chileans and of Chile as a nation and a state attains sufficient strength to guarantee return to its traditional and exemplary republican democratic path. Under those conditions, elections—the sooner the better."

The new interior minister, Gen. Oscar Bonilla, asserted Sept. 14 that the coup had been staged to "safeguard the destiny of the country" against 10,000 foreign "extremists" who allegedly entered the country under Allende's government and supported a government plan to violently seize full power and institute a dictator-ship. The junta Sept. 19 added the charge that Allende had "sacked and robbed" Chile during his three years in office.

The junta received the support Sept. 13 of the two major political opposition parties, the Christian Democrats and the Nationals. The Christian Democrats made it clear that they expected an early return to constitutional rule.

Ex-President Eduardo Frei, a senator and the acknowledged Christian Democratic leader, said in a phone call to a son overseas Sept. 14 that his party had been guaranteed new elections within 6–12 months. He supported military charges that the Allende government had been preparing its own armed uprising, as did Christian Democratic party President Patricio Aylwin Sept. 18.

The leading opposition newspaper, El Mercurio, one of only two permitted to publish by the junta, praised the coup Sept. 13, declaring: "The intervention of the armed forces saved Chileans from the imminent Marxist dictatorship and from political, social and economic annihilation." Twenty-six newspapers and magazines had been closed by the junta for allegedly opposing its goal to "depoliticize" Chile's mass media.

Marxist parties banned; new Constitution planned. The military junta Sept. 21 outlawed the nation's Marxist political parties and declared the non-Marxist parties "in recess to let the country catch its breath politically." It also announced plans for a new Constitution giving the armed forces a role in future legislative bodies.

Gen. Augusto Pinochet Ugarte, junta president, charged at a news conference that the Marxist parties were responsible for the Sept. 11 military coup "because their behavior, their lack of morals and ethics, the fraud they perpetrated on the people were bringing about chaos and the downfall of the nation."

At a separate news conference, Gen. Gustavo Leigh Guzman, air force commander and also junta member, said a "committee of distinguished jurists" was working on a new Constitution, "based on a general outline indicated by the junta," which would assure the armed forces of a wider role in national affairs and "representation in legislative bodies." Congress had been closed indefinitely by the junta on the day of the coup.

The junta moves, though not the junta itself, were criticized Sept. 22 by Sen. Patricio Aylwin, president of the Christian Democratic party, who had supported the coup. Aylwin told a news conference his party was "categorically and clearly against" any attempt to use the military government "to turn back history and establish the model of a permanent reactionary dictatorship."

"Christian Democrats do not accept directives concerning changes in the constitutional Chilean regime that do not come from the people," Aylwin asserted. "No one can impose a constitutional regime, and certainly not by force of arms." He added that his party did not believe "that political parties can be suppressed by decree, nor do we believe that ideas can be suppressed by governmental decisions."

The junta took other action in a number of areas. Among the developments:

Economy—Pay raises scheduled by the ousted government for Oct. 1, to offset effects of Chile's runaway inflation, were canceled by the junta Sept. 30. Finance Minister Rear Adm. Lorenzo Gotuzzo said the move was necessitated by the nation's "economic prostration." The national currency, the escudo, was devalued by 143% Oct. 1.

Chile asked the International Monetary Fund and the World Bank Sept. 27 to help rescue it from "the brink of bankruptcy." Gen. Eduardo Cano, new president of the Central Bank, told the annual meeting of the two lending agencies in Nairobi, Kenya that Chile would "create the conditions that will form an environment in which external assistance can prove effective."

Foreign Minister Rear Adm. Ismael Huerta said Sept. 28 that "the door is open" for a resumption of negotiations on compensation for U.S. copper companies whose Chilean properties were nationalized by the Popular Unity government. However, he asserted Chile's copper mines would remain in government hands, and the country would "maintain sovereignty over its natural resources" while welcoming foreign investment in other areas.

The massive El Teniente mine was placed under the direction of new managers. Jorge Sibisa, the new general manager, said Sept. 28 that he had fired 316 workers who were "political agents," and another 467 workers hired during the previous six months. A report by the Washington Post Sept. 30 said the mine was operating full-time, with no apparent discord among workers.

The vast majority of state-run factories and businesses were placed back in the hands of the executives who ran them before the late President Salvador Allende was elected, the New York Times reported Sept. 25. Agencies administering food and price controls were abolished, new delegates were named to most state economic agencies, and pledges were made to restore to its owners land that the junta said was illegally expropriated under Allende.

Factories not returned to the private sector, such as the large textile plants, were placed under the control of military personnel.

Labor—The pro-Allende Central Labor Federation (CUT), the nation's largest labor group with some 800,000 members, was abolished Sept. 25. The junta charged CUT had "transformed itself into an organ of political character, under the influence of foreign tendencies alien to the national spirit."

Government—All mayors and city councilmen were removed from office Sept. 25.

Education—The junta obtained the resignations of all university rectors Sept. 29 as part of a plan to eliminate "the grave and conflicting problems that have practically impeded the normal development of academic activities." Concern for the Chilean tradition of university autonomy was voiced Sept. 30 by Edgardo Boeninger, resigning rector of the University of Chile, and by El Mercurio, the nation's leading newspaper.

A new education minister, Rear Adm. Hugo Castro Jimenez, was appointed Sept. 27. He replaced Jose Navarro Tobar, one of two civilians in the Cabinet named by the junta Sept. 13. Navarro, who resigned for "personal" reasons, would become Chile's ambassador to Costa Rica.

U.S., others recognize junta. The U.S. officially recognized the Chilean military junta Sept. 24. Panama, Haiti, Venezuela and South Korea followed suit that day, and other countries did so later.

The Soviet Union and its Eastern European allies refused to recognize the junta, with the Soviet Union breaking diplomatic relations Sept. 21. Moscow accused the junta of "arbitrariness, lawlessness and mockery" toward Soviet institutions in Chile, citing the alleged searching and beating of Soviet sailors during the military coup and hostile acts against Soviet citizens in the country. Yugoslavia broke relations with Chile Sept. 27.

Adm. Merino, junta member, charged Sept. 25 that 16 Soviet citizens, in Chile to help build housing, had been training Chileans in urban guerrilla warfare. The junta continued its campaign against "foreign extremists," urging citizens in radio broadcasts to turn in "foreign extremists who have come to kill Chileans." It broke relations with North Korea Sept. 23.

Casualty reports. The junta claimed Sept. 18 that 95 persons had been killed, 300 wounded and 4,700 arrested since the coup Sept. 11, but other sources asserted the toll was much higher. A government official had said Sept. 17 that 5,200 persons, including foreigners, would receive courts martial under wartime laws for alleged subversive activities.

Amnesty International, the London-based organization working to free political prisoners, charged Sept. 15 that Chilean authorities were systematically arresting and executing backers of the Allende government and that "hundreds" of workers already had been killed. One Chilean doctor reported 5,000 dead and 1,000 wounded at his hospital, Amnesty International asserted.

Unofficial estimates of the number of prisoners taken by the junta varied from 3,500 to 20,000. The high figure came from Jose Gerbasi, correspondent of El Nacional of Caracas, who reported Sept. 18 that 10,000 prisoners were being held in the national stadium in Santiago, 6,000–7,000 in other stadiums, and others in military installations. Those arrested included officials and former officials of Allende's government, including Jose and Jaime Toha, Clodomiro Almeyda and Orlando Letelier, according to a report Sept. 15.

Two British citizens arrested and held for two days said Sept. 19 that thousands of Chileans and foreigners were being subjected to "systematic brutality" in the national stadium. One of the Britons, Adrian Jansen, said there had been "Bolivians, Haitians, Nicaraguans, Brazilians, Uruguayans, Paraguayans and Guatemalans in our cell, and they were terrified." His companion said they saw "prisoners, mostly Latins, kneeling on the ground with their hands up in the air, being kicked and beaten on the calves. Another group came into our cell and appeared to have been badly beaten up."

Jansen said he had heard firing while he was in the stadium "which could only have come from inside." There were numerous reports of executions of foreigners; one Venezuelan student, Enrique Maza Carvajal, had been executed in the first hours after the coup Sept. 11, according to El Nacional of Caracas Sept. 19.

A U.S. Senate subcommittee on refugees held hearings on Chile's refugee problem Sept. 28. Sen. Edward M. Kennedy (D, Mass.), chairman of the subcommittee, deplored the Nixon Administration's "policy of silence" on the human problems resulting from the Chilean coup, and said Washington should be "in no hurry to provide economic assistance to a regime which has come to power through a violent military coup—especially after years of denying such bilateral assistance and impeding multilateral assistance to a democratically elected government."

Chile Sept. 26 released six U.S. citizens taken prisoner during the coup. Two of them claimed at Kennedy's subcommittee hearings to have heard but not seen the execution of several hundred prisoners in the national stadium in Santiago.

The body of a man identified as a missing U.S. student, Frank Teruggi Jr., of Chicago, was reported found in Santiago Oct. 3. Teruggi had been arrested by soldiers Sept. 20.

Foreign embassies in Santiago were reported concerned about the fate of their nationals in Chile under the new government, fearing many would be executed for alleged "extremism." A number of embassies also harbored Chileans seeking political asylum; Mexico, which withdrew its ambassador from Chile Sept. 14, said the next day that 332 Chileans were asking asylum in its embassy, and Argentina said Sept. 18 that 300 Chileans had taken refuge in its embassy. Some governments airlifted refugees out of Chile, but the junta informed them Sept. 23 it would no longer give Chileans safe-conduct passes for political asylum abroad.

The Chilean National Committee for Aid to Refugees, under the auspices of the U.N. high commissioner for refugees, had reached an agreement with the junta to establish 15 reception centers in Santiago and 11 in the provinces where foreign refugees would be assisted in putting their identification papers in order, or in leaving the country, it was reported Oct. 2. U.N. officials emphasized they could protect only foreigners, and not Chileans, who under international law were not considered refugees until they left the country.

Rev. Juan Alcina, a Spanish priest of the Catholic Action Workers Movement, was reported arrested Sept. 18 and found shot to death several days later. A Chilean priest, Miguel Woodward, who worked in a slum district of Valparaiso and taught at the Catholic University, reportedly died after being arrested and beaten "savagely."

The government called on Chileans to turn in all arms, allowing them to deposit them in churches to protect their identities. The Roman Catholic Church had offered to cooperate with the junta in the "reconstruction" of Chile, but was alarmed by the junta's increasing repression, particularly its arrest and expulsion of foreign priests, it was reported Oct. 1.

An office within the church reportedly had been set up to look into abuses of human rights by the junta and acts of violence toward workers, who generally supported the Allende government, and toward religious institutions.

The church hierarchy was reported concerned over the junta's dismissal of the rector of Catholic University, who had been appointed by the pope.

2,796 deaths reported. The U.S. magazine Newsweek reported in its Oct. 8 issue that, according to the daughter of a staff member of the Santiago city morgue, 2,796 corpses had been received and processed by the morgue Sept. 11–25. The junta claimed Sept. 25 that only 284 persons had been killed since the coup, but unofficial death estimates ranged as high as 5,000.

Newsweek correspondent John Barnes reported slipping into the morgue on two separate occasions and seeing at least 270 corpses. On the first occasion he saw 200 bodies, reporting that "most had been shot at close range under the chin. Some had been machinegunned in the body . . . They were all young and, judging from the roughness of their hands, all were from the working class . . . Most of their heads had been crushed."

As for corpses not delivered to the morgue, Barnes reported: "No one knows how many may have been disposed of elsewhere; a gravedigger told me of reports that helicopters have been gathering bodies at the emergency first-aid center in central Santiago, then carrying them out to sea to be dumped. One priest informed me that on [Sept. 15] he had managed to get into the city's Technical University, which had been the scene of heavy fighting . . . He told me he saw 200 bodies . . ."

Barnes reported that nearly all the victims came from the slums around Santiago. National police reportedly raided slums and took away local leaders, who later appeared on death lists issued by the government.

Leftists arrested. Luis Corvalan, secretary general of the Communist party, was arrested in Santiago Sept. 27. The junta announced Oct. 3 that he would be tried before a military court for treason, subversion, infraction of the arms-control law and alleged fraud by Communists in state-controlled industries. Conviction carried a possible death penalty.

(Corvalan's arrest led to widespread fear he would be summarily executed, and caused a shouting and shoving incident at United Nations headquarters in New York between the Chilean and Saudi Arabian delegates to the General

Assembly. The tussle, between Raul Bazan of Chile and Jamil Baroody of Saudi Arabia, followed an appeal to U.N. Secretary General Kurt Waldheim by the Soviet delegate, Yakov Malik, to intercede to save Corvalan's life. Waldheim later contacted the Chilean government and learned that Corvalan had neither been tried nor sentenced.)

Corvalan was one of 17 former government and Popular Unity coalition officials most sought by the junta. The junta Sept. 28 offered to reward citizens turning in any of the officials with the equivalent of $1,500, plus any money carried by the officials. The list included CUT President Luis Figueroa and Socialist party Secretary General Carlos Altamirano.

The junta disclosed Sept. 22 that 30 "very important persons," officials at the upper levels of the Allende government, were being held at a naval base prison on Dawson Island, in the Strait of Magellan. Interior Minister Gen. Oscar Bonilla said Sept. 29 the detainees included Clodomiro Almeyda, Jose Toha, Anibal Palma (previously reported dead), Carlos Matus, Luis Matte, Sergio Bitar, Fernando Flores and Jose Cademartori, all former Cabinet ministers, and Daniel Vergara, former interior undersecretary. Red Cross officials were allowed to visit the Dawson Island prison, it was reported Oct. 2.

Santiago Mayor Julio Stuardo, a Socialist, was arrested Oct. 1. The governor of Talca Province, German Castro Rojas, was executed Sept. 27 for allegedly killing a policeman and attempting to blow up a dam on the day of the military coup.

Meanwhile, soldiers and national police continued what they called Operation Cleanup, intended to eliminate Marxist influence from Chilean life. Left-wing students and workers were arrested, and Marxist literature was burned in Santiago. The manager of the government newspaper La Nacion, Oscar Waiss, was reported under arrest Oct. 4. (La Nacion had been handed over to the Chilean Journalists' Federation, and would resume publication under a new name, La Patria).

The leader of the neo-fascist Fatherland and Liberty party, Roberto Thieme, was released on bail along with four aides Sept. 26. They had been arrested before the coup for admitted terrorism and sabotage against the Allende government.

Radicals, API banned. A decree by the military junta Oct. 14 banned all seven parties of the deposed Popular Unity (UP) government, including the Radicals and the Independent Popular Action party (API), two groups not included in the junta's earlier ban on Marxist parties.

Gen. Gustavo Leigh Guzman, air force commander and junta member, had said Oct. 8 that the non-Marxist parties which had opposed the UP and supported the military coup, would remain "in recess" for the present. "This is not a time for discussions, dialogues, meetings, forums or Congressional debates," Leigh asserted. "We must pull this country out of its present chaos and clean it of undesirable, negative and dangerous elements. Only after achieving this will we study the suitability of authorizing political parties."

The junta's apparent determination not to restore political or civil liberties in the near future reportedly alarmed its moderate civilian supporters, despite a new assertion by ex-President Eduardo Frei that the armed forces had "saved" Chile from a "Marxist dictatorship." Frei, leader of the Christian Democrats, said in an interview in the Madrid newspaper ABC Oct. 10 that "this is a time in which politicians must be quiet."

The junta continued to receive the strong support of the neo-fascist Fatherland and Liberty party and of the right-wing National party, which suggested the regime found its own political movement similar to Brazil's governing ARENA party. The president of the Supreme Court, Enrique Urrutia Manzano, added his support for the junta Oct. 18, saying he trusted "the goodwill of the military leaders" to restore legal norms and institutions after it "re-educated" the "many people who have been led morally astray."

Arrests, executions continue. Arrests and executions of leftists continued during October and November as the junta tried to stamp out all remaining resistance. Executions announced officially included that of Jose Gregorio Liendo

("Comandante Pepe") Oct. 3. Liendo had led peasants and leftists in seizures of private farms in the South.

The junta announced 43 executions Oct. 19–Nov. 5, bringing the official total to 94. Unofficial reports continued to put the total much higher, and to estimate the overall number of deaths since the coup at more than 2,000, roughly four times the number estimated by the junta.

The junta Oct. 24 ordered an end to summary executions, but said military tribunals would continue to hand down death sentences for crimes such as treason, armed resistance and attacks on security officials. More than 30 of the officially announced executions were said to have been summary, and another 100 persons had been killed by police and soldiers while reportedly "trying to escape."

The junta claimed Oct. 6 that 513 persons, including 37 policemen and soldiers, had been killed since the coup Sept. 11. This number too was disputed by numerous sources. The New York Times reported Oct. 12 that more than 2,000 persons might have been killed during the period.

Authorities reported Oct. 6 that 1,094 leftists had been rounded up in southern Chile in massive police and troop raids. Large arms caches were also reported confiscated. The army maintained tight control of Concepcion, the reputed MIR stronghold, where many of the raids took place. In Santiago, the curfew was extended by two hours (to 8 p.m.–6 a.m.) Oct. 4.

The leaders of two of the banned Marxist parties, Carlos Altamirano of the Socialists and Oscar Garreton of MAPU, were declared common criminals by the junta Oct. 8 and denied the right of political asylum. The two and Miguel Enriquez, leader of the extremist Revolutionary Left Movement (MIR), were court-martialed in absentia for allegedly encouraging mutiny in the navy.

MIR Secretary General Pablo Henriquez Barra was reported arrested in Concepcion Province Oct. 12.

(Governments abroad continued to voice concern over the safety of Communist party Secretary General Luis Corvalan, arrested Sept. 27 but not yet court-martialed. Corvalan denied in an interview with the Associated Press Oct. 5 that the UP had planned to eliminate military and opposition leaders and institute a dictatorship. "My conscience is quite clean," he said, "because as the entire world knows, [the UP] organized a revolution without violence, without recourse to arms.")

327 persons were released Oct. 12 from the prison in Santiago's national stadium. Officials said some 3,000 prisoners remained there. The junta announced Oct. 14 that 1,316 persons had been given safe conduct to leave the country, and 386 were still hiding in foreign embassies. An airplane with 116 refugees aboard had left for Mexico Oct. 13.

Military courts began trials Oct. 17 for some 1,200 prisoners accused of "political activism" in factories, illegal possession of arms, resisting the armed forces and police, making personal profits while in public office, and other alleged crimes. Some defendants were sentenced to life imprisonment.

The junta continued to clear out the temporary prison camp in Santiago's national stadium, moving all but some 1,000 prisoners to city jails by Nov. 5. Arrests continued, however, as authorities fought what they called "pockets of resistance" remaining in some parts of the country. A resistance group in Valparaiso was reported smashed Oct. 24.

The junta claimed Oct. 26 that all prisoners remaining in the Santiago stadium were Chileans, the last 200 foreigners having been turned over to the national refugee organization for removal from the country. Foreign Minister Ismael Huerta had asserted Oct. 19 that of 5,000 persons seeking asylum in foreign embassies since the coup, only 119 had been denied safeconducts out of the country; those denied passage reportedly were former high officials in the Allende government being investigated for possible wrongdoing.

The junta confirmed Oct. 19 that a second U.S. citizen, Charles E. Horman of New York, had died since the coup. Horman was reported arrested Sept. 17 was later found shot dead.

The Latin American School for Social Sciences, founded in 1957 by the United Nations Educational, Scientific and Cultural Organization and the Inter-

American Development Bank, disclosed Oct. 21 that it had suspended its activities and sent home its foreign students for fear of their safety under the new regime.

Luis Ramallo, interim secretary general of the school, said two of the school's Bolivian students had been killed while in military custody. Twelve other persons connected with the school had been arrested since the coup and five remained in custody, despite oral assurances from authorities that the school would not be "harassed," Ramallo asserted.

Three foreign priests—two Spaniards and a Frenchman—were expelled from Chile Oct. 20 for alleged "extremist activities." Some 50 foreign clerics had been forced to leave the country since the coup, according to Roman Catholic Church sources in Santiago.

Torture charged—A three-man commission of foreign jurists charged Oct. 13 that an investigation they carried out in Santiago revealed confirmed cases of torture and summary executions since the military coup.

A commission member, Leopoldo Torres Boursault of Spain, secretary general of the International Movement of Catholic Jurists, said: "We have found cases of mistreatment of all kinds. In some cases we have interviewed the victims themselves, and in other cases the information has come from persons of absolute moral integrity, including diplomats and clerics."

Prisoners, often foreigners, were beaten, burned with cigarettes, immersed in water and given electric shocks, the commission reported. Others were summarily executed, with authorities announcing later they had been shot trying to escape.

"We send 30 to 40 missions around the world yearly and we have not seen in recent years a situation so grave as that in Chile—not even Brazil or Greece," said another commission member, Joe Nordmann of France, secretary general of the International Association of Democratic Jurists.

The commission met Oct. 12 with the junta president, Gen. Augusto Pinochet Ugarte, who denied any violation of human rights and asserted: "We must defend ourselves."

The commission also took up the problem of foreign political refugees. More than 800 political refugees had found asylum in United Nations-sponsored sanctuaries, and there was fear the junta might send them back to their own countries, where they faced arrest. The commission pointed out to Pinochet that such action would violate international conventions.

Torres and the third commission member, Muchel Blum of France, secretary general of the International Federation of Human Rights, spoke in Washington, D.C. Oct. 17 with members of the U.S. House Foreign Affairs Committee and with members of the staff of Sen. Edward M. Kennedy (D, Mass.), chairman of a Senate subcommittee on refugees.

The U.S. Senate had passed an amendment to a foreign aid bill Oct. 2 prohibiting aid to Chile until the new government guaranteed the right to seek political asylum, the right to leave the country for political asylum abroad, and humane treatment in jails and prison camps. The Nixon Administration granted Chile a $24 million credit Oct. 5 for wheat purchases, provoking an angry reaction from Kennedy, who noted the loan was "eight times the total commodity credit offered to Chile in the past three years when a democratically elected government was in power."

Criticism of the junta's treatment of both Chilean and foreign prisoners continued in foreign countries despite junta assertions that human rights were being respected and prisoners were being tried for violations of the law and not for their political beliefs.

The Inter-American Commission on Human Rights, an agency of the Organization of American States, disclosed Oct. 25 that it had sent two notes to Gen. Pinochet asking him to respect the human rights of Chileans and foreigners in his country.

The Council of the Inter-Parliamentary Union, meeting in Geneva Oct. 26, unanimously approved a resolution denouncing the junta for allowing summary executions, arresting members of Congress, and "inverting the evolution toward greater economic, social and cultural progress undertaken by the Allende presidency." The Council urged all governments to suspend all political, economic and military assistance to Chile.

Reports of abuse of human rights continued to come from foreign newsmen. Swedish journalist Bo Sourander, arriving in Stockholm Oct. 25 after being expelled from Chile, asserted prisoners in Santiago were beaten savagely and tortured, and Brazilian police interrogators had been allowed into Chile to question Brazilian political refugees arrested after the coup.

A French journalist, Pierre Kalfon of the French newspaper Le Monde, was expelled from Chile Oct. 21. He said he was deported for reporting a press conference in which three international jurists reported extensive abuse of human rights by the junta.

Other junta action. Among other junta actions:

Economy—Prices of essential articles were raised by 200%–1,800% Oct. 15 to allow them to reach their "real" level and help spur an increase in local production.

Regulation of agricultural prices was begun, and subsidies were instituted for tea, bread, noodles, sugar and vegetable oil. Workers were awarded special monthly bonuses and family supplements, but their workweek was increased by four hours.

The economy minister, army Gen. Rolando Gonzalez, was replaced Oct. 11 by Fernando Leniz, president of the El Mercurio newspaper chain, who became the second civilian member of the Cabinet. Gonzalez, who reportedly underwent surgery recently, would become ambassador to Paraguay.

The junta had said Oct. 4 that its principal financial adviser would be Rene Saez, a former general manager of the state development corporation and administrator of Alliance for Progress programs.

The rate of inflation would reach an unprecedented 1,200% by the end of 1973, Gen. Gustavo Leigh Guzman, air force commander and junta member, said Oct. 16. The official inflation rate was 323.5% through July, Guzman said, but this was based on figures falsified by the UP. "We are in for some very, very hard times," Guzman asserted. "Next winter we will undoubtedly have to ration electrical power and face other shortages. We don't want to make false promises."

The Central Bank president, Gen. Eduardo Cano, said Chile's foreign debt stood at $4 billion, it was reported Oct. 26. The country's trade deficit was $500 million.

Gen. Augusto Pinochet Ugarte, army commander and junta president, said Oct. 19 that the regime would return to their previous owners most of the more than 300 Chilean and foreign companies seized without compensation by the Allende government. These reportedly included some 40 firms in which U.S. interests had invested. Pinochet stipulated, however, that the companies must give up claims against the government for damages or losses to their installations while under government control.

Chile's new ambassador to the U.S., retired air force Gen. Walter Heitmann, said Nov. 5 the government was willing to "renegotiate the indemnization" of the major U.S. copper companies expropriated under Allende. He added, however, that compensation to the companies should be fixed by the Chilean government and should be reinvested in Chile. He suggested a compensation payment of $60 million.

Education—Retired military officers Oct. 3 assumed the rectorships of the University of Chile and Catholic University in Santiago. Gen. Cesar Ruiz Danyau, former air force commander and transport minister, took control of the first school, and navy Rear Adm. Jorge Sweet of the second.

Housing—Interior Minister Gen. Oscar Bonilla Oct. 22 called conditions in Santiago's shantytowns, or poblaciones, "a national catastrophe," and announced a program to improve them. He said a "pilot study" of some 200 poblaciones had solved their basic problems in a week, and in one shantytown, formerly called Poblacion Ho Chi Minh, the Housing Ministry had already installed electric lights, telephone service and a water pump, and had begun building a school.

The Chilean authorities were replacing Marxist leaders of the poblaciones with non-Marxist junta supporters, in many cases Christian Democrats, the New York Times reported Oct. 16. Many of the former poblacion leaders had been arrested and some had been reported executed.

The junta also had radically altered delivery of food and medical services in the shantytowns, formerly under left-wing control. Government warehouses that had distributed food and household goods at cheap, subsidized prices had been closed in favor of more expensive private groceries and other shops. The clinic system created by the UP to bring medical facilities into the poblaciones was being dismantled in favor of the large, central hospital system backed by conservative medical authorities.

Civil liberties—A decree Oct. 17 forbade all political activity by individuals, parties or other organized groups.

Pinochet said in an interview with the newspaper El Mercurio Oct. 27 that the state of siege would continue for at least eight more months. He admitted some armed resistance to the junta continued, particularly in the South.

Government—The junta announced Oct. 26 a sweeping reorganization of virtually all public services and enterprises in which the state had a majority interest. Dismissals of thousands of public employes had been reported since the coup, according to press accounts Oct. 17. More than 500 persons, including 155 journalists, reportedly had lost their jobs in the state and private press and broadcasting.

The junta announced its intention Oct. 29 to establish a national youth secretariat to "promote the great moral values of the Chilean nation" and "open broad and renewed horizons to all youth."

Press—Four foreign newsmen were expelled by the junta Oct. 15 for allegedly sending false dispatches abroad. They were listed as Philippe Labreveux, of the Paris newspaper Le Monde, who had left Chile the previous week; Grazie Mary Cervi (believed to be Italian journalist Mario Cervi, who also had left); Leif Person, a Swede; and Peter Sumberd, otherwise unidentified.

(A Brazilian journalist, Flavio Vanderley of the Rio de Janeiro opposition weekly Opiniao, was reported missing Oct. 18. A spokesman for the airline Swissair reportedly said he had been arrested.)

Defense of Coup & Junta

Junta defended at U.N. Foreign Minister Ismael Huerta defended the military junta before the United Nations General Assembly Oct. 10, charging foreign reports of abuse of human rights in Chile constituted a "most false, most malevolent, most vicious and very well-orchestrated campaign."

The delegations of Cuba, the Soviet Union, Algeria, Tanzania and at least 16 other nations walked out of the Assembly as Huerta rose to speak, but there was some applause from Latin diplomats. Eight demonstrators in the public gallery were evicted during Huerta's address after they shouted anti-junta slogans.

Huerta asserted the armed forces had overthrown the late President Salvador Allende and his Popular Unity coalition (UP) to avert what he called a totalitarian takeover largely instigated and supported by Cuba. To support this contention, Huerta read and later distributed to newsmen a handwritten letter which, he said, had been sent to Allende by Cuban Premier Fidel Castro July 29.

In the alleged letter, Castro offered his cooperation "in the face of the difficulties and dangers obstructing and threatening the [Chilean] process." He wrote of the need for Allende to "gain time to organize forces in case the fight breaks out " and urged the president not to "forget for a second . . . the vigorous support offered by the working class."

Huerta charged foreign agents sent principally by Cuba had smuggled into Chile enough Soviet- and Czech-made weapons to equip 20,000 men. He added that more than 13,000 foreign extremists had been admitted to the country under Allende to establish "a parallel army to oppose the regular armed forces." These foreigners, Heurta charged, had become directors of public offices, taken illegal control of factories, and in a few cases, joined Chilean delegations in international negotiations.

Huerta later held a press conference in which he outlined "Plan Z," which, he claimed, had been devised by Cuba and the UP to seize "absolute political power" in Chile. The plan, to have been carried out Sept. 17–19, while troops were occupied in national independence anniversary celebrations, allegedly involved assassination of the armed forces commanders, political leaders, and business and management organization executives.

In response to questions about the military takeover of Chilean universities, Huerta said the junta sought to return the schools to their "teaching and investigative functions." He barred any future participation in the universities by Marxists. In response to questions about the junta's expulsion of several foreign journalists, Huerta said: "Chile opens its doors to newsmen and to all who wish to verify the truth."

Cuban response—Cuban Ambassador Raul Roa returned to the General Assembly after Huerta's address and delivered a bitter denunciation of the Chilean junta and the U.S., which he accused of directing the overthrow of Allende.

He called Huerta "a sergeant of Goebbels," and asserted the Chilean had been telling Nazi-style "big lies" while the junta committed Nazi-style atrocities.

Chilean Ambassador Raul Bazan rose after Roa concluded and repeated Huerta's charges against Cuba. He then attacked Premier Castro personally, asserting Castro had made it his "daily pastime" to watch the execution of political opponents and to invite foreign diplomats to the spectacle.

The attack on Castro caused Roa to shout at Bazan and rush to the podium with a few other Cuban representatives to silence the Chilean. The Cubans were stopped by U.N. guards and other delegates. Eyewitnesses said later that some of the Cubans had carried pistols under their jackets and one had warned, "Be careful, I am armed!"

Junta White Paper justifies coup. The military junta issued a 264-page White Paper Oct. 30 purporting to explain why it overthrew the Popular Unity (UP) government of the late President Salvador Allende Gossens.

The report asserted the armed forces had taken power because Allende had sought to "decapitate" them and because he had presided over the "economic, social, institutional and moral ruin" of Chile.

The bulk of the document was devoted to "Plan Z," the alleged Marxist plot to assassinate military and opposition political leaders during national independence celebrations Sept. 17–19. However, the report provided little actual documentation of the alleged plan, failing to state where it was discovered, to list persons or organizations directly linked to it, or to provide strong evidence of its endorsement by Allende.

Certain documents in the White Paper indicated the Socialist and Communist parties had discussed in detail the possibility of a coup and the armed action to be taken against it. However, one Socialist document asserted a well-organized coup would be impossible because of political divisions among military officers and the presumed impossibility of keeping the revolt a secret during its planning stages.

The report asserted large caches of arms had been discovered in Allende's private residences ("enough to equip without difficulty about 5,000 men"), and that the president had used his home on the outskirts of Santiago as a guerrilla training camp. Photographs of the alleged caches were included in the White Paper.

'72 military plotting revealed. Gen. Augusto Pinochet Ugarte, junta president, revealed that the armed forces had plotted to overthrow the government of the late President Salvador Allende since mid-1972, and had decided to seize power May 28, not immediately before the Sept. 11 coup, as previously claimed, the Washington Post reported Dec. 29.

U.S. policies linked to coup. U.S. Rep. Michael J. Harrington (D, Mass.) said in Santiago Oct. 27 that U.S. economic policies of "deprivation" had set in motion the events that led to the Chilean military coup.

Harrington asserted that three days of intensive contacts in Chile, including a two-hour meeting with three of the four military junta members, had reinforced his view that "United States economic policy was the really damaging part of our relationship" with the deposed government of President Salvador Allende.

He stressed "the enormous pressures [the U.S.] brought to bear" on the late President by curbing credits, expressing "chilling interest" in the private sector, and failing to continue economic programs. "We lost a major opportunity in not trying to deal with the freely elected government," Harrington declared, asserting the U.S. could have demonstrated pluralism by cooperating with Allende's Marxist experiment.

Harrington said the junta members had "tried to convey" to him "a strong sense of legitimacy for what they had done," but had been evasive when he expressed "concern over the suppression of the rights of expression and political parties."

Harrington was a member of the House of Representatives' Subcommittee on Inter-American Affairs, which received secret testimony Oct. 11 on Central Intelligence Agency (CIA) operations in Chile during Allende's presidency. The testimony, by CIA Director William E. Colby and agency official Frederick D. Davis, was obtained by journalist Tad Szulc, who reviewed it in an article in the Miami Herald Oct. 22.

Testimony by Colby and Davis, at times unclear and contradictory, touched on "the CIA's own very extensive role in Chilean politics, but it also helps in understanding and reconstructing the [Nixon] Administration's basic policy of bringing about Allende's fall one way or another," according to Szulc.

"The [CIA] activities described range from the 'penetration' of all the major Chilean political parties, support for anti-regime demonstrations and financing of the opposition press and other groups to heretofore unsuspected agency involvement in financial negotiations between Washington and Santiago in late 1972 and early 1973 when Chileans were desperately seeking an accommodation," Szulc wrote.

"There are indications that the CIA, acting on the basis of its own reports on the 'deterioration' of the Chilean economic situation, was among the agencies counseling the White House to rebuff Allende's attempts to work out a settlement on the compensations to be paid for nationalized American property and a renegotiation of Chile's $1.7 billion debt to the United States," he continued.

"The Nixon Administration's firm refusal to help Chile, even on humanitarian grounds, was emphasized about a week before the military coup when it turned down Santiago's request for credits to buy 300,000 tons of wheat [in the U.S.] at a time when the Chileans had run out of foreign currency and bread shortages were developing," Szulc noted. "On Oct. 5, however, the new military junta was granted $24.5 million in wheat credits after the White House overruled State Department objections. The department's Bureau of Inter-American Affairs reportedly believed such a gesture was premature and could be politically embarrassing.".

Colby reportedly told the subcommittee that the CIA and the National Security Council had felt it was "not in the United States' interest" for Allende's government to be overthrown. He made the comment in response to a question about a similar statement reportedly made by Jack Kubisch, assistant secretary · of state for inter-American affairs.

A letter Oct. 8 from Richard A. Fagen, professor of political science at Stanford University, to Sen. J. William Fulbright, chairman of the Senate Foreign Relations Committee, reported that Kubisch had told a group of U.S. scholars, "It would have been better had Allende served his entire term, taking the nation and the Chilean people into complete and total ruin. Only then would the full discrediting of socialism have taken place. Only then would people have gotten the message that socialism doesn't work. What has happened has confused this lesson."

Arrests, resistance continue. Arrests of supporters of the ousted government continued in Santiago as further resistance to the junta was reported in the South.

The junta announced the arrest of eight "Communists and extremists" in the capital Nov. 14, and of 20 alleged Marxists there Nov. 22.

In the South, some 1,000 specially trained anti-guerrilla troops began operating at the beginning of November in the area between Concepcion and Osorno, it was reported Nov. 17. Seven guerrillas were reported killed in an unsuccessful attack Nov. 11 on an army regiment in the southern city of Temuco.

The junta said Nov. 22 it had awarded safe-conducts out of the country to 4,342 of the 4,480 Chileans who had taken refuge in European or Latin American embassies in the capital. It added it had expelled 487 other Chileans and had allowed out 182 foreigners hiding in facilities of international organizations.

The national stadium in Santiago was reported cleared of prisoners Nov. 11. Red Cross official Robert Gaillard-Moret, allowed to visit the country's major prison camps, said he had found prisoners in good health and under humane treatment.

The Washington Post reported Nov. 8 that Pedro Ramirez, mines and later housing minister in Allende's Cabinet, had disappeared after being held by authorities for a week. Ramirez, a son-in-law of Radomiro Tomic, former Christian Democratic presidential candidate, had been virtually the only high official of the Allende government not arrested during the first month after the military coup.

Another leftist, Dewest Bascunan, director of the bi-monthly magazine Andino, had been found dead after attempting to flee to Argentina, the Santiago newspapers El Mercurio and La Prensa reported Nov. 8.

The junta Nov. 15 announced confiscation of all goods and property belonging to the outlawed Marxist parties and other left-wing groups.

Former Bolivian official abducted— Jorge Gallardo Lozada, former Bolivian interior minister, reportedly was kidnapped from his exile home in Santiago and returned to his country on orders of the Bolivian government.

Gallardo's wife, Maria Eugenia Paz, said Nov. 5 that her husband had been seized the week before by two men in civilian clothes—one armed with a submachine gun—and two soldiers. The Chilean Bureau of Investigations denied knowledge of the incident, but the Bolivian government admitted Gallardo had returned to Bolivia two days after his abduction, according to a report Nov. 23.

Mrs. Gallardo insisted her husband had "retired from politics" and that his abduction was "an act of vengeance" by the Bolivian government for a book he had written in 1972. The book, "From Torres to Banzer—Ten Months of Emergency in Bolivia," treated the overthrow of the government of Gen. Juan Jose Torres, under whom Gallardo served, by Gen. Hugo Banzer Suarez, the current president, and implicated the U.S. Central Intelligence Agency and the Brazilian government.

Universities purged. Thousands of leftist students and professors had been suspended from universities, and many faced possible permanent expulsion, it was reported Nov. 14.

Military rectors had closed whole departments or universities that they considered leftist strongholds, and had encouraged right-wing students and professors to denounce Marxist colleagues. Most departments of the University of Chile had been assigned a "prosecutor," usually a law professor, to receive written or oral denunciations. The denounced were not allowed to face their accusers.

The eastern campus of the University of Chile in Santiago had been closed because of alleged Marxist penetration of its social science and political science departments, and some 8,000 students there, mostly leftists, had been suspended. At the University of Concepcion, the most important academic center south of the capital, some 6,000 of 16,000 students and hundreds of professors had been suspended.

About 70 students and 44 of the 360 professors had been suspended from the University of Chile Law School. Some 1,500 students in the university's schools of fine arts, music and architecture also had been suspended along with about 100 professors.

Teachers' colleges to be reorganized— The junta Dec. 13 appointed a commission to direct the reorganization of the nation's teachers' colleges. The reorganization was to "end the situation of anarchy in the technical, administrative and pedagogic aspects of teacher training," and "re-establish the principles of order, discipline and morality," the official decree said.

Cuban, Soviet ships held in Panama Canal. Freighters owned by the Cuban and Soviet governments were detained by U.S. authorities in the Panama Canal Zone in October and November at the request of Chilean companies demanding delivery of cargo they claimed to have paid for previously.

A Cuban freighter, the Imias, was detained by U.S. federal court order Oct. 2 at the request of Chile's National Sugar Industry and its Vina del Mar Refining Co., which claimed two other Cuban vessels, the Playa Larga and the Marble Island, had failed to deliver more than 18,000 metric tons of sugar purchased for more than $8 million.

The Playa Larga had been unloading its sugar in the Chilean port of Valparaiso Sept. 11, the day of the Chilean military coup, and had escaped with much of its cargo after being bombed and strafed by Chilean air force rebels. It had met the Marble Island a day later in the Pacific and warned it not to proceed to Chile. The Chilean firms had attempted to have the Marble Island detained Oct. 1 in the Panamanian port of Balboa, at the entrance to the Canal, but the vessel had escaped.

Panama officially protested the detention of the Imias Oct. 4, asserting that under international law the U.S. had no legal jurisdiction over a vessel owned by a foreign government.

A Soviet freighter, the William Foster, was detained in the Canal Oct. 13 by order of U.S. federal Judge Guthrie Crowe, at the request of two Chilean firms claiming to have paid $309,000 for some of its cargo, including electrolytic zinc. This was protested by the Panamanian National Assembly Oct. 18.

An out-of-court settlement was reached on the William Foster at the behest of the U.S. State Department, it was reported Nov. 7. The vessel was freed after it agreed to transfer its Chilean-bought cargo to another Soviet vessel for shipment to Chile via Peru.

The Imias was freed by court order Nov. 13, also at the request of the State Department.

Constitution draft approved. The military junta Nov. 29 approved a draft for a new Constitution which would establish an "organic democracy" and assure "the incorporation of all sectors of activity in the process of collective decision-making."

According to Enrique Ortuzar, president of the jurists' commission that drafted the document, the new Constitution would contain a mechanism to prevent the election of a minority government—such as the one overthrown by the junta—and would provide for resolution of conflicts between the executive and legislative branches by plebiscite.

Like the previous Constitutions of 1833 and 1925, Ortuzar said, the new one would "maintain and strengthen public liberties, without discrimination; guarantee equality before the law, and the freedoms of conscience, worship, learning and expression. It will also respect the right to property."

The document would reaffirm the importance of political parties, but these could act "only within their proper orbit," Ortuzar said. Parties would not be allowed to "intervene" in "public administration or in elections or labor conflicts in universities, educational establishments, economic associations or labor unions," he asserted.

Parties which "oppose the democratic system of government will be declared unconstitutional," Ortuzar siad, apparently referring to the now outlawed left-wing organizations. Persons who "agitated against the democratic regime" and "defended crime and political violence" would "not be able to exercise any public function," he added.

The Constitution would guarantee the independence of the judiciary and the comptroller general's office, he said. The armed forces and national police would remain "essentially professional, hierarchical, disciplined, obedient and non-deliberative," always understanding that "their obedience is to the entire institutionality of the country and that it can never mean, as the previous regime intended, a political subjugation to the president of the republic."

The role of the military would continue to be the protection of Chile's internal and external security, in defense of which the armed forces and police had "freed the nation from the international communism which was destroying it," Ortuzar asserted.

Swedish envoy expelled. The government Dec. 4 declared Swedish Ambassador Harald Edelstam "persona non grata" and accused him of exceeding his authority as a foreign diplomat. He was the first non-Communist envoy to be asked to leave Chile since the military coup Sept. 11.

Edelstam had said he and four embassy secretaries had been beaten Nov. 25 by soldiers and police who arrested a Uruguayan woman under their protection.

Edelstam asserted he and his aides were assaulted at a clinic in Santiago as they tried to prevent authorities from seizing Consuelo Alonso Freiria, who had sought asylum three weeks earlier in the Cuban embassy, under Swedish protection since Chile and Cuba broke relations Sept. 13. Alonso had been recovering from an emergency operation when the incident occurred. She was taken by the authorities to a prison clinic.

The Chilean Foreign Ministry denied Nov. 26 that there had been violence at the clinic but criticized Edelstam for trying to prevent Alonso's arrest. It alleged Edelstam had acted "improperly" because Alonso had given up diplomatic asylum in leaving the Cuban embassy. Edelstam asserted the army had approved her move from the embassy, and she thus remained under Swedish protection.

Swedish Foreign Minister Sven Andersson and United Nations high commissioner for refugees, Prince Sadruddin Aga Khan, formally protested the incident Nov. 26.

A high Chilean police official, Jaime Vasquez, alleged Nov. 28 that Uruguayan Interpol officers had identified Alonso as Mirta Ercilia Fernandez, widow of a Tupamaro guerrilla leader, and said she was wanted in Uruguary for "terrorist conspiracy and falsification of public documents."

Alonso was allowed to leave Santiago for Stockholm Dec. 3 after authorities determined that she had not participated in domestic "subversive" activities. The police Dec. 1 had given the press a sworn statement by Alonso confirming that she was actually Mirta Ercilia Fernandez, widow of a Tupamaro leader, as the police had claimed, and had entered Chile illegally.

Edelstam had vigorously defended the rights of political refugees in Chile since the military coup Sept. 11. He was credited with single-handedly preventing troops from storming the Cuban embassy and with protecting the estimated 20–32 Chilean and foreign refugees who had sought asylum there. He also was a major backer of the international effort to win guarantees for the security of opponents of the new military junta.

Troops had surrounded the Cuban embassy Nov. 6 and had arrested a Swedish newswoman and two Chilean chauffeurs of the Swedish embassy attempting to enter the building. Edelstam protested the action the next day and secured the release of the journalist—Margarethe Sourander, wife of Swedish newsman Bo Sourander, arrested and deported earlier—and the drivers. He complained that Swedish embassy automobiles were searched illegally and that he was forced to sleep at the Cuban embassy every night "to protect the refugees."

The Chilean government asserted the Cuban embassy had been surrounded because persons inside it had fired on security forces outside. Edelstam denied this.

Edelstam left Santiago Dec. 9. Arriving in Stockholm the next day, he charged that some 15,000 persons had been killed in Chile since the coup, 7,000 had been arrested and 30,000 left homeless. He noted that arrests were continuing and alleged that political prisoners were being tortured.

Swedish Foreign Minister Sven Andersson Dec. 4 had protested Edelstam's expulsion and commended Edelstam for working "more than any other person [in Chile] to save refugees." Sweden said Dec. 5 it would not name a new ambassador to Chile. Swedish aid to Chile was canceled Dec. 11.

Miriam Contreras, personal secretary to the late President Salvador Allende and one of the 10 persons most sought by the government, had taken asylum in the Swedish embassy, according to government sources Dec. 5. Orlando Cantuarias, a former Cabinet minister and vice president of the Radical party, left the embassy Dec. 9 and surrendered to police.

Estimates of the number of Chilean and foreign refugees remaining in Western European and Latin American embassies in the capital ranged from 500–700, reported by the Washington Post Dec. 11, to some 2,000, reported by the French newspaper Le Monde the same day. Le Monde reported the junta had decided to give no more safe-conducts abroad to refugees in embassies of countries that had not signed asylum conventions with Chile. These reportedly included most Western European nations.

The Geneva-based Intergovernmental Commission on European Migrations said Nov. 30 that some 1,200 refugees of 28 nationalities had been transferred from Chile to 26 countries since the coup. The majority, about 800, went to Western Europe, and the others to Latin American states. Sweden, the Netherlands and France were the European nations most willing to take refugees from Chile, according to Le Monde Dec. 5.

The U.S. had offered to allow foreign refugees stranded in Chile after the military coup to enter the U.S. under a special "parole" arrangement suspending certain immigration restrictions, it was reported Dec. 1. The offer—initially suggested by Sen. Edward M. Kennedy (D, Mass.)—had been made more than a month before, but fewer than 30 persons had accepted it.

The Latin embassies with most refugees were those of Argentina, Mexico and Venezuela. Some reports said the refugees remained there because Chile would not grant them safe-conducts, and others asserted the nations in question were reluctant to admit leftists because of their own domestic conditions. The Washington Post reported Dec. 11 that Chileans in the U.S. said the junta had denied safe-conducts to 200–300 Chilean refugees who had been at one time or another leaders of the ousted Popular Unity coalition.

The Bogota newspaper El Tiempo Nov. 29–30 criticized the treatment by the Chilean junta of refugees in the Colombian embassy in Santiago. It also charged Colombian actions to protect refugees had been "weak and irregular."

The wife of Oscar Garreton, leader of the left-wing MAPU party and one of the junta's 10 most wanted persons, had charged Nov. 29 that the junta had offered safe-conducts to a dozen refugees in the Colombian embassy in exchange for Garreton, who was also in the embassy.

In a related development reported Dec. 6, three persons were wounded and captured when they tried to scale the fence around the Panamanian embassy in Santiago and gain asylum there. Panama, Honduras and Costa Rica reportedly had been the Latin countries most willing to take Chilean refugees.

The junta told European embassies in Santiago Dec. 10 that it would not grant courtesy safe-conduct abroad to persons who took political asylum in the embassies after Dec. 11. Military guards were strengthened outside all embassies Dec. 10 to prevent political refugees from gaining entrance.

The Times of London reported Dec. 12 that more than 2,000 foreign refugees remained in hostels set up by the United Nations High Commissioner for Refugees. Their political background reportedly made them unwelcome in their own countries, and some lacked the official visas necessary to leave Chile.

West German Chancellor Willy Brandt said Bonn would give asylum to more Chilean refugees than any other European nation, it was reported Dec. 11. He said 40 refugees from Chile had arrived in West Germany Dec. 7.

Ex-minister wounded. Ex-Agriculture Minister Rolando Calderon was shot in the head Dec. 19 by a sniper who fired into the Cuban embassy in Santiago, where Calderon had taken refuge after the military coup. He was not wounded seriously, but was taken to a military hospital after receiving safe conduct from the junta.

Torture reports continue. The Mexico City newspaper Excelsior Dec. 7 printed photographs of what it called four separate instances of torture of detainees at the national stadium in Santiago, which until recently was used to hold persons arrested after the military coup.

The French weekly Politique Hebdo, cited by the Cuban press agency Prensa Latina Nov. 9, alleged political prisoners in Chile were forced to walk on hot coals or with broken glass in their shoes, and were subjected to other "scientific" tortures administered with the aid of "specialists" from Brazil and Uruguay.

Prensa Latina also reported that executions of leftists were continuing. (The government later stopped announcing executions to improve its image abroad, the Miami Herald reported Dec. 10.) The junta announced one execution Dec. 1, bringing the official total to 95. Socialist Congressman Luis Espinoza Villalobos was shot to death Dec. 4 while "attempting to escape" from a military patrol transferring him from one prison to another.

The French newspaper Le Monde reported Nov. 29 that at least 18 doctors had vanished, been arrested or executed since the military coup. Five had been executed, including Enrique Paris, a member of the Communist party's central committee; 10 had disappeared, including former Health Minister Arturo Jiron and National Health Service Director Sergio Infante; and three had been arrested, including Alfredo Jadresic, former dean of the medical faculty of the University of Chile at Santiago.

Persecution of leftist doctors had been organized within the medical profession, Le Monde reported. A commission had been named at each health center to classify personnel politically and report to military authorities. Denunciations were encouraged, and all doctors in directorial positions were replaced with supporters of the new government. Many doctors detained during or immediately after the military coup had been abused, and one—Martin Cordero, now living in London—had been tortured, Le Monde reported.

Other arrests continue—The government announced the capture of 10 "extremists" in Concepcion Nov. 28 and of seven "extreme left terrorists" in Curico and Concepcion Provinces Dec. 9. Seven prisoners had been condemned to life imprisonment by a military court in Talca Nov. 8.

Communist party Secretary General Luis Corvalan and several other political prisoners—including former Cabinet minister Pedro Felipe Ramirez, previously reported disappeared, and Anselmo Sule, former Radical party president—had been transferred to the prison on Dawson Island, in the Strait of Magellan, where high

officials of the ousted government were held, Le Monde reported Nov. 30.

Other political prisoners were at Chacabuco and Pisagua, in the north, and on Quiriquina Island, in front of the Talcahuano naval base in the south. Some 500 prisoners on Quiriquina were being forced to build their own prison, El Nacional of Caracas reported Dec. 9.

Sources within and outside Chile reported that former Interior Undersecretary Daniel Vergara, held on Dawson Island since the coup, had died Dec. 9 of gangrene from an unattended wound suffered during the coup. The navy asserted Dec. 11 that Vergara was alive at a naval hospital at Punta Arenas, where he was being treated for an infected hand.

Two other former government officials, Werber Villar and Rigoberto Achu Liendo, both Communists, were killed in northern Chile Dec. 14 while allegedly trying to escape from authorities, according to the French newspaper Le Monde. The army announced Dec. 22 that five "terrorists" had died in a gun battle with troops in Santiago after they were discovered trying to blow up a city power supply line.

The navy confirmed Dec. 19 that two more persons had been condemned to death, presumably for "terrorist" activities, bringing the official number of executions to about 100.

Carlos Altamirano, secretary general of the outlawed Socialist party and one of the junta's 10 most wanted men, said in a message broadcast by Havana radio Dec. 18 that all democratic forces in Chile should unite for "a long struggle, inevitably victorious," against the junta. The junta had denied earlier reports that Altamirano had surrendered to undergo medical treatment.

Mrs. Allende sees Trudeau. Hortensia Bussi de Allende, widow of President Salvador Allende, met with Canadian Prime Minister Pierre Trudeau in Ottawa Nov. 30. At a subsequent press conference she urged Canada to aid Chilean political refugees and cut off loans to and trade with Chile's "fascist" military junta.

Since her husband's ouster and death Sept. 11, Mrs. Allende had visited several Latin American and European cities to seek help for Chilean political refugees and political prisoners.

Chileans abroad to lose citizenship. A spokesman for the junta told United Press International Dec. 10 that Chileans abroad who attacked "the essential interests of the state" would lose their citizenship.

The spokesman said there were some 50 persons "directing the campaign against Chile abroad," including Hortensia Bussi de Allende, widow of President Salvador Allende; Volodia Teitelboim, former Communist senator; and Armando Uribe and Carlos Vasallo, former ambassadors to East Germany and Italy, respectively.

Other foreign developments—A Chilean mission led by Leon Vilarin, a leader of the truckers' strike that helped precipitate the military coup, was expelled from Venezuela Dec. 3. The group was on an international tour to explain the current Chilean "reality" and offset bad publicity being given the junta in the foreign press. The mission and the Chilean Foreign Ministry accepted Venezuela's explanation that the expulsion was dictated by security considerations for the Venezuelan presidential election Dec. 9.

Vilarin's group proceeded to the Dominican Republic, where its scheduled press conference Dec. 5 was boycotted by the national newsmen's union. The union denounced the mission for "making propaganda" for Chile's "ferocious and brutal military dictatorship."

The Congo Republic broke relations with Chile Dec. 7.

Private U.S. loans increase. Loans to Chile by private U.S. banks had increased sharply since the military junta overthrew the left-wing government of the late President Salvador Allende, the New York Times reported Nov. 12.

Manufacturers Hanover Trust Co. of New York announced a $24 million loan to the Bank of Chile Nov. 9, and banking sources quoted by the Times said Manufacturers Hanover had extended an additional $20 million loan to the Central Bank. Financial sources in Santiago added that eight to 10 U.S. banks and two Canadian banks had offered Chile commercial loans totaling about $150 million since the armed forces took power.

In a related development, an international bank syndicate including three U.S. banks—Bankers Trust, Irving Trust and First National City Bank—and several Canadian banks had opened a $170 million credit line to Chile, according to the Andean Times' Latin America Economic Report Dec. 14.

U.S. government loans also were made available after the coup. The U.S. Agriculture Department disclosed granting a $28 million loan to Chile to buy U.S. corn, it was reported Nov. 16. The U.S. earlier had provided a $24 million credit for wheat purchases.

Copper negotiator named. The government Dec. 13 named Julio Philippi, a former finance minister, as its representative for projected talks with U.S. copper firms whose property was expropriated by the ousted government.

Economy Minister Fernando Leniz, announcing the appointment, stressed that it meant only that the government was willing "to discuss the issue" of compensation to the U.S. companies.

The U.S. had agreed to renegotiate its share of Chile's foreign debt—whose total, according to the junta, was $3.2 billion—without prior compensation to U.S. copper companies for property expropriated without payment under Allende, it was reported Nov. 16. This concession followed a visit to the U.S. by Foreign Minister Ismael Huerta, who defended the junta at the United Nations and conferred with officials of Kennecott Copper Corp., Anaconda Co. and other firms.

The junta already had offered to compensate the copper companies, but it had virtually no cash to do so; reserves in the Central Bank reportedly totaled only $3.5 million.

U.S. debt repayment pact. The U.S. State and Treasury Departments announced Dec. 21 that the U.S. and Chile had reached agreement on repayment of $124 million in Chilean debts over the next eight years.

Chile reportedly agreed to pay $60 million over a four-year period beginning with a $16 million payment Dec. 28, and another $64 million over six years beginning Jan. 1, 1975, adding a 6% yearly interest rate.

The Wall Street Journal reported Dec. 28 that Chile had sent the U.S. $19.5 million for the first installment, with the extra $3.5 million to be kept in reserve.

Economic developments. The government Nov. 28 devalued the escudo and reduced taxes on imports.

The newspaper La Segunda reported Nov. 23 that the state development corporation CORFO had drawn up a list of 88 businesses and industries to be returned to their owners because they had been "illegally" confiscated by the Allende government.

Military authorities announced that 115 nationalized companies, including 12 controlled by foreign capital, were being returned to their former owners, it was reported Dec. 11. Among the first returned were four U.S.-owned motion picture distributors.

Two U.S. firms, General Tire International and Dow Chemical, said Nov. 7 they had been invited to resume operations in Chile.

The first strike since Allende's overthrow, by some 200 manual workers on Santiago's subway system demanding higher wages, was broken when army troops occupied the site and warned that strikers would be dismissed immediately, it was reported Nov. 23.

The government Dec. 5 decreed a ban on domestic beef sales to last Dec. 8–18.

The junta Dec. 19 announced its 1974 wage policy. It set a single pay scale for public employes, including the armed forces and police, and provided for 500% wage increases, based on salaries earned in January 1973, for private sector employes. Pensions and annuities were similarly increased, and family bonuses were doubled.

The government's special economic adviser, Orlando Saenz, had resigned on grounds he had completed the task entrusted to him, the London newsletter Latin America reported Dec. 14.

October inflation up 87.6%—The cost of living in Chile rose by 87.6% in October,

increasing the rate of inflation for the first 10 months of 1973 to 449.2%, according to the National Statistics Institute Nov. 13.

The institute said the October figure reflected price increases ordered by the junta shortly after the military coup to put the economy on a more "realistic" basis. The junta had estimated inflation might reach 1,200% by the end of 1973.

The junta was being forced to print large amounts of new currency to meet many of its financial commitments, despite having criticized the Allende government for doing so and thus adding to inflation, the Andean Times' Latin America Economic Report noted Nov. 16. The 70% increase in the money supply from September to the end of 1973 would be higher than for any period under Allende before May.

Land reform ends—Chile's land reform program, begun in 1960 under conservative President Jorge Alessandri, was ended Dec. 19 when the military junta decreed that land could no longer be expropriated.

Most land designated for agrarian reform by previous governments reportedly was being turned over to peasants with individual deeds of ownership, to be purchased over 30-year periods.

The Agrarian Reform Institute Nov. 16 began returning to their former owners agricultural properties of less than 40 hectares expropriated by the ousted government.

Voting records voided. The junta Nov. 19 nullified all electoral records, including recent voter registrations, while it studied creation of a new system to prevent vote fraud and guarantee the "seriousness and efficiency" of the electoral process.

An Interior Ministry decree announcing the action charged "investigations pursued by public and university organizations have proved the existence of grave and extensive vote fraud," particularly in the March congressional elections, in which the deposed government did better than expected.

The junta had claimed in its recent White Paper justifying the military coup, that an investigative commission of the Catholic University had found the government benefited from numerous irregularities in the elections, including double registration of voters and ballots cast for deceased persons.

The junta Nov. 12 dissolved as "unnecessary" the Constitutional Court, established by the ousted government to resolve disputes between the executive and legislative branches.

The junta announced Nov. 14 that public employes would be barred from participating in politics and would be observed regularly by government inspectors to see that they worked "in a real spirit of discipline."

Santiago elections barred. An edict signed by Gen. Sergio Arellano, commander of the Santiago Province emergency zone, prohibited "elections of any type—be they in unions, economic associations, politics, schools or any other groups." Vacancies in elected offices would henceforth be filled in consultation "with the corresponding representative of the military junta." The edict, issued Dec. 16, applied only to Santiago Province.

Newspaper closed. Interior Minister Gen. Oscar Bonilla said Nov. 28 that the left-wing tabloid Clarin, closed since the coup, would not reappear. Three other leftist papers—El Siglo, Puro Chile and Ultima Hora—previously had been closed permanently.

1974: Aftermath

Repression Charged

During 1974 the Chilean military junta faced continued charges that it was guilty of wholesale killings, political arrests and torture of prisoners. Controversy flared in in the U.S. late in 1974 over testimony that the CIA had spent $8 million to "destabilize" the government of the late Salvador Allende. The junta, meanwhile, reached settlements on payments to be made to U.S. companies for expropriated copper properties, and it made progress in negotiating foreign loans and renegotiating foreign debts.

Altamirano accuses junta. Ex-Sen. Carlos Altamirano, the leftist most sought by the military junta, appeared Jan. 2 in Havana, where he attended celebrations marking the 15th anniversary of the Cuban revolution.

Altamirano said at a press conference the following day that since the September 1973 coup 2/3 of Chile's Socialist national and regional leadership had been killed or imprisoned, but the party remained alive and committed "to fight until the complete defeat of the fascist military junta."

Altamirano charged that since the coup, more than 15,000 persons had been "assassinated," more than 30,000 arrested

for political reasons, thousands tortured, more than 200,000 dismissed from their jobs and more than 25,000 expelled from universities.

He charged that many priests had been killed or imprisoned and 175 had been deported. Altamirano praised the many priests who had helped leftists escape from Chile but denounced the Roman Catholic hierarchy for not speaking out against the junta's "atrocities."

Jara murder charged. Victor Jara, a well-known leftist folk singer, was murdered in the national stadium in Santiago after the military coup, according to an article by a Chilean refugee in Argentina printed by the Buenos Aires newspaper La Opinion Jan. 3.

Torture charges continue. Amnesty International charged Jan. 20 that the military junta had allowed widespread torture of political prisoners under the guidance of "foreign experts," specifically Brazilian police agents.

Amnesty Secretary General Martin Ennals said in a letter to Gen. Augusto Pinochet Ugarte, junta president, that an Amnesty commission that had visited Chile in November had interviewed political prisoners who showed "visible signs of torture" and prison guards who freely admitted the training of Chilean interrogators by Brazilian agents. The guards reportedly referred to a four-day training course given by the Brazilians in the Chilean Defense Ministry building.

Ennals charged recent reports from Chile indicated torture of political prisoners and other abuses of human rights were continuing.

The Amnesty team—Frank C. Newman, of the University of California Law School at Berkeley; Bruce W. Sumner, presiding judge of the Orange County, Calif. Supreme Court, and Roger Plant, an Amnesty staff researcher—spoke with prisoners and guards in the National Stadium in Santiago, since then vacated of prisoners. According to Ennals, they were given "considerable liberty" to conduct their inquiry.

The commission's findings, released at United Nations headquarters in New York Jan. 18, were rejected by the junta, which said the commission had refused to go outside Santiago and thus could not make a well-founded judgment on Chile as a whole. A spokesman for the commission said the inquiry had been limited because its members were short of time.

Excerpts from the Amnesty report:

SOME INTRODUCTORY QUESTIONS

1. In Chile are there prisoners of conscience? The answer is Yes.

Because of their beliefs are people threatened with detention, though they have neither used nor advocated violence? The answer is Yes.

In our opinion the statement in the UN General Assembly on October 9, 1973, that "We do not persecute anyone for political reasons in Chile," was not accurate.

2. Are prisoners treated humanely? The answer is No.

Far too many detainees have been kept incommunicado, their families advised as to neither the fact of arrest nor the place of detention....

3. Is torture used?

In our opinion the 2d statement in the UN General Assembly on October 9, 1973, that "We have no tortures in Chile," also was not accurate.

Yet as of November 8, when we left, we believe that, in the Santiago area, at least, the use of torture had decreased....

4. Are people being executed? The answer is Yes.

In our opinion the 3d statement in the General Assembly on October 9, that "We do not murder anyone in Chile", was inaccurate if Ambassador Bazan meant to imply that since September 11 the Government forces have killed no one without just cause,

without trial. (Cf. to his letter of September 25 to the UN Secretary General, SG/SM/1893, p. 2: "(H)uman rights will be faithfully observed in Chile.... Regarding the insidious rumours about tortures and mass or arbitrary executions in Chile, my Government denies them with its utmost vigor...")

Near the end of October the government decreed that summary executions should cease. Since then executions are said to be pursuant to sentence of the courts martial. Often at night we heard gunfire; no one suggested to us during our stay that people thus were executed. Many people believe, though that killings of "fleeing prisoners" have not in fact been justified....

6. Was international law violated by the arrests, detentions, interrogations, and killings that have taken place since September 11?

The answer is Yes....

It was reported in Peru that Alejandro Jiliberto, administrative undersecretary of the outlawed Socialist Party, had been tortured and lay near death in a Santiago military hospital, according to the Cuban press agency Prensa Latina Jan. 16.

The French newspaper Le Monde confirmed Jan. 24 that Jiliberto, a former legislator, had been arrested at the end of December 1973 and was in grave condition.

(The Geneva-based International Commission of Jurists declared May 16 that three of its members had visited Chile for 10 days in April and found that Chilean political prisoners were systematically subjected to "various forms of ill treatment, sometimes amounting to severe torture.")

Torture report disclosed—The Mexican newspaper Excelsior May 16 published excerpts from an extensive report on torture of Chilean political prisoners. The document had been prepared by a Chilean interchurch group called the Comite de Cooperacion Para la Paz (Committee of Cooperation for Peace).

The committee was sponsored by Chile's Roman Catholic, Protestant and Jewish religious leaders. Its report, not intended for publication, was obtained by Excelsior director Julio Scherer Garcia during a recent visit to Chile. Scherer wrote the May 16 article and subsequent reports on other aspects of repression by the junta.

The report cited at least 134 cases of

torture of political prisoners and 12 cases of death by torture since the September 1973 military coup. "The tortures noted here," it declared, "are only those that leave no margin of doubt. They have been recalled by those who suffered them, or recounted by those who witnessed them."

The cases were cited by date, location and type of torture. The tortures included beatings, burns, immersion in water, electrical shock and simulated executions.

A spokesman for the junta charged May 17 that the Excelsior story was "a grave distortion of reality" based on "material of dubious quality." Chile's censored press denounced the Mexican newspaper, with El Mercurio, Santiago's leading daily, accusing it of starting "a new campaign against the junta."

Excelsior published another article by Scherer May 19 reporting that since the military coup 25% of Chile's university professors had been fired and 20,000 students suspended or expelled for political or moral reasons.

France takes 1,000 refugees. The French newspaper Le Monde reported Jan. 3 that France led all nations in accepting refugees from Chile, having welcomed some 1,000 persons fleeing the military regime. The figure was confirmed the next day by French Premier Pierre Messmer.

The Geneva-based Intergovernmental Committee on European Migration had reported Jan. 2 that since mid-October 1973, 2,225 refugees, about half Chilean, had left Chile for other countries. Most reportedly went to Western Europe, with the largest number, 442, going to Sweden, and the next largest, 385, to France.

Vuskovic, Del Canto leave. Two officials of the ousted government, former Economy Minister Pedro Vuskovic and ex-Interior Minister Hernan del Canto, were allowed to go into exile after spending several months in foreign embassies in Santiago.

Del Canto flew to Colombia April 13 and Vuskovic to Mexico April 21.

The Mexican government had given top priority to obtaining Vuskovic's release, the Washington Post reported April 22.

Mexican Foreign Ministry sources said Mexico had conditioned future purchases of Chilean goods on Vuskovic's emigration.

The governments of Colombia and Venezuela had accused the junta April 9 of procrastinating in granting safe-conduct passes to persons who had taken asylum in their embassies in Santiago.

Colombia, Mexico withdraw envoys. Colombia officially withdrew its ambassador from Chile May 20 and rejected the credentials of Chile's new ambassador in Bogota May 22. Mexico had withdrawn its ambassador from Santiago April 19.

The Colombian action, which the Chilean junta called "deplorable," followed the junta's refusal to grant safe-conduct passes abroad to the refugees who remained in the Colombian embassy in Santiago. The Mexican move followed strained relations between Mexico and Chile since the September 1973 coup.

Kennedy denounces junta. U.S. Sen. Edward M. Kennedy (D, Mass.) excoriated the military junta Feb. 3 and urged President Nixon to "condition any U.S. military or economic assistance on the junta's respect for human rights and progress in the restoration of constitutional government."

"More than four months after the violent overthrow of the Allende government," Kennedy said, "the junta continues its gross violations of human rights. Reports in many quarters—including our own government as well as the most respected international humanitarian organizations—suggest continued repression, the denial of safe-conduct passes to many political refugees, new waves of arrests, the torture of prisoners, and executions at an alarming rate."

Kennedy, chairman of the Senate Judiciary Subcommittee on Refugees, released a partially censored version of a Jan. 28 State Department letter replying to a series of questions he submitted to the department on conditions in Chile. Specific estimates of deaths during the military coup were deleted, but Kennedy said they were "in the thousands."

U.N. unit asks rights observance. The United Nations Human Rights Commission sent a message to the military junta Feb. 28 asking it to end "all violations of human rights, committed in defiance of the principles enunciated in the United Nations Charter and in other international documents . . ."

The Commission said it had "examined with profound uneasiness the numerous reports from diverse sources according to which flagrant and massive violations of human rights have been committed in Chile." It asked in particular that the junta release five important political prisoners—Clodomiro Almeyda, Luis Corvalan, Enrique Kirberg, Pedro Felipe Ramirez and Anselmo Sule—whose "situation has been reported as dangerous."

The message resulted from a compromise in which the Soviet Union agreed to drop a resolution condemning the suppression of human rights in Chile, in return for which Chile dropped a resolution denouncing Moscow's treatment and exiling of writer Alexander Solzhenitsyn.

Chile reportedly agreed to release the men, two of whom—Corvalan, head of the outlawed Chilean Communist Party, and Kirberg, a former university rector—the Soviets were particularly concerned about.

The message followed an emotional appeal to the Commission Feb. 25 by Hortensia Bussi de Allende, widow of Chilean President Salvador Allende. She asked the Commission to condemn the Chilean junta for "genocidal repression."

Although U.S. immigration authorities allowed Mrs. Allende to make the U.N. appeal, they prohibited her from traveling to Washington, D.C., where she was scheduled to appear at a press conference on Chile organized by Sen. Edward M. Kennedy (D, Mass.), the Cuban press agency Prensa Latina reported Feb. 26.

Kennedy was among several U.S. legislators who sponsored a Capitol Hill forum on Chile financed by the Fund for New Priorities, the Washington Post reported March 11. He told the forum that several international investigations and "the innumerable personal accounts that have been submitted to my office

disclose the grossest violations of human rights" in Chile.

Continuing Chilean repression had created unease among U.S. government officials, according to Latin America March 22. The Central Intelligence Agency estimated 11,000 persons had been killed in Chile between the coup and the end of November; State Department officials were prepared to accept estimates of up to 20,000 and conceded that killings were continuing at a rate of 20–50 a week, Latin America reported.

Political arrests continued, keeping pace with releases of political prisoners, and included members of apolitical religious groups. The junta announced March 22 that it had transferred to the Pisagua prison camp, in the northern desert, five leaders of the Silo movement who had been held in Santiago for more than a month. Siloists advocated a communal, nonmaterialistic way of life; the junta accused them of being "servants of international communism" seeking to implant "malignant ideas in youthful minds" and destroy the traditional family system.

An earlier police raid on the Santiago temple of the Divine Light Mission resulted in the arrest of 208 disciples of the young Indian guru Maharaj Ji, the New York Times reported March 24.

A State Department official said April 15 that the U.S. had expressed concern over reports of human rights violations in Chile, the Washington Post reported April 16. Chilean Foreign Minister Ismael Huerta, in the U.S. April 15, said he was unaware of the expression of concern.

Toha suicide reported. The military junta announced March 15 that former Interior and Defense Minister Jose Toha Gonzalez, a close aide of the late President Salvador Allende, had hanged himself in a Santiago military hospital.

The announcement was challenged by Chilean and foreign leftists, ecclesiastical authorities and independent observers, who doubted that Toha, who apparently was dying of stomach cancer, was strong enough to hang himself. Former Chilean Socialist Party leader Carlos Altamirano charged in Paris that Toha had been murdered after being subjected to more than six months of "extreme physical and psychological tortures."

The primate of Chile's Roman Catholic Church, Raul Cardinal Silva Henriquez, celebrated a requiem mass for Toha in the Santiago cathedral March 17, a service never celebrated for suicides. An estimated 3,000 mourners followed the funeral procession, and many shouted leftist slogans banned after the September 1973 military coup. Former Socialist Sen. Aniceto Rodriguez was prevented from delivering the funeral oration by military authorities.

Among the mourners were members of the former opposition political parties, including Tomas Pablo, ex-president of the Senate, and Fernando Castillo Velasco, former rector of Catholic University. Some sources reported a number of arrests after the ceremony.

Junta President Gen. Augusto Pinochet Ugarte March 20 rejected charges that Toha had been murdered and denounced Carlos Altamirano as "a mollusk trying to leave tracks which he couldn't establish in Chile."

Toha's death followed by two days the death of air force Gen. Alberto Bachelet, the highest-ranking military officer awaiting trial for his services to the Allende government. The junta claimed that Bachelet had died after a heart attack, but sources cited by Le Monde March 24 said he had been tortured.

'Poblaciones' conditions poor. Conditions in Santiago's "poblaciones" (shantytowns) had deteriorated markedly since the military coup, with a reappearance of delinquency, heavy liquor traffic and disease, Le Monde reported Jan. 5.

Left-wing leaders who had helped organize the poblaciones, eliminating crime and improving health and housing conditions, had either disappeared or been arrested or killed since the coup, Le Monde reported. One leader, a woman linked by the press to Alejandro Villalbas (Comandante Mickey), leader of the Nueva Habana poblacion, had been tortured, according to Le Monde.

Local clinics had been dismantled, leading to a reappearance of diarrhea in infants, and the price of public housing had been raised so high that members of poblaciones could no longer afford it, Le Monde said.

Pinochet assumes executive powers. Gen. Augusto Pinochet Ugarte assumed sole executive powers as president of Chile June 26. The other three members of the ruling military junta were assigned subordinate advisory and legislative roles in his government.

According to press reports, the development reflected Pinochet's growing power and the apparent failure of the collective military leadership.

A decree published June 25 proclaimed Pinochet "supreme chief of the nation" for an indefinite period, with "special powers" to:

Dictate decrees to "execute the law;" control the armed forces and the judiciary; name Cabinet ministers, diplomats, provincial chiefs and judges; hire and fire government employes, and control the nation's budget; maintain diplomatic and commercial relations with other countries; declare a state of emergency in the event of foreign invasion or internal commotion; order the arrest and transfer of persons anywhere in Chile, and pardon convicted criminals.

Legislative power was assigned to the commanders of the three armed forces and the national police. Pinochet remained army commander; the other service chiefs were navy Adm. Jose Toribio Merino, air force Gen. Gustavo Leigh and police Gen. Cesar Mendoza. Merino was placed in charge of economic legislation, Leigh of social policy and Mendoza of agriculture, according to the London newsletter Latin America June 28.

Domestic Dissent

Opposition to the junta's allegedly repressive rule was expressed publicly during 1974 by an increasing number of church and political spokesmen.

Church magazine criticizes junta. The Roman Catholic review Mensaje, founded by Jesuits, asserted in its most recent issue that "force" would not enable Chileans to build a "fatherland" where "justice and brotherhood exist not only in speeches but in actions," it was reported Jan. 25. This was considered the first overt criticism of the junta by a sector of the Chilean church, which was divided by the military coup.

In a similar development Jan. 22, El Mercurio, the nation's leading newspaper, criticized the junta's strict censorship of the media. The critique was printed in full in the paper's Valparaiso edition but censored in the Santiago edition. It said, among other things, that Chileans must be allowed "to face the truth." El Mercurio had vigorously supported the junta since the coup.

Christian Democrats criticize junta. Leaders of the Christian Democratic Party made their first major criticism of the military junta's social and economic policies but denied that they had broken with the armed forces.

The criticism was contained in a letter to the junta president, Gen. Augusto Pinochet Ugarte, from party President Patricio Aylwin and First Vice President Osvaldo Olguin. It was dated Jan. 18 and reported by the foreign press Feb. 8.

"A lasting order cannot be created on the basis of repression," the letter declared. "Many Chileans have been or are being deprived of their jobs, detained, censored, threatened or pressured in different ways without any justification other than the ideas or opinions which they profess, or which are attributed to them."

The letter denounced the "denial of any real possibility of adequate defense for accused persons; preventive detention of undetermined length for people who are not tried by competent tribunals; and the use of moral or physical pressures to obtain confessions." These constituted "a denial of justice and a grave violation of human rights," the letter charged.

The letter also protested the suspension of political party activity and denounced "a systematic and malevolent campaign against the Christian Democrats." It added: "We are convinced that the absolute inactivity of the democratic sectors facilitates the underground efforts of the Marxist groups. Without guidelines from their leaders, our rank and file members and sympathizers are at the mercy of rumor, trickery and infiltration."

As for economic matters, the letter protested junta policies that, it said,

placed the heaviest burden on the poor. "The remunerations of workers barely permit them to feed themselves and in many cases do not allow them to meet the vital needs of their families," the letter declared. "We do not exaggerate when we say that there are many who are hungry. Meanwhile, there are businesses whose profits exceed all expectations. No one can ignore the injustice of this situation and the dangers which it entails."

Aylwin met with Interior Minister Gen. Oscar Bonilla Jan. 28 and 29. He said in a subsequent private memorandum that Christian Democratic leaders wanted the period of military rule "to be as brief as possible" but understood "that it cannot be too brief, that it can last two, three or maybe five years," the New York Times reported Feb. 8.

Bonilla was said to have replied to the Christian Democratic criticism by asserting that repression was necessary to defeat groups which proposed violence and "have the arms to do it," according to the Miami Herald Feb. 10. Defense Minister Patricio Carvajal said Feb. 11 that the junta's ultimate objective was "to prevent a return to the polluted democracy which allowed a minority of demagogues as dupes to take command of the nation."

Even the right-wing National Party, a vigorous supporter of the junta, had protested the repression, the Washington Post reported March 23. Former National Sen. Francisco Bulnes said he had protested the suspension of political activities and other arbitratry measures, but had been ignored by the junta.

Cardinal Silva threatened. Raul Cardinal Silva Henriquez, archbishop of Santiago and primate of Chile's Roman Catholic Church, said in a sermon April 14 that he had received threats against his life and was being protected by bodyguards.

Silva sharply criticized the military junta, asserting it had not listened to the church's protests against continuing repression. "That is why we cry today, with the pain of a father who sees the break-up of his family, the struggle of his children, the death of some and the imprisonment and suffering of many among them," Silva said.

The junta asserted April 14 that Silva's life had been threatened by "leftist extremists."

Bishops criticize junta. Chile's Roman Catholic Church issued a statement April 24, criticizing the military junta for its economic policies, political repression and violations of human rights.

The declaration, titled "Reconciliation in Chile," was endorsed by a majority of the nation's bishops. It was distributed by Raul Cardinal Silva Henriquez, primate of the Chilean church, who said he had received a telegram from Pope Paul VI urging Chile's bishops to continue their efforts toward national conciliation and pacification.

"We are concerned, in the first place, with the climate of insecurity and fear [in Chile], whose roots we believe are found in accusations, false rumors and the lack of participation and information," the bishops declared.

"We are also concerned with the social dimensions of the current economic situation . . . [including] the increase in unemployment and job dismissals for arbitrary or ideological reasons," they continued. "We fear that, by accelerating economic development, the economy is being structured in such a way that wage earners must bear an excessive share of sacrifice without having the desired level of participation . . ."

After expressing concern over the junta's educational policies, which allegedly denied "enough participation by parents and the academic community," the bishops protested against "the lack of effective legal safeguards for personal security that is evident in arbitrary or excessively long detentions in which neither the persons concerned nor their families know the specific charges against them; in interrogations that use physical and moral pressures; in the limited possibilities for a legal defense; in unequal sentences in different parts of the country; in restrictions of the normal rights of appeal."

The bishops said they did not doubt the "righteous intention nor the good will of our governors. But as pastors, we see objective obstacles to reconciliation among Chileans. Such situations can be overcome only by the unrestricted respect for human rights as formulated by the United Nations and the Second Vatican Council."

The criticism was rejected by Gen. Gustavo Leigh, air force commander and junta member, who said of the bishops: "I have great respect for the church, but like many men, without realizing it, they are vehicles for Marxism."

Anti-church campaign denounced. Chile's Roman Catholic bishops issued a declaration May 29 charging a "hateful campaign" had been unleashed against them, particularly against Raul Cardinal Silva Henriquez, the church primate, and Fernando Ariztia, his auxiliary bishop.

Silva had been bitterly attacked in letters printed in Chile's censored newspapers throughout May, while he was on a trip to the U.S., Europe and the Vatican. Following his return, he was honored at a mass June 5 in the Santiago cathedral, where he was cheered by thousands of poor and lower middle class residents, including relatives of political prisoners and supporters of the ousted Popular Unity government.

A spokesman for the junta said May 25 that it had broken up a subversive group of priests and members of the outlawed Revolutionary Left Movement who allegedly received coded orders from Moscow. The junta said the next day that a leader of the group, Deacon Mario Irarrazabal, had been arrested and expelled from Chile, and four other priests, all members of a group called "Christians for Socialism," had been ordered seized and deported.

U.S. Properties & Foreign Loans

Dow units returned. The U.S. firm Dow Chemical Co. said Jan. 4 that the junta had formally returned to it two Chilean affiliates "requisitioned" by the ousted government in October 1972.

The units, reportedly worth more than $32 million, were Dow Quimica Chilena S.A., a polystyrene producer 100% owned by Dow, and Petroquimica Dow S.A., a low-density polyethylene and polyvinyl chloride producer owned 70% by Dow and

30% by two Chilean government agencies.

The junta said Jan. 4 that it would return to their previous owners all commercial banks nationalized by the ousted government.

Cerro compensation pact. Cerro Corp. announced March 12 that Chile had agreed to pay at least $41.9 million for its Chilean copper interests, which were nationalized in 1971.

Under an agreement signed in Santiago by representatives of the U.S. firm and the Chilean military junta, Cerro would receive a $3.2 million cash payment—already delivered—and nearly $38.7 million in 17-year notes carrying a 9.165% interest rate. The notes, guaranteed by Chile's Central Bank, would be free of Chilean taxes.

The settlement appeared to cover most of Cerro's interest in Compania Minera Andina S.A., the expropriated firm. Cerro's 1972 annual report said its investment in Andina totaled $39.7 million, including equity, notes and interest.

The agreement also provided for Cerro to purchase "copper-bearing materials" which could not be processed in Chile. As Cerro sold these materials, the proceeds would be applied to repayment of the notes, in inverse order of maturity.

Cerro was the only one of the three major U.S. copper firms in Chile maintaining cordial relations with the deposed government after its properties were nationalized. Cerro had continued to provide technical assistance to the Chilean operators of Andina's Rio Blanco mine.

Anaconda settlement. The military government and Anaconda Co. of the U.S. announced July 24 that they had reached a settlement over the 1971 expropriation of Anaconda's two Chilean subsidiaries.

The subsidiaries, Chile Exploration Co. and Andes Copper Mining Co., operated the Chuquicamata and El Salvador copper mines. Chile had purchased 51% of the companies in 1969 under President Eduardo Frei and had nationalized the other 49% two years later under the late President Salvador Allende.

Under the settlement, Chile immediately paid Anaconda $65 million—$59 million for the Allende seizure and $6 million for the Frei purchase—and signed $188 million worth of promissory notes guaranteed by the Chilean Central Bank. The notes bore an annual interest rate of 10% and were payable in equal installments semiannually over a 10-year period beginning Feb. 1, 1975.

Anaconda said all prior claims and controversies between it and the Chilean government were resolved, including all claims for Chilean taxes, all legal actions in Chile and the U.S. and all claims regarding notes issued to Anaconda's subsidiaries at the end of 1969.

The settlement also left Anaconda free to continue arbitration of its claim against the Overseas Private Investment Corp. (OPIC) regarding the 1971 expropriation. OPIC was a U.S. government agency that insured U.S. businesses abroad.

OPIC and the Chilean government June 19 signed an agreement rescheduling payment of a $22 million Chilean debt to the agency. Approximately $19 million of the debt, plus interest, covered installments due under a series of promissory notes guaranteed by OPIC. The notes originally had been held by Braden Copper Co., the Chilean subsidiary of Kennecott Copper Corp., and had been sold to private investors.

Kennecott announced it would continue to press its claim for compensation for the 1971 seizure of its Chilean properties with the military junta's copper negotiator, Julio Philippi, it was reported July 29.

Chile's large copper mines—formerly operated by Kennecott, Anaconda and Cerro Corp.—reported that production in January–June had increased by 44% over the same period of 1973, according to the newsletter Latin America July 19.

Chile had already paid OPIC more than $1.5 million in a first step toward repaying OPIC $8.2 million to cover defaults by the ousted government to Braden Copper Corp. and the Bank of America, it was reported Feb. 11. The full payment would be made over the next seven years.

Foreign loans & debts. Chilean Central Bank President Gen. Eduardo Cano returned from a visit to Brazil with $50 million in credits from the Brazilian government, it was reported Jan. 10. Late in 1973 he had signed two agreements with Argentina for loans totaling $20 million.

The International Monetary Fund Jan. 30 approved a stand-by arrangement allowing Chile to borrow the equivalent of $94.8 million over 12 months to overcome a serious foreign exchange deficit. The credit was granted after IMF officials in Washington, D.C. conferred with members of a Chilean economic mission that had arrived in the U.S. Jan. 28.

Finland canceled a credit pact signed with the Allende government in August 1973 for an ambitious forestry development program, it was reported Feb. 1. Finland said conditions in Chile "have changed so much that the continuation of cooperation does not correspond with the spirit nor the aims of the agreement."

A disputed $22 million loan to help finance the Chilean junta's agricultural recovery program had been "rammed through" the Inter-American Development Bank by the U.S. over the opposition of several Latin American nations, the Washington Post reported April 2. The credit was approved without the usual technical review of the application, to which Mexico and Venezuela, among other nations, objected. The money would be used to provide credits for farmers, farm cooperatives and agricultural organizations to purchase equipment, seed, fertilizers and insecticides.

The Inter-American Development Bank April 25 approved a $75.3 million loan to help build a hydroelectric power plant in Antuco, south of Santiago. The loan was an expanded version of one denied to the ousted government in 1972. U.S. support for the loan was attacked April 26 by U.S. Sen. Walter Mondale (D, Minn.), who noted Chile was a military dictatorship under investigation by the Organization of American States.

The junta had signed an agreement with General Motors Corp. April 11 for General Motors to resume manufacturing automobiles in Chile.

Japan's Marubeni Corp. granted a $12 million loan to Chile's state electricity firm to purchase four gas turbine generators for the mining and industrial areas of northern Chile, it was reported May 3.

'Paris Club' renegotiates debt—Chile's 12 creditor nations agreed March 25 to refinance 80% of Chile's foreign debt falling due between Jan. 1, 1973 and Dec. 31, 1974.

The accord, following an agreement in principle Feb. 23, covered more than $750 million, including $200 million already consolidated by the ousted Popular Unity government, according to Chilean economic adviser Raul Saez.

The creditor nations, known as the "Paris Club," were the U.S., West Germany, Belgium, Canada, Denmark, Spain, France, Japan, the Netherlands, Sweden, Great Britain and Switzerland.

The agreement, keyed to Chile's commitment to compensate U.S. copper companies, allowed Chile to repay only 5% to 10% of $1 billion due in 1974. However, Chile would have to repay other outstanding debts, and they reportedly would raise 1974 repayments to $200 million.

The Netherlands, a minor creditor, had tried unsuccessfully Feb. 21 to persuade the major creditors to withhold agreement until the Chilean junta liberalized its domestic policies. The U.S., Great Britain and West Germany rejected the proposal as an "introduction of political questions in a financial negotiation."

Despite its estimated $4 billion foreign debt, Chile had taken an estimated $570 million in foreign loans since the September 1973 military coup, it was reported March 15.

Britain ends aid, arms sales. Great Britain's Labor government March 27 cut off aid and military sales to Chile to underscore its "desire to see democracy and human rights fully respected" by the military junta. The junta responded March 29 by threatening to suspend copper shipments to Britain.

British Foreign Secretary James Callaghan told the House of Commons March 27 that new arms export licenses would not be granted to Chile and that existing contracts were being "urgently" reviewed. He referred to a $120 million contract under which Britain was building two warships—one already delivered—and two submarines for the Chilean navy.

Overseas Development Minister Judith

Hart announced the same day that there would be no new aid to Chile and that current aid was being halted except for support for Chilean students and graduates coming to Britain and financing for completion of one or two minor technical assistance projects. British aid to Chile in the six months ending March 31 was estimated at $1,632,680.

Chilean Mines Minister Gen. Arturo Yovane said March 29 that he would recommend that the junta suspend all shipments of copper to Great Britain. He expressed surprise over the British move, asserting that "Chile has always cooperated with Great Britain without considering momentary circumstances," and that "the matter of [Chilean] political prisoners has been cleared up."

(But he said April 10 that Britain would deliver to Chile the three remaining warships it had agreed to build under a contract signed with the government of President Eduardo Frei in 1969. These would be the last British arms deliveries to Chile, Callaghan said.)

Foreign investment invited. The military junta July 11 enacted a new Statute of the Foreign Investor drafted specifically to attract foreign capital to Chile.

The law declared that foreign investment was indispensable for an accelerated rate of economic growth in Chile, and barred discrimination between national and foreign investments. It established a Foreign Investment Committee to oversee new transactions between Chile and foreign firms.

Foreign companies would be allowed to send "invested capital, utilities or benefits" out of the country. However, "foreign investment in areas reserved by law to national companies" would not be accepted, the law stated.

U.S. Aided Allende Downfall?

Covert CIA action reported. A major controversy was touched off in Washington Sept. 8 by testimony that the Nixon Administration had approved covert activities by the Central Intelligence Agency in Chile in 1970–73 in an effort to undermine the government of the late President Salvador Allende Gossens.

To finance these activities, more than $8 million was authorized by the so-called 40 Committee, a high-level intelligence panel chaired by Secretary of State Henry Kissinger in his capacity as national security adviser to former President Nixon, according to testimony by CIA Director William E. Colby to the Subcommittee on Intelligence of the House of Representatives' Armed Services Committee.

Colby's testimony, given in executive session April 22, was revealed in a confidential letter from Rep. Michael J. Harrington (D, Mass.), a critic of U.S. Chilean policy, to Rep. Thomas E. Morgan (D, Pa.), chairman of the House Foreign Affairs Committee. The letter was leaked to the New York Times and the Washington Post.

Harrington asked Morgan to open a full investigation into the CIA's role in the September 1973 military coup in which Allende died and his elected government was overthrown. He said he had appealed to other legislators including Sen. J. William Fulbright (D, Ark.), chairman of the Senate Foreign Relations Committee, and Rep. Dante Fascell (D, Fla.), chairman of the House Foreign Affairs Subcommittee on Inter-American Affairs, but none had been willing to pursue the matter.

Colby's testimony was made available to Harrington by Rep. Lucien N. Nedzi (D, Mich.), chairman of the intelligence subcommittee. Harrington reported the testimony from memory, having been allowed to read it twice but not to take notes. According to his letter, Colby testified that:

■ In 1969, before Allende's election, the 40 Committee authorized about $500,000 to "fund individuals who could be nurtured to keep the anti-Allende forces alive and intact." (The CIA, Colby testified, had spent $3 million to help Christian Democrat Eduardo Frei defeat Allende in the 1964 presidential election.)

■ During the 1970 election, the committee approved $500,000 to help "opposition party personnel."

■ After the election, which Allende won by a plurality, the committee earmarked $350,000 in an unsuccessful effort "to bribe the Chilean Congress" to choose Allende's opponent in the runoff vote.

■ After Allende's inaugural, the committee authorized $5 million for "more destabilization efforts during the period from 1971 to 1973."

■ About $1.5 million was earmarked by the committee to help opposition parties in Chile's 1973 Congressional elections, in which Allende's coalition improved on its 1970 vote percentage. "Some of these funds were used to support an unnamed but influential anti-Allende newspaper," according to Harrington's account.

■ In August 1973, during the wave of strikes that precipitated Allende's downfall, the committee authorized $1 million for "further political destabilization activities." The program was called off when Allende was overthrown, but the funds were spent after Chile's military government was installed, Colby testified.

The CIA's activities in Chile, Harrington wrote, "were viewed [by the Nixon Administration] as a prototype, or laboratory experiment, to test the techniques of heavy financial investment in efforts to discredit and bring down a government."

Disclosure of Colby's testimony brought immediate protests from a number of sources, including Democratic legislators and newspaper editorials. The New York Times said Sept. 8 that Colby's testimony indicated the State Department and the White House had "repeatedly and deliberately misled the public and the Congress about the extent of U.S. involvement in the internal affairs of Chile."

Sen. Edward M. Kennedy (D, Mass.) charged Sept. 9 that CIA funding of Allende's opponents "represents not only a flagrant violation of our alleged policy of non-intervention in Chilean affairs but also an appalling lack of forthrightness with the Congress." He noted that the CIA activities disclosed by Colby had been "denied time and time again by high officials of the Nixon and now the Ford Administrations."

Sen. Frank Church (D, Ida.), chairman of the Senate Foreign Relations Subcommittee on Multinational Corporations, which investigated attempts by International Telephone & Telegraph Corp. (ITT) to subvert Allende's government, said to news personnel Sept. 11 that he was "incensed" by Colby's testimony. During the ITT hearings, two State Department officials—Charles A. Meyer, former assistant secretary of state for Latin American affairs, and Edward M. Korry, former ambassador to Chile—had testified under oath that the U.S. had maintained a policy of non-intervention toward Chile under Allende. They also refused to answer specific questions about what they said were privileged communications on U.S. policy toward Allende.

The staff of Church's subcommittee, headed by chief counsel Jerome Levinson, issued a report, leaked to the press Sept. 16, recommending that perjury investigations be initiated against Meyer, Korry and former CIA Director Richard Helms, who testified during 1973 hearings on his confirmation as ambassador to Iran that the CIA had not passed money to Allende's opponents.

The staff report also accused Kissinger of "deceiving" the Senate Foreign Relations Committee in secret testimony Sept. 17, 1973, shortly after the Chilean coup. Kissinger had minimized the role of the CIA in Chile's 1970 election, asserting the agency's objectives were "to strengthen the democratic political parties and give them a basis for winning the election in 1976." The report recommended that the record of hearings for Kissinger's confirmation as secretary of state be reopened and that he be asked to give a "rationale" for covert CIA activities in Chile.

(Kissinger's direct involvement in efforts to undermine Allende was described in "The CIA and the Cult of Intelligence," a book by two former U.S. intelligence officials, which was published in June after being partially censored at the CIA's request. A deleted passage in the book quoted Kissinger as telling the 40 Committee on June 27, 1970: "I don't see why we need to stand by and watch [Chile] go Communist due to the irresponsibility of its own people," the New York Times reported Sept. 11.)

The State Department, meanwhile, stood by its previous assertions that the U.S. had not intervened in Chilean internal affairs after Allende's election. State Department spokesman Robert Anderson Sept. 9 backed the testimony of Korry and Meyer before the Senate multinationals subcommittee. Korry defended his testimony Sept. 15, asserting the U.S. had pursued "an extraordinarily soft line" toward Chile during Allende's first year as president, during which Korry was U.S. ambassador.

Colby refused to comment on his reported testimony, although he did not deny that Harrington's account of it was accurate. He emphasized Sept. 13 that the CIA's covert activities in Chile were approved by the National Security Council and thus reflected "national policy." He added that "the chairman or various members of" key Congressional committees had been kept informed of these activities.

Ford admits U.S. role. At a televised news conference Sept. 16, U.S. President Gerald R. Ford conceded that the U.S. had engaged in covert activities against the Allende regime.

Ford was asked: "Is it the policy of your Administration to attempt to destabilize the governments of other democracies?"

Ford responded that it was "a very important question:"

"Our government, like other governments, does take certain actions in the intelligence field to help implement foreign policy and protect national security. I am informed reliably that Communist nations spend vastly more money than we do for the same kind of purposes. Now, in this particular case, as I understand it and there's no doubt in my mind, our government had no involvement in any way whatsoever in the coup itself. In a period of time, three or four years ago, there was an effort being made by the Allende government to destroy opposition news media, both the writing press as well as the electronic press. And to destroy opposition political parties. And the effort that was made in this case was to help and assist the preservation of opposition newspapers and electronic media and to preserve opposition political parties. I think this is in the best interest of the people in Chile, and certainly in our best interest."

The State Department and White House refused to elaborate on Ford's claim that the Allende government had sought to destroy opposition parties, newspapers and electronic media. Acting White House Press Secretary John W. Hushen said he stood by Ford's statement and any further comment would have to come from the State Department. State Department spokesman Robert Anderson said Ford's statement "speaks for itself."

Kissinger role in aid embargo cited— Secretary of State Kissinger personally directed the Nixon Administration's program to curtail economic aid and credits to Chile during Allende's presidency, according to government sources quoted by the New York Times Sept. 15.

The Nixon Administration had repeatedly denied there was any program of economic sanctions against Allende, asserting his government's inability to get loans and credits reflected its poor credit risk.

During Allende's tenure in office, the Times sources said, Kissinger, then President Nixon's national security adviser, directed a series of weekly meetings at which Administration officials worked out a policy of economic sanctions. The officials reportedly included assistant secretaries in the State, Defense and Treasury Departments, and national security aides of Kissinger.

"The whole purpose of the meetings in the first couple of months after [Allende's] election was to insure that the various aid agencies and lending agencies were rejiggered to make sure that [Allende] wasn't to get a penny," one source told the Times.

Brazil anti-Allende aid reported. A Washington Post report Jan. 8 asserted that private groups in Brazil gave financial and other support to the civil resistance movement that helped topple the government of the late President Salvador Allende Gossens.

The article, by correspondent Marlise Simons, was reported by El Nacional of Caracas Jan. 9. It said there was no evidence the Brazilian government participated in the anti-Allende activity, although the local intelligence services must have been aware of it.

Two Brazilians, Glycon de Paiva and Aristoteles Drummond, admitted helping anti-Allende forces and said other private groups gave arms, money and political advice to Chilean opponents of Allende, Simons reported. De Paiva was linked to Brazil's Institute for Research and Social Studies (IPES), which, according to Simons, organized, financed and coordinated activities by businessmen and military officers in 1961–64 to help oust the Brazilian government of Joao Goulart. De Paiva was also a consultant to several U.S. and multinational corporations, the Post reported.

De Paiva reportedly said that after Allende's election in 1970 a number of Chilean businessmen asked his advice, and he explained how civilians could prepare the conditions for a military coup against the president. He recommended they create political and economic chaos, fomenting discontent and fear of communism among workers and managers, blocking legislation by leftist parties, organizing demonstrations and resorting to terrorism if necessary.

On de Paiva's recommendation, a Chilean version of IPES, the Center for Public Opinion Studies, was created in Santiago by middle-class economic associations and businessmen and landholders. The center became a principal source of anti-government strike strategy, rumor campaigns, shock troops for street demonstrations, and the women's movement against the government, Simons reported.

Simultaneously, the opposition Christian Democrats founded the Social and Economic Studies Corp., funded by local as well as Italian and West German Christian Democrats, which, according to sources, employed psychologists and sociologists to plan the ouster of Gen. Carlos Prats, who until his resignation as army commander was Allende's firmest supporter in the armed forces, Simons reported.

Anti-Allende activists, particularly the neo-fascist Fatherland and Liberty Party, received funds and arms from Brazilians, the Post reported. Brazilians also helped finance the anti-government strikes immediately preceding the coup, according to the Post.

Orlando Saenz, until recently the military junta's principal economic adviser, successfully raised money abroad to pay the strikers not to work.

Index